I Hear Voices

Terrace Books, a trade imprint of the University of Wisconsin Press,
takes its name from the Memorial Union Terrace, located at
the University of Wisconsin–Madison. Since its inception in 1907,
the Wisconsin Union has provided a venue for students, faculty, staff,
and alumni to debate art, music, politics, and the issues of the day.
It is a place where theater, music, drama, literature, dance, outdoor activities,
and major speakers are made available to the campus and the community.
To learn more about the Union, visit www.union.wisc.edu.

I Hear Voices

*A Memoir of Love, Death,
and the Radio*

Jean Feraca

TERRACE BOOKS
A trade imprint of the University of Wisconsin Press

Terrace Books
A trade imprint of the University of Wisconsin Press
1930 Monroe Street, 3rd Floor
Madison, Wisconsin 53711-2059
uwpress.wisc.edu

3 Henrietta Street
London WC2E 8LU, England
eurospanbookstore.com

Printed in the United States of America

Library of Congress Cataloging-in-Publication Data
Feraca, Jean.
I hear voices: a memoir of love, death,
and the radio / Jean Feraca.
p.   cm.
ISBN 0-299-22390-6 (cloth: alk. paper)
1. Feraca, Jean.
2. Radio broadcasters—United States—Biography.
I. Title.
PN1991.4.F39A3   2007
384.54092—dc22   2007011786
[B]

ISBN 978-0-299-28574-6 (pbk.: alk. paper)
ISBN 978-0-299-28573-9 (e-book)

Chapter 1, "My Brother/The Other," first appeared in the *North American Review*.
Chapter 8, "Roger and Me, Too," first appeared, in a shorter version, in *2 Bridges Review*.
Poems first appeared in the following publications: "Bacchus at St. Benedict's," *Isthmus*; "January
    Thaw," *The Southern Review*; "Troubled Sleep," *Green River Review*; "Waking Early after Heavy
    Snow," *The Iowa Review*; "Postpartum," "Nursing My Child through His First Illness," and
    "Crossing the Great Divide," *South From Rome: Il Mezzogiorno*; "The Zealot," "Of Bread," and
    "Sailing to America," *Crossing the Great Divide*; "August I," "August II," "Mater Dolorosa," "A
    River of Ice," and "Happiness," *Rendered into Paradise*.

Three great mysteries there are in the lives
of mortal beings:
the mystery of birth at the beginning
the mystery of death at the end;
and greater than either,
the mystery of love.
Everything that is most precious in life
is a form of love.
Art is a form of love, if it be noble;
labor is a form of love, if it be worthy;
thought is a form of love, if it be inspired.

Benjamin Cardozo, U.S. Supreme Court Justice,

officiating at a wedding in 1931

Contents

Acknowledgments

This is not the book I intended to write. It is a much better book. For that, two people are primarily responsible: Molly Peacock, my friend and collaborator, who guided me through the first two chapters and cleared the way forward, and Raphael Kadushin, my editor at the University of Wisconsin Press, who shaped, chapter by chapter, all that followed. Without his subtle and wise influence, this would have been a collection of essays rather than a story of emergence. I am also grateful to Steve Salemson, my first contact at the Press who encouraged the idea of a book in the first place, to Norbert Blei, my generous friend who held up markers when I got stuck, and to Wisconsin Public Radio for granting the leave of absence that made the work possible.

When I first embarked on this project, I imagined writing a book about my experiences as the host of *Conversations with Jean Feraca,* the talk show I coproduced with Carmen Jackson that was broadcast every weekday morning from 9 to 11 on Wisconsin Public Radio from 1989 to 2002. To the loyal members of my audience who might be disappointed not to find yourselves in these pages, I say, look again. For above all, it is to you I am most grateful, first, for welcoming me when I was newly arrived, a stranger to the culture of the Midwest, and secondly, for teaching me to be myself on the radio, to be real. This would not have been a story of emergence without you. Through you, I learned to think not just for myself but to listen to all sides. Through you, I discovered the collective genius of everyday people, and the power of radio to cross the great divides. You enlarged me. You grew me beyond my own boundaries. You grew my program until it outgrew itself, and then turned into something virtually limitless: *Here on Earth: Radio without Borders.*

Many of the people I have written about in these pages appeared first as guests on my program, some several times—my brother, for one, who put me in my place the first time I introduced him as an expert in Lakota Sioux religion by announcing, "You already made a mistake!"; Suzanne Sklar, my dearest friend, the Blake scholar, who entertained and inspired us many times over, recounting her madcap adventures in places as far-flung as Siberia and Vanuatu; Donald Hall, my beloved teacher, who interpreted the poetry of his late wife, Jane Kenyon, my former classmate; Mary David Walgenbach and Joanne Kollasch, the brave Benedictine nuns who have since separated from canonical Roman Catholicism and renamed their center Holy Wisdom Monastery, who introduced their ecumenical vision on the radio. Linnea Smith, "La Doctora," described the primitive conditions of her Amazonian medical practice on the radio, thereby inspiring Rotarians from Duluth to build her a state-of-the-art clinic. My sibylline friend Willow Harth launched "Hands across the Heartland," a campaign that sent five hundred tons of food and medicine to Moscow to "end the Cold War with hot soup." Alan Attie and I actually began our courtship on the radio the night he talked about winemaking, and continued thereafter, when we grinned and blushed our way through a program about the connections between poetry and science. To him, I also owe thanks for being, much to my surprise, as excellent and exacting an editor as he is a geneticist. To my amazing and forbearing sons, Giancarlo Casale, who served as my Middle East correspondent in Turkey, and Dominick Fernow, the artist, I owe my very self, for in giving birth to them, they have as surely given birth to me.

I Hear Voices

1

My Brother/The Other

the mystery at the beginning

My brother Stephen died of lung cancer on June 29, the feast of St. Peter and St. Paul. To watch somebody with a life force that verged on the diabolic reduced to a box of ashes overnight was a shock. I'm grieving.

I was with him for five days before he died, all by myself toward the end, when my son, Dominick, staggered into the waiting room from a brutal two-week hike with the Boy Scouts in the Southwest in time to deliver an eagle feather into my brother's hands just hours before he died.

It wasn't as if we didn't know he was dying. The question was, did he know? He had been dying all his life. He was born dehydrated, and my mother couldn't nurse him. If it hadn't been for penicillin, he would have died of pneumonia in the hospital. He went under the knife so many times in his adult life he was like St. Sebastian, full of arrows. They opened him up last Christmas and found the tumor too close to his heart to operate. But this was his third cancer. There was something about the way he stood up to it that made us think maybe the old reprobate might just scrape by.

I remember him standing in the middle of that miserable apartment of his in Arlington, Virginia, rocking slowly back on his heels as he came to terms with his diagnosis: stage 3 lung cancer, inoperable. *"Iu sunu Calabrez,"* he finally said in that dialect he loved to affect, his teeth clenched, his jaw thrust out, "I survive everything." And that was that. It might have been the last time he gave his cancer any real thought. He reminded me of that brigand Norman Douglas wrote about in *Old Calabria* who grinned at the crowd and spat in defiance as they hauled him off to the gallows with his two amputated hands strung around his neck.

I sat in the back seat of the car on the return trip from his first visit to the oncologist. His friend John was driving. My brother took a draft on his cigarette. "Well," he finally announced dryly in that gravel-grit voice of his straight out of *The Godfather*, "it's either radiation, or it's decapitation . . ." He paused. "And if it's decapitation . . . they cut off your head and replace it with the head of an Irishman. And that's when you know you're not just brain-dead. You're dead-dead." He flicked his ash.

He had always nurtured a professional hatred for the Irish. Irish kids, the sons of cops and firemen in Riverdale where we lived in the Bronx, had once ambushed him on his way home from school and pelted him with rotten eggs. Irish nuns at St. Margaret's School had tormented him and his hooligan friends. He used to make me eat a cold boiled potato on St. Patrick's Day. But I'd catch him hanging out in Irish bars where he loved to tell his filthy jokes. "How is an Irishman like a banana?" His green eyes gleaming, his lip curling in derision, he delivered the punch line with an almost savage satisfaction: "He's born green, lives yellow, and dies rotten."

He had started smoking at the age of eleven. Butts he picked up in the street. Unfiltered Pall Malls. Then regular Chesterfields. And finally, Marlboros, which he consumed at a rate of two or three packs a day. He never stopped. Not even after throat cancer and two operations. He was deeply addicted. The walls of his room, already dingy with age when he moved in, took on layer upon layer of a yellow mucilaginous slick until the room seemed to recede into a cavernous gloom. There he lived out his last days as if chained to a beast with whom he was condemned to share his meat. Whenever he had strength enough to drag his carcass to the table at the one window in the room where he would work on his book, he would sit and smoke day after day, scratching away in that tall slanting script of his my mother used to call Chinese. "I'm so mad," he would fume when he couldn't work. "I haven't got time for this! I have a book to write!" He had taken an early retirement from the Bureau of Indian Affairs, where he had worked principally on treaty claims, in order to write his own books. Since retiring, he had produced a screenplay and two works of nonfiction: *Why Don't They Give Them Guns,* a critical account of his years with the bureau; and *Wakinyon,* a study of Lakota religion originally published as a monograph and considered a classic in its field. He was hard at work on a third book by the time he got sick again.

There was a lot of power in that room, surrounded as it was by all his artifacts and icons. It was divided equally along the same fault lines that split his psyche: Columbus and the Indians. His life was like a palimpsest, a manuscript that had been used to tell two stories, one inscribed right on top of the other, so that both stories blurred together and became distorted. The Columbus story derived from the Old World, the story of the Indians was from the New World, each equally compelling, both permanently at war. He was true to both of them, but they disavowed each other. This set up in him a kind of dissonance that festered and boiled over.

In the Columbus story, he was an Italian American who had been born on the Fourth of July in 1934 in New York City and raised in the Bronx, the only son of second-generation immigrants from the south of Italy. His lifelong fascination with ancestry and the folk culture of the Mezzogiorno in Calabria and Basilicata, the two provinces from which our parentage derived, made him the family throwback. During the years when he lived with his wife and children in Reston, Virginia, he became famous for the huge bashes he threw every Columbus Day and for the Italian street festivals he organized on certain feast days throughout the year, somehow managing to persuade his ultra-middle-class neighbors to parade his almost life-size statue of St. Frances of Paola through the streets to Lake Anne. Whenever he came to visit us in Wisconsin for the holidays, he always carried big stiff slabs of salted codfish with him in his suitcase to make the *baccalà* on Christmas Eve, deliberately reinstating a peasant tradition my mother had strictly outlawed when we moved out of the Bronx and into Scarsdale. My nerves were always set on edge for the three days it took for the fish to purge in the kitchen sink under a constant trickle of water while the house filled up with the stink of the fish. My brother had so identified with his heritage that he even tried to move back to a little town on the coast of Calabria after his divorce, a misadventure that lasted only six months.

Underneath the Columbus story was an older story that bled through from below. It surfaced when he was only five years old and my mother happened to show him a picture of a Plains Indian warrior in a warbonnet and full battle regalia mounted on horseback, an image that left an indelible imprint on my brother's soul. It must have stirred and triggered in him some prenatal memory that set his whole life's course. By the age of ten he was filling up our back porch with old clothes that came from clothing drives he organized for Holy Rosary Mission on Pine Ridge Reservation in South Dakota. He was only a teenager when he made friends with several full-bloods who lived in New York City. One of them was Chief Hill Canoe, who worked as a silversmith in a little shop on Forty-Second Street, just a block up from the entrance to Grand Central Station. I remember the day he took me downtown to meet his friend. "This is my little sister, Jeannie," he said, introducing me to a tall, handsome, dark-skinned man with a weathered face, long gray braids, and a headband. He was wearing a western shirt and a lot of turquoise jewelry. "Jeannie, shake hands with Chief Hill Canoe." Another one of my brother's friends was Louie Mofsie, who could do the hoop dance with sixteen hoops, a feat he performed every year on one of my father's flatbed trucks in front of the grandstand on Fifth Avenue in the Columbus Day Parade. Stephen had a crush on Louie Mofsie's sister. When he graduated from Manhattan Prep, we held a pow-wow in the backyard, and all the Mofsies came: Louie, his sister, and his mother. Mrs. Mofsie taught us all how to do the rabbit dance. We held hands and danced in a circle, and the sound of the drums could be heard all over the neighborhood.

As my brother got older, his psyche became a battleground where the Indian Wars were never settled. He became more and more diffi-cult, flying off the handle at the slightest provocation. We learned to live with him the way the Neapolitans live with Vesuvius, never knowing from one minute to the next just when he might blow. He was a living contradiction. Whatever could be said of him, the opposite was also true. He was kindhearted, but he could be equally cruel; he had the manners of a courtier when he wanted to be charming; he was downright gallant one minute, shockingly crude the next. He was a romantic and a cynic, a skeptic and a true believer. His knowledge of the history of North American Indians was encyclopedic; he was trained as an anthropologist in the scientific method, but, underneath it all, he practiced magic.

While he was still working toward his Ph.D. at Columbia University, he suddenly quit to take a job with the Bureau of Indian Affairs, where he stayed for the rest of his professional life, doing community development work at first with the Sioux on Pine Ridge Reservation in South Dakota and later with the Seminoles in Florida before taking a desk job in the Washington bureau to adjudicate treaty claims. He began working with the Sioux while he was still in college, spending his summers on Pine Ridge, where he learned how to speak Lakota and earned the trust and respect of many tribal elders. As a student of the Lakota religion, he was allowed to take part in ceremonies that up until that time no other white man had ever witnessed. He was even adopted into the tribe by Mrs. Mary Fast Horse, a saintly woman who was respected by her people as a tribal elder and a renowned herbalist. I met her once on Pine Ridge after my brother's first child was born and he asked me to be her godmother. I was seventeen years old at the time. The old woman greeted me at the door of a dark, one-room shack and ushered me inside, where there was a wood-burning stove, a calendar tacked to the wall, and a picture of President Kennedy. She was still living in the old way, with no electricity or running water. My brother revered her.

What Stephen wanted above all was to help Indians to recover their tribal traditions and reclaim the honor they had lost as hunters, warriors, and shamans, a project that was doomed from the start. When, instead, they stayed drunk and dissolute, he, too, became drunk and dissolute. One of his major projects, the establishment of a fishhook factory that was intended to bring employment to the reservation, failed miserably. He suffered another major blow with the rise of the Red Power movement in the 1960s, finding himself shunted aside and rejected as a white man, forced to watch from the sidelines while others with far less knowledge rose into positions of leadership. That just about finished him off. In my brother's canon, ignorance was punishable. "Goddamn Indians," he would fume while he whittled, working himself into a lather as the shavings piled up. "Bunch of savages. . . . When our people come to power, every Indian tribe will have its own resident guinea anthropologist to teach them about their culture and traditions, and no goddamn Indian will ever be allowed to write one single word." He said this while he growled, spitting out every word through clenched teeth as if he were spitting poison darts.

He worshiped Crazy Horse and Sitting Bull, Lorenzo de Medici and Mussolini; he preached benign dictatorship and practiced a form of petty tyranny at home. "He was never any good at anything that mattered," his daughter once said of him. "A great artifaker," was what he called himself, speaking of his uncanny ability to re-create Indian artifacts, but really the same was true of his own makeup. Only a very few of us could see through his bluff. "Steve is like America," his friend Cesare said. "Love him or leave him." His wife left him. His children left him. But I always adored him, and so did my two sons.

The great strain he was under, struggling always to keep his two stories separate and distinct from one another, was evidenced in the rigid way his living room was organized. It was more like a museum than a home. The Indian artifacts were all nailed up along one wall, labeled and dated. There was a gallery of photographs: Sitting Bull, the Osceola brothers, a picture of me as a kid posing with two Seminole girls in ribbon dresses, Mrs. Mary Fast Horse, his beloved Indian mother on Pine Ridge. Intermixed among the photographs was a deerskin drum with a red star he had stretched himself, a ceremonial pipe, a pair of richly beaded Sioux moccasins, and a Nez Perce purse that featured an antlered deer on one side. These objects all had resonance. They were totemic. Apart from them, my brother had no real possessions. He had lived like a mendicant, with one bookcase full of books and a single suit of clothes. These were his only riches. They had followed him everywhere throughout the many twistings of his nomadic life.

The back of the room was all Italian. Big topical maps of Calabria and Basilicata covered nearly the whole of the back wall, hanging from ceiling to floor. In front of the maps stood a pedestal with a bronze bust of Saverio, our paternal grandfather, which had been made from a death mask and subsequently rescued from the family mausoleum after it began to corrode. Saverio, who looked just like my father with a moustache, dominated the room, staring out over our heads with all the blank magisterial indifference befitting an Italian family patriarch. And gleaming from a shelf in the corner to the right of the bust was a bronze mortar and pestle that had once belonged to our great-grandmother on my mother's side, so both families were represented. In the opposite corner, leaning on a staff, was the life-size statue of St. Francis of Paola my brother had carved himself. It had big staring eyes that seemed to follow you everywhere. I stayed in that room for a week, sleeping on the couch while I nursed my brother through one of his postoperative spells. I felt the power in those eyes.

Over the months, as Stephen went in and out of the hospital, all these objects began to disappear. One after another, he gave them away in what seemed like a never-ending potlatch, the only tangible sign he ever gave that he really did know he was dying. Big yellowish squares and rectangles kept opening up in the ever-darkening wall until all that was left was a gallery of ghosts. Like phantom limbs they spoke of old pain and old loss, and they opened in me a host of corresponding holes.

I think my brother was never truly free from pain in his whole life, except, perhaps, just before he died. Of course, the morphine helped. But in the hospital, I saw him turn to my friend, Willow, who appeared like an angel at his deathbed, and say to her with a deep sigh, "I'm so glad you came. I have never been so comfortable."

He was stoic throughout his last ordeal. He was like a Sioux; he never complained. He never stopped trying to finish his book. "I'm working! I'm working," he would insist, whenever I asked. The book was to have been a sequel to *Wakinyon,* his classic on Lakota religion. After an absence of many years, he had made the arduous journey back to Pine Ridge to learn from tribal elders their views about the changes that had taken place in traditional religious practice. The Sun Dance was now gone. In its place he discovered a proliferation of little sun dances, many of them conducted by fraudulent medicine men who were self-appointed and seeking to make a profit from New Age initiates. Worse, he discovered evidence of witchcraft on the reservation and was horrified at this inversion of the sacred order. It was courageous work, in personal terms as well as professional, a project near to his heart that he desperately wanted to complete.

When the pain got so bad that he couldn't sit up, he would lie down on his couch and paint. Before his hair had a chance to fall out he shaved his head and threatened to have a portrait of Mussolini tattooed onto the back, and then he walked around in a battered Calvin Klein cap that was entirely out of character. He was undergoing a double course of chemo and radiation, and I was worried that it was too much. "Yeah," he said in his raspy voice as he was grinding down a pipestone, "It's overkill. That's what they call it. I go to the clinic twice a week. There's a Sicilian woman who sits in the doorway at the top of the stairs sharpening a bread knife. She's dressed all in black, and over her head there's a big sign that says 'Overkill.'"

When my niece called with the news that the cancer had cracked one of Stephen's ribs and then, within the same week, she called again to report that he had suffered a brain seizure, I called my friend Willow. She was on the plane with me the next day, headed for D.C.

Willow is a kind of sibyl. She's a delicate, blue-eyed Fay Wray blonde with a spring-trap mind. Willow grew up as a free spirit on a Navajo reservation, an environment that nurtured her intuition and deepened her dream life. Stephen fell violently in love with her one Christmas when she read him his tarot cards. He was a doorway she simply walked through. "You're someone who is covered with wounds," she told him, much to his astonishment. He had drawn the Ten of Swords. She could see right through all of his defenses and subterfuges. He had been born under the sign of Cancer, a tender being, soft-bodied under all that armor. Being seen and received, he was utterly disarmed. He knew the language of the old magic as she did; he recognized her power.

Over the years, whenever Stephen came to visit, there developed between them an improbable Beauty and the Beast romance. She once took him to see the Indian mounds on the shore of Lake Mendota where she watched him walk in deep meditative silence before stooping down to pick up a piece of wood he carved into a bird whistle for her with his pocket knife right there on the mound. She said he was pure Indian in that moment. There was an uncanny link between them. They seemed to be conjoined, animus to anima, shaman to shaman. Once he presented her with a strange gift of three small arrows he had painted yellow and wrapped up in a rabbit skin with his Indian name scratched on the inside. Instantly, she recognized it as the psychic weapon she had dreamed about the night before. "Your brother is really scary," she said to me. Stephen was forever urging Willow to visit him, but she was attached to another man, a psychologist who had once loaned Stephen a winter coat. "Allyn Roberts," Stephen used to say softly in his raspy whisper. "He's such a nice man. Too bad I have to kill him."

I had packed a bottle of one of my husband's treasured vintage reds, a Rothchild cabernet, and a crazy quilt made by Mrs. Fast Horse my brother had given me years ago. Willow had dreamed of Mrs. Fast Horse the night before we left. In the dream, the old Indian woman had entered Stephen's room, drawn by the quilt. She had strung a necklace of turquoise all around his bed, and the beads had turned to stones, and then to boxcars, and the train had circled and rumbled all around him until it was spinning in a circle, and then the spinning circle had turned into a white rattlesnake. "I'm not sure what that means," she feigned.

Willow made me tell her my stories: My big brother by ten years, he was always good to me. He defended and protected me in family quarrels and the occasional street scuffle. When I was a kid, he carved me a child's bow and arrows from ash tree saplings he had cut down in Van Cortland Park. Yippee, his hunting dog, an English fox terrier, very smart, used to follow him into the park to hunt rabbits and squirrels. He taught me to shoot into the bull's-eye of a target he nailed into one of the oak trees in our backyard in Riverdale. He taught me how to do the deer dance and insisted that I practice every day when I came home from school, running upstairs to his room to find him. There was an alcove attached to his bedroom where I used to love to hang out. It was chock full of all kinds of fascinating things that were always kept in meticulous order: comic books, Chinese coins, drawing pencils, flints and arrowheads and rabbits' feet. He was a tough and exacting first teacher who instilled in me the same standards of excellence to which he himself scrupulously adhered.

We performed in minstrel shows together. While he beat out the rhythm on one of his hand-stretched drums and sang in a high nasal voice, Indian style, I danced the deer dance, all decked out as an Indian brave in a costume he had conjured out of ribbons, beads, and turkey feathers. The last thing he did before each performance was tie a head-band around my head and paint each of my cheeks with two yellow streaks and one red dot. I wore a breechcloth, a vest, and a turkey feather bustle he helped me fix around my waist. I was supposed to shake a rattle in my right hand while fluttering a turkey feather fan in the left. That took some doing. I don't think I ever got it right. Best of all were the real beaded buckskin moccasins Chief Hill Canoe had made just for me that I wore with strings of bells around my ankles so that whenever I moved, I jingled. We performed this brother-and-sister act many times together on stages and auditoriums throughout the Bronx until I finally got too big to be passed off as an Indian brave.

He was shaking all over, huddled up in a fetal position when we got to the hospital. I was frightened. "I tried to warn you, " Willow said. "This is what I saw in the dream." She was calm. She knew exactly what to do. "Tell the stories," she whispered as she began crooning to him and rubbing his feet. "Stephen . . ." I hesitated, afraid he had already slipped beyond hearing, "remember when I was a kid and you taught me how to do the deer dance . . ."

A while later I opened up the wine and poured a little into a Dixie cup that I held up to his lips. He sipped it. And a little more, until, slowly, he began to revive.

The next day he was sitting up in bed when we came in carrying the quilt, holding it up for him to see. His eyes widened. "Where did you get that?" he rasped. Suddenly, his face crumpled and he began to cry, but just as quickly, he caught himself. He reached out his right arm, the finger pointed. "Wash it," he commanded. "Wash it. Cold water. Now." The two of us looked at each other. "Now."

The water splashed dark as it pooled in the bottom of the hospital slop sink we discovered in the back of a utility closet. We poured in the red liquid antiseptic. He was right, of course. After hanging for over ten years on my office wall, the quilt did need to be washed. The water ran clear after several rinses, but soaking wet the quilt was very heavy. We struggled with it, wringing out the long snake before filing back into his room to hold it up for his inspection. Again, the finger pointed. "Dry it. Dry it." Again, we exchanged glances and then looked outside at the roof. It was a warm day, but windy. He shook his head. We ended up draping it in long loose swags over the shower rod in the bathroom, where over the course of the next day it did dry out. And so it was that he prepared his own shroud.

Oh, what a time it was! Caruso crooning from a tape recorder. A Laotian man who kept calling him "Babe" on one side of his bed, and Willow on the other side, who finally climbed right into bed with him, while I kept spooning scrambled eggs into his mouth whenever I thought he wouldn't notice. He was in his element. He had always loved being the center of attention.

He kept coming and going, in and out of consciousness. On June the twenty-fifth, the anniversary of the Battle of the Little Big Horn, my son, Giancarlo, who was born on that day, called from Greece. Stephen was in a coma. I put the receiver to his ear and yelled, "It's Giancarlo on the phone." He had always been crazy about Giancarlo. His murky green eyes flickered open. "Uncle Stephen!" I could hear my son shouting from halfway across the world. "This afternoon I'm going to be on Mount Olympus at three o'clock with my friend Dimitri. We're going to eat barbequed lamb tripe and drink Retsina, and I'm going to salute you!" From somewhere deep inside his chest came a rumbling that emerged from his throat as barely more than a whisper. "Beautiful!" he managed it, his finger pointing. "Beautiful! I'll be there." He had rallied again.

What a lucky bastard he was, when I think about it. To live your whole life a prodigal and a reprobate only to die like a saint. He really did look like one of the desert fathers when we walked into his room and found him swaddled in nothing but a sweaty sheet. He had always been afraid he would die alone. He had been disinherited by my father after a terrible quarrel. Stephen hadn't come to my father's funeral. That was a disgrace. Ten years went by when none of us talked to him, not even me. During that time, his wife left him; his children became estranged. Yet there he was, surrounded by his tribe: sisters, daughter, sons, lovers, friends of every hue and stripe, his family reunited, even Jo Anne, his gentle ex-wife.

He had married the beautiful woman on the reservation who smiled as she handed him packs of Chesterfields over the counter at the Wounded Knee Trading Post her parents ran. It was his first summer on Pine Ridge. He was still a *wasichu,* a white boy, learning to speak Lakota and drumming with the Sun Dance men. Jo Anne looked like a classic Indian princess and was a mixed breed who had grown up on the wrong reservation. Her grandmother, a full-blooded Chippewa from the Iron Range, had married a German trapper and walked west with him. My parents were aghast when they found out that their son wanted to marry an Indian, and refused to attend the wedding. But my father, who always defended his son in those days, relented at the last minute, bought himself an airplane ticket, and flew to Rapid City by himself—a breach my mother never forgave. He came back from South Dakota to tell us that he had been honored among elders, that he had sat on the ground with men at the wedding feast and had eaten dog stew.

Time and again, Stephen would tear at his mask and try to get out of bed. The day before we arrived, his doctor had written him off, announced there would be no more treatments. In his rage, Stephen ripped the IVs out of his arm, threw the telephone out the window, cord and all, got out of bed, and had started to get dressed. They tried to move him to a hospice, but he had uttered such black-hearted curses that he frightened the nun away. He was halfway down the hall and headed out the door before they tackled him and strapped him back into bed. Even after he'd stopped eating, when there was nothing but sugar water in his veins and he was drowning in morphine, he was still trying to leave that hospital, so strong was his will. I would take his two arms in mine, feeling the mortal strength of his grip, and together we would pull. I could feel how badly he wanted to get up out of that bed, right until the very end.

He humbled himself like a sun dancer. He cried and apologized to everybody, including my dear husband, whom he had once called a dirty Jew. "I'm so sorry," he began, the instant Alan's bearded face appeared above the bed. Penitent, his mouth quivering, his head rolling from side to side, he repeated it over and over. "I'm so sorry. I'm so sorry." We were all astonished that he would bare his soul to us like that, stripped clean. "It broke my heart," my husband said.

"Pity me, pity me," the sun dancer sings as he enters the arena, a skirt around his loins, a bone whistle in his teeth. Stephen's daughter had said, "I want my father to die right." She meant a priest. But it was to us that he confessed. He was becoming authentic.

That night he thrashed and tore off his mask, and in his oxygen deprivation he began to regress and go through his life review. "I'm so sorry," he told Jo Anne, who stayed with him all night. "I'm sorry" became his mantra. He was a model of penitence, wringing out his soul, purging his demons. We were witnessing the suffering of a man who had sinned grievously against his own conscience. I watched how his suffering refined him, how the small head seemed to rise above the thin neck, the broad shoulders, the lean body. I had imagined him going out like Blackbeard, but he looked more like St. Jerome.

Who would have expected such naked contrition? He had been in sweat lodges on Pine Ridge. He had waited in the dark while the *yuwipe* man slipped his bonds like a Houdini. Now it was his turn to escape.

"Where's Dominick?" he kept asking, searching for the one face that was still missing from the circle. "Dominick's coming. He's on his way." Again, the whispered question, more insistent, "Where's Dominick?"

It wasn't until everybody but me had left that Dominick finally arrived, staggering into the hospital waiting room with his huge backpack still on his back, having traveled all the way from New Mexico where he had been on a hiking expedition with his Boy Scout troop. He was exhausted, still wearing his scout uniform and a rain hat with a bedraggled eagle feather tucked into the brim. His troop had stopped at a trapping lodge somewhere along the trail, where he had won the eagle feather in a poker game. "Uncle Stephen taught me how to play poker," he explained. "I remember how he gave me an eagle feather when I was a little kid. Now I would bring one to him."

It became a quest, an idée fixe, to bring his uncle that feather. Everything had gone wrong on the trip. It was as if the troop had been cursed. They were plagued by lightning storms, torrential downpours, cold, mud, mosquitoes, and bears. They had gotten lost. They were soaked to the bone with no way to get dry. Quarrels had broken out. Dominick had to run off the trail a dozen times to rescue the feather each time it blew off. Back at base camp, he had called home and discovered that his beloved uncle was dying. It took him a halting twenty hours on the train to get from Denver to Chicago. By the time he reached O'Hare, he found the airport burning, the whole terminal deserted and filled with smoke that had been caused by an electrical fire. All flights had been cancelled. He was resolute. He waited for hours.

By the time Dominick arrived my brother was unconscious, about to be transferred to a hospice. The orderlies loaded him into the back of an ambulance and the two of us climbed on board. One of the attendants, a big burly woman, turned to us as we lurched down a street full of trolley tracks and potholes. "You do know he's DNR," she said pointedly, and then, seeing our blank looks, she added, "Do Not Resuscitate." We could easily have lost him en route; the road was so rough, we were afraid his lungs might collapse right then and there. But he made it.

Dominick stuck right by his side in the hospice, the feather still clutched in his fist, hovering over his uncle in the hope that he might still regain consciousness. He was right there at the ready the instant the green eyes fluttered open. "Uncle Stephen, Uncle Stephen," he began, holding out the eagle feather in his hand. "I brought you this eagle feather. I came all the way from New Mexico to bring it to you. I won it in a card game. I came through fire to bring it to you."

I was watching from the other room; I saw the effort it took; the heavy chest lifted slowly from the backrest, the leaden arms extending, the slow hand that trembled as it reached out to take the feather, the arms that closed around the boy and his tribute. They held that last embrace until, once again, my brother's body fell back slack against the bed, his head settled into the pillow, and his eyes closed, this time for good.

That night, Dominick and I both slept on the floor of his room, Dominick at the foot of his bed, with me at his side. We were like loyal dogs. Every so often throughout the night his nurse whose name was Carol MacCloud came into the room with her stethoscope to check his vitals and renew his morphine. She had promised to wake us if she noticed any change. On the floor beside him, his breath was a light blanket that fell over us, rising and falling, rising and falling. I dozed as I listened: in . . . (pause) . . . out . . . (pause) . . . in . . . (pause) . . . out . . . (pause). Oddly enough, I felt strangely soothed by the sound, harsh as it was, but so present as it persisted throughout the night, each exhalation following on its inhalation, the long drafts regularly placed, perfectly balanced, continuing without any alteration or hesitation. It was like praying the rosary; each breath, as it passed, was another bead to finger. He was knitting me into his rhythm, the little hitches every now and then only a thickening of the strand, shadings in this finest of yarns.

I felt a little guilty lying there on the floor drawing so much comfort from the sound of my brother's labored breathing, the nurse entering and leaving, her ministrations measured, practiced, merciful, renewing his medicine, bringing a steady supply of ampoules that were carrying him into Lethe. I remembered how he always knew how to comfort a new puppy on its first night home. "Just put a clock in his box with a dirty sock," he would say. "He'll sleep just fine."

I remembered, too, how he had hooked a rug from nails on a spool when he was a boy, lifting off the thread from each nail head until the hank grew to a fantastic length, a quarter mile or more, as the story was told. And here he was, hooking the rug of his life off the spool one stitch at a time while the hank went on disappearing slowly down the hole. I had never before realized how each of us has just so many breaths, a finite number, an allotment assigned to us like the number you get in a bakery or a butcher's shop. And the more we use them up, the more each one of these breaths becomes a thing unto itself, discreet as a shaped note. In . . . out . . . in . . . out . . . all through his last night on earth. Nothing to suggest that the end was near. No faltering. No stumble. No slowing down at all. And then it stopped. I felt like a diver who had just let go of the boat. I looked at the clock. Ten minutes to six. The machine that was regulating his oxygen intake stopped too and began to beep, awakening Dominick, who rushed to his side. He took one last half breath and died in Dominick's arms. When the nurse came in she was just as surprised as we were that the end had come. She checked his pulse, looked up at us, and declared, "He was a brilliant warrior."

Dominick shaved him. Together, we removed his hospital gown. I washed his hands and feet, taking liberties with my brother's body I never would have dreamed of taking while he was alive. All the while, he was giving off heat in waves that kept rising off his forehead as if it were coming up from some deep source, like coal compressed under many layers, buried in his core. His nurse said he had spiked a fever in the middle of the night. His last fever. He was still burning, still purging. The heat intensified before it began to diminish, giving rise to a series of transformations that seemed alchemical. The same process by which he himself had spent hundreds of hours rendering, bending, and polishing hardwoods and catlinite, always the dourest of substances, was now at work on him. It was as if, in that hour after death, he was carving himself. The bones began to shine through, rarified and fine. The skin changed color, turning a dark granular gold, like wet granite, and then began to sink below its own surface as it clarified. It was as if you could see right down into it, the way river stones in a clear stream draw your mind down to their depths. His heat was purgative, erasing all traces of the anguish and torment that had characterized his last days — his whole life, in fact. In their place, a deep peace came to settle into him like a great stone that had finally found its groove. It seemed to suggest that his suffering, the very cruciform of his life, had been redemptive after all. The work was unfinished, but the man was complete.

We wrapped him in the crazy quilt his Indian mother had stitched. Underneath, we tucked in a sketch of Mussolini that Dominick had once drawn for him together with a holy card of St. Pellegrino, the patron saint of malignant growths, and a puppy picture from his calendar, just for luck. He had always loved dogs. We found a spool of thread. Dominick sewed the eagle feather into the quilt right above his chest where I tied a red rose and a bit of lavender, which was the closest thing to sage I could scavenge in the garden.

We prayed over him. We sang "On Eagles Wings." We tried to close his mouth, and then, mysteriously, it closed itself, but only halfway, so that he looked as if he were about to make one last pronouncement.

After they came to pick up the body, it was still morning. Having nothing more to do, and with time on our hands, we wandered off to the Corcoran Museum, where I found myself in the same room with two paintings of St. Peter—one by El Greco, and the other by Goya. Goya's Peter was a round-faced peasant with a broom-straw beard and a monk's cowl that brought to mind my brother's humble saints. El Greco's Peter was an aristocrat, lean and lantern-jawed, with a tragic, stricken look; his huge, luminous eyes were cast upward, brimming with grief and remorse. In his hand, he held a clutch of keys. Who better, I thought, to post at heaven's gates? Who better to judge penitence than one who was himself a penitent? Peter, the great betrayer who had denied Christ three times. It wasn't the saint in Peter that had earned him the keys to the kingdom of heaven; it was the sinner.

It was Tuesday, the twenty-ninth of June, the feast day of St. Peter and St. Paul.

My brother was nowhere to be found at his funeral. In St. Anne's Roman Catholic Church in Reston, Virginia, where a few old friends and neighbors had gathered with the family, there was no coffin, no corpse to be blessed, no pall bearers in black suits straining under their load. His spirit was not in the prayers of the funeral mass, not in the priest's perfunctory remarks, not in the singing of "The Old Ruddy Cross," not in the tenor's red tie that was printed with bottles of Tabasco sauce.

Nobody in my family had ever before been cremated. When I walked into the church and discovered the wooden box no bigger than a book that held his ashes, I cried out in shock and disbelief. It was a harrowing thing, to grasp so suddenly that he was really gone, vanished altogether from the face of the earth. The same fevered body we had so lovingly tended and wrapped only the day before had been rolled into the flames to be consumed and had quite literally gone up in smoke. Someone—maybe one of his sons—had placed a bow and a quiver of arrows crosswise on top of the box. The bow was exquisitely made, a thing of striking elegance with clean, simple lines. There was an aliveness about it. Clearly the work of my brother's hands, it seemed to signify an essence of the man he was, taut, notched, stained, and ready to fly. I thought of Rumi's words, "Your real country is where you're heading, not where you are."

My brother had wanted his ashes scattered over the Bay of Naples. That was impractical. They were buried, instead, in the Herndon cemetery in Virginia in a family plot tended by his ex-wife. His grave was left unmarked until a year later when his daughter arranged for a headstone bearing both his names, Italian and Indian, to be put in place: Stephen E. Feraca, and Wachiyapi, which in Lakota means "We depend on him."

Back home in Wisconsin, I set up a little altar in the middle of the living room in memory of my brother. In the center was his carving of Sant'a'Roc', Saint Rocco, with his wounded knee and his dog. In front of the statue, I placed a flower from my brother's grave in a vase, a scrap from the hem of Mrs. Fast Horse's quilt, a bit of kala, the seaweed used for forgiveness in family rituals Willow had brought me from Hawaii, my copy of *Wakinyon*, and a photograph taken the day he gave me away at my wedding when he looked like a statesman in a dead man's borrowed jacket and a new Italian silk tie.

Whenever I feel the need to connect with my brother, I call Willow. She puts my intention into her "hopper" and a dream usually arrives within a day or two. Stephen appears very relaxed and at ease in Willow's dreams. He is always smoking. Once he showed up wearing nothing but a top hat and a long white shirt, smoking with Chief Tamanend, and Geronimo, and some scary Aztec. In another dream he was dressed impeccably in a royal blue Italian silk suit. That was during a time when I was troubled by nightmares after my mother died, and Stephen delivered precise instructions on how to lay my mother's ghost to rest. Through Willow's intercession, I even consulted him about writing this book. That was more difficult. Willow came back in a few days with a report. "You have to interpret this message yourself because Stephen doesn't speak English anymore," she said. "He is no longer hanging around and was very hard to find. He looked great. His mood was ebullient, and he was smoking up a storm. He said, 'You tell my sister to get a life, and start enjoying herself. Tell her to stop beating a dead horse.' Then he took a long drag on his cigarette and said with a smirk, enjoying his joke as he blew out the smoke, 'Tell her to lighten up.'"

2

"Dolly"

the mystery at the end

My mother was a monster who lived well into her nineties. Toward the end of her life, much to my surprise, I grew to love her. I loved her fiercely, in fact. It was the monster in her that kept her alive, and the monster that made me love her. I had moved far away, but a turn of events brought us together again, let me face her, let me, finally, in a strange way, love her to death.

But in childhood, we all hated her—my brother, my sister, and I. When we moved out of our cozy neighborhood in the Bronx into a big sprawling house my father built in Scarsdale, she spent the better part of every day cleaning house in her nightgown, climbing a kitchen stool to scrub the walls she cursed, and polishing the oak floors down on her hands and knees until they seemed to burn. She was angry and spiteful most of the time, and none of us quite knew why. Once, she threatened to scald me with a steam iron. Another night she picked up a pitchfork and carried it out of our two-car garage, intent on sticking it into her brother-in-law.

My sister, Rosemary, who had my father's dark movie-star looks, said she was glad she didn't take after our mother. She remembered the welts, the hair pulls, the nights she cried herself to sleep. My brother,

Stephen, called my mother a witch and tried to throw her down the cellar steps. She even called herself a witch, as if it were a credential. She could read our hearts and spell out their secrets; she had a knack for finding lost objects and had a way with animals. "I'm a witch," she used to say. "I come from a long line of witches." Her mother, our grandmother, consulted a dream book and practiced *malocchio*, the cult of the evil eye. Her grandmother, our great-grandmother, cursed her second husband from her deathbed, a man who had fleeced her of her fortune. "I'm dying," she told him, "but one year from today, I'm gonna take you with me." He died a year to the day.

My mother was christened Rose, but everybody called her "Dolly" because of her fair skin, her perennially pink cheeks, and her startling sapphire-blue eyes, so rare in southern Italian families. She was a true Leo, arriving in the swelter of mid-August in 1906 in New York City, the eldest of three children born to Frank and Jenny Sinisgalli, her mismatched parents who always hated each other. Like all Italian men, Frank hoped that his firstborn would be a boy, and so when my mother was born he dispatched the band he had hired to play. That was the first event of note in my mother's long life. When Jenny miscarried their second child and it turned out to be male, Frank insisted that the fetus be kept in a pickle jar on top of the living room mantel until, after two years, Jenny finally took it down in disgust and buried it in the cemetery, hiding the jar under her coat in the trolley.

The boy they both longed for finally arrived, weighing in at a hefty thirteen pounds. He was nursed until he turned five. Always big, and never very bright, Sonny was kicked in the head by a horse, so the story went, and grew up to be a mama's boy who never left home except to fight in World War II. Next came Tootsie, my mother's baby sister, who was born on Christmas Eve. Everybody loved Tootsie. An invalid for most of her life, Tootsie was pretty and sweet with a temperament as meek as milk. Poor thing, she was diagnosed with breast cancer and underwent a double mastectomy when she was only sixteen years old. She married my uncle Victor, but when the cancer recurred she went back home to be nursed by her mother until she died.

Growing up with a baby sister everybody adored and an only brother who was petted and spoiled, Dolly got short shrift as the only one of the three who was endowed with a sturdy constitution. The roses in her cheeks bloomed all year round, and she never succumbed to chicken pox or mumps or any of the other childhood diseases that infected her siblings. The year she turned a chubby eighteen she was dubbed Miss Health Girl of 1924, much to her mother's satisfaction. Dolly "was made out of number two," as Jenny always said with immigrant pride.

When Dolly and Sonny and Tootsie were still quite young, a gaggle of their newly orphaned aunts and uncles trooped into the Sinisgalli household to be raised by their big sister. It wasn't as if Jenny didn't have enough to do what with her own brood. This was an invasion on a grand scale. It placed a terrible strain on the family's scant resources, swelled their two-story Bronx walk-up to bursting, and added all sorts of tensions to daily life.

Morris and Tina, Jenny's youngest charges, caused all sorts of trouble, defying their big sister and refusing to go to school, so she took to thrashing them with a rubber hose when they ran around the streets truant. In the chaos that ensued, Dolly wanted to run away from home. She daydreamed about joining the circus to become a lion tamer and acted it out by dressing her cat in doll's clothes and training it to walk across a tightrope until it fell to its death in the alley from a second-story window one day, dressed in pink gingham and a hat to match.

Dolly was fed on nanny goat beans by her aunt Tina, the leader of the incorrigibles who got the bright idea of gathering them from the family goat that was kept in the backyard, and wrapping them up in shiny aluminum foil so they looked like candy. Maybe that's why my grandmother said my mother was made out of number two. Another one of her aunts allegedly bled to death on the kitchen table while undergoing a tonsillectomy that was performed with a buttonhook. Whoever the surgeon was, we never knew. The incident was never properly reported. But we guessed it might have been my great uncle, Dominick, the future surgeon, who entered medical school when he came of age and fell in love with my mother, the niece he was allowed to take to dances "to protect him from all those man-hungry nurses." Dolly and

Dominick made a handsome couple and won first prize in a tango competition. "He used to like to stroke my cheek, and say, 'Skin like a baby,'" my mother reported with that fond faraway look that used to come into her eyes whenever she spoke of her uncle.

One day, while my mother was still a teenager, her father got fed up, clapped his fedora on top of his bald head, and left home, never to return. His desertion was counted an official abandonment in the family, roundly denounced, but never completely regretted. My mother never grieved for her father, not even after he died. He was mean and stingy, she often told us. He kept the piano locked to keep his daughters from practicing and threatened to send them to work in a beading factory, a sweatshop fate that was suffered by many an Italian girl deprived of an education.

But Jenny had different ideas. She had never had anything but contempt for the husband she always referred to as Beesha-Beesh— "Piss-Piss," I think it meant. He was a tailor from the old country to whom she had been hastily married off in the vacuum left by her father's death. In their wedding portrait, she's the one who is tall and broad chested, towering over the little man beside her who was standing on a stool just to be able to come up to her shoulder. Jenny wasn't just tall; she was stately, with a mass of dark glossy hair that was piled on top of her head and a figure so commanding, even at sixteen she was formidable.

"Mama should have been a man," Tootsie used to say. "She was as good as ten men," my brother, who adored her, always said. Jenny was possessed of a courage and cunning that seemed leonine. Her feats of daring were repeated time and again and became famous in the family lexicon. As a girl she had tangled with Casey Stengel, the legendary future manager of the New York Yankees, a neighborhood bully who used to beat her up and call her a "guinea" until the day she pushed him down an excavation pit. She even tangled with the parish priest, who also called her a "guinea," plucking his beard in the confessional and dashing out of the church and into the street. Coming of age in Italian Harlem, Jenny became known as The Belle of 109th Street. Arturo Toscanini wanted to marry her, but she turned him down after her mother told her he was a bum who would always be on the road. Watching how she raised her young family in the Bronx, the neighbors kept a respectful distance and called her a *diavola femmina,* "devil woman." She used to catch mice and spin them by the tail before hurling them live from the upstairs window. She took a fiendish delight in teasing her daughters with live eels. She once saved a woman from rape and routed a robber in her nightgown, chasing him down the street with the same length of hose she used to beat up her brothers and sisters.

Jenny had an eighth-grade education. As soon as it was clear that Beesha-Beesh had rounded the corner and was gone for good, she got herself a real estate license, ordered business cards printed up with her initials, "J. R. Sinisgalli," and sent my mother to New Rochelle College with her earnings. It was also rumored that she made money as a loan shark.

My mother wanted to become an elementary school teacher, but Jenny wouldn't hear of it. "Nothing doing," she said. "You're going to be a high school teacher." So, Dolly, who slimmed down during her college years, became known as Miss Skinny Belly at Evander Child High School, where she taught French and Spanish, gave elocution lessons, and doubled on the playground as a gym teacher. Every morning she would walk to school along sidewalks that my father had chalked during the night with love poems signed with his epithet, "Alter Ego."

My parents met at my father's house on Grote Street in the Bronx on a Sunday afternoon while they were both in college. His mother wasted no time, plucking him by his sleeve and dragging him into the living room to meet the "Nice-a gell." That was all it took. He was instantly smitten. Lovesick in the weeks that followed, he took to prowling around in his father's Pierce Arrow when he couldn't sleep, shining his headlights into Rosy's bedroom window in the middle of the night. He courted her at the Bronx Zoo, and took her for long drives in the Pierce Arrow along the winding Bronx River Parkway on Sunday afternoons. One evening, he brought her home ten minutes late from the ice-cream parlor. Jenny was waiting at the top of the stairs, where she slapped her daughter so hard across the face that, in shock, my father fainted.

They were married at the end of December 1929 at the start of the Great Depression, an era that became the governing metaphor of their long years together. My father had just earned his law degree from Fordham University, but law degrees were suddenly not worth the paper they were printed on, so he went to work full time for his father in the building industry in New York City. The new couple moved into a fifth-floor walk-up in a building owned by my grandfather on Bryant Avenue in a Jewish neighborhood in the south Bronx. The Great Depression played them at least one lucky card in that they were able to furnish their apartment with finely handcrafted furniture they bought at rock-bottom prices from dealers who were going bankrupt. They picked out a Spanish oak dining room table with hob-nailed leather-backed chairs, a handsome carved mahogany sofa and matching armchair, an eight-piece Italian marquetry bedroom suite with matching baroque mirrors, and bureaus topped with inch-thick Carrara marble, all of it heavy enough to sink a ship. In its very solidity, its dense resistance to loss or diminishment, the furniture set down an Old World standard that would persist through the decades, and a heaviness that would increase, stubborn, dour, irremediable. It would follow them from New York to Arizona and back again to New York. It would finally outlast them to be handed down to their children, engendering quarrels and setting one generation against another. It augured at the outset their mutual misery, in each other and in life itself.

He would be subject to chronic depressions and end up disappointed in almost everything: business, marriage, family, the American Dream, the human condition. She would be subject to manic rages, exacerbated by a mental disorder that would go untreated and undiagnosed until late in life, long after he was gone. "Your mother is like a pressure cooker," he would say. "The heat builds up and builds up until, bah-bah-bah-BOOM, there she blows!" Whenever she would explode, he would button himself into his overcoat, clap on his fedora, and walk resolutely out the door to wait out the storm.

I don't know what went wrong with that marriage. I know their love was genuine, at least at the start. But my father was an Old World Italian patriarch; he made sure he kept the reins tight on his high-spirited wife, and I can only guess that, passed from a domineering mother to a domineering husband, sat on and fettered all her life, she simply rebelled. No matter what my father decided, on principle, my mother was opposed. Even on those special occasions when he'd present her with a double strand of pearls or a diamond pendant, she'd always find a way to spoil it and throw it back at him. Their marriage was an alpha/alpha pact, a standoff, with each of them determined to keep the other from gaining an inch. By the time we were living in Scarsdale, things had gotten so bad between them that I once watched them spit in each other's faces right in front of me. My mother spat first.

"I'd rather fight than switch," she used to say with a swagger, borrowing the quip from the famous Tareyton cigarette ad that always featured a woman with a black eye. Forever at a disadvantage in the power struggle, she fought dirty and sometimes resorted to sabotage. I remember how she cackled the day my father, ever dignified, came in through the front door with his head held high and suddenly took off, stepping onto a rug that had abruptly turned into a flying carpet on top of her newly waxed floor. "He had the rug pulled right out from under him," she'd scream every time she told that story. My mother had a wicked sense of humor. But it was hell living with the two of them and their forty-year cockfight.

Once or twice a year, on a Sunday morning, my father would walk into the kitchen with his beat-up leather-bound copy of *The Golden Treasury of English Poetry* tucked under his arm. This was a ritual we all knew by heart, and the repertoire never varied. Standing in the middle of the room, he would commence a recitation of his favorite poems, always beginning with "The Highwayman," which he followed up with Gray's "Elegy in a Country Churchyard," Wordsworth's "Ode to Toussaint l'Ouverture," and an obscure little poem called "Day." I think it was by Robert Browning. His deep voice would reverberate, rising as it grew more excited, "Faster and more fast / o'er night cup's brim, / day boils at last, BOILS PURE GOLD." And there at the climax his hand shot up with one oracular finger that pointed.

Seated at the kitchen table in a corner of the room, my mother was poised and ready, with her darts all lined up. "The Highwayman came riding, riding UP to the old inn door," my father would begin, always with the same inflection. "Up to the old inn DOOR," my mother, the elocution teacher, would correct. He would lower his book and scowl, glaring over his horn-rimmed glasses at his wife, his complexion darkening like the sky before a storm. "Teacher, teacher," he would hiss, "why can't you ever shut up?"

Every time he said "Toussaint l'Ouverture," no matter how hard he tried, he always massacred the French. I could feel him cringe as he approached it, knowing full well he was heading straight into an ambush. "Too-cent LOO-vercher." He hesitated, expecting the blow. Miss Prissy, the French teacher, never let it go. " Tee-OOH-saw "Lee-OOH-vair-tee-OOOER," she drew it out, pursing her lips. And on it went. My father would rhapsodize and soar; my mother would pull his chain and bring him smack back down to earth. He was as hot as she was cold; as much as I loved him for his ardor, I hated her for her exactitude.

It wasn't until much later that I came to understand this ritual as a kind of dance, a pas de deux between my father the poet and my mother the critic, each indispensable to the other. As it turned out, I needed them both. From my father, I learned the heat and art of transport. From my mother, cold planetary detachment. He taught me to love beautiful language. What she modeled was clarity and a necessary reserve. She could sling her barbs, be merciless and exacting, but only by keeping her distance. It was a lesson that went deep, repeated year after year like a seasonal liturgy. It served me well. Later on, when I became a poet myself, it taught me how to ride out the elation/depression roller coaster ride that inevitably attends the writing of a new poem. Then, when I entered public broadcasting and became a radio talk show host, it taught me how to be both inside and outside the conversation at the same time. I could do-se-do with a guest whose work I admired, but I also knew when to pose the question with the razor edge, expose the flaw in the argument, keep my distance, and move on.

The roar of the Hoover, the stink of Lysol, the endless array of toxic agents she amassed that were stashed away in dark and secret places, malodorous purgatives and medicinals locked behind the bathroom cabinet: alcohol, mercurochrome and iodine, witch hazel and spirits of camphor; naphtha, ammonia, and benzene underneath the kitchen sink where a tall brown bottle was kept, marked with a skull and crossbones; this was my mother's arsenal. Allied with things that had names like Arm & Hammer and Twenty-Mule-Team Borax, my mother took on power and a lethal aura.

When we fell ill, she melted methane crystals into a porcelain basin and made us kneel over the stove to breathe in the swimmy fumes; she rubbed us down with purple Vicks and put us to bed with mustard-colored woolen rags plastered across our chests; when our fingers got infected, she made us dip them into boiling water laced with boric acid; she painted our thumbs with something red and bitter as gall that burned our lips and tongues and forever spoiled the pleasure of sucking.

She had a special fondness for mothballs and used to drop them into odd places like the china cabinet and the back of the spinet piano. One Easter Sunday, with the family gathered in the dining room around the heavy Spanish oak table that was set with silver cut-glass goblets, my father lifted his wine to offer the toast, took a sip, spluttered and choked on the little white ball floating in the burgundy. "You and your damn mothballs," he spat, setting the glass down in a hurry.

It was "Goddamn this" and "Jesus Christ Almighty that" in the chronic rages of our household, and I, the pious Catholic schoolgirl, was mortified. Everything about my home life seemed profane. My mother was nothing like the Blessed Virgin Mary the nuns taught us to pray to or the virgin martyr saints we were supposed to emulate. These were all heroic and larger than life, but my mother's life was small. I watched my father get dressed every morning in one of his Rogers Peet suits, put on his fedora and his overcoat, and set out into the great world. His life had purpose and moment. Her life was degraded. I watched her crawl around on her hands and knees cleaning the house, sweating as she wiped down the cellar steps or cleaned up the dog's mess, lifting her head to lash out in fury at one of us from time to time. I asked myself, how could this abject thing, this bestial servile creature that goes about on all fours, be my mother? I was an Ariel trapped by Sorax, the witch who was Caliban's mother. I wanted to be a missionary in Africa or China, lead a crusade, or start a new religious order. All my mother wanted was a clean house. We children, with our messy hobbies and our sloppy dogs and our friends who were forever trooping through the house with their muddy boots, were the enemy of her empire. This was the 1950s, a whole decade before Betty Friedan would ignite a revolution among American housewives, but it was clear to me even then, judging from the way my mother behaved, that the menial work to which the underclass of women had been consigned rendered them subhuman, crippled their souls, and kept them in a permanent state of humiliation and outrage.

Cleaning house was my mother's way of avenging her ruined life. She cleaned with a furious energy that never abated, the work itself refueling her anger so her heels went slapping up and down the halls against her sling-back shoes long into the night. My sister and I were her Saturday slatterns. How I hated aping her servility, swabbing floors on my hands and knees, dusting baseboards and the rungs under chairs that were seldom sat in, vacuuming up specks from the oriental carpets, the caretaker of my mother's museum. It was all the labor of Sisyphus, no sooner completed than repeated.

When summer finally came, my mother would invariably choose one of the hottest days in late June when it was ninety degrees and 95 percent humidity to decide it was time to reline the bedroom closets. All day I would be made to stand on a slippery stepladder in the swelter of the closet, woozy from the stifling heat and the stink of the tarpaper, my nose just inches from the ceiling while lines of sweat crawled down my face and neck and the thumb tacks between my clenched lips kept dropping to the floor, my arms aching from holding up the heavy hammer and the big unwieldy sheets of tarpaper. Meanwhile, to add to my torment, the sounds of children at play would come wafting through the open window where the ancient tulip tree was in full bloom.

I hated housecleaning for most of my life. I was so bad, in fact, that it finally became a matter of official court record. In a hearing during my divorce in Kentucky, with custody of my then two-year-old son at stake, my father-in-law testified that as a young housewife I would start to vacuum and abruptly leave off, throwing the vacuum down and retreating to my study to work on a poem. My mother, who was brought from New York to testify on my behalf, chose this occasion to level the playing field. With head held high and one eyebrow cocked, she damned me with faint praise, looking down her nose to tell the judge, "Yes, my daughter can keep house . . . but her standards aren't up to mine." After a week of testimony, the judge handed down his decision. Finding me "intelligent, ambitious, and therefore unfit," he awarded custody of our son, Giancarlo, to his father. I was completely devastated. With my father's help I filed an appeal, and two years later, the Kentucky State Supreme Court overturned the lower court's decision, ruling in my favor.

When I was nearing twelve and beginning to develop breasts, my mother sat me down at the kitchen table and prepared to tell me the facts of life, acting under duress from my older sister, Rosemary. "Jeannie," she began with a deep sigh, "I'm sorry to have to tell you this. Men have it easy in this life, but somehow the good Lord in His wisdom decided that women should have to suffer." Another sigh. "So we all have this cross to bear . . ." Needless to say, when my period finally arrived, I was completely terrified, refused to say a word to anybody, and rigged myself a makeshift sanitary belt with crooked safety pins and my gold Girl Scout scarf.

My mother never nursed us. She had inverted nipples, a genetic defect I was fortunate not to inherit. Nursing my son gave me my first surge of confidence as a mother, something my mother never knew. When my brother was born dehydrated and started to die in the hospital, the nurses pumped my mother's breasts so hard they squeezed out blood instead of milk. But I doubt my mother would have liked the messy business anyway. She was fastidious. Even the feeling of raw meat on her hands when she rolled meatballs repulsed her. "I was never a cow," she used to say with a hint of pride, as if that lifted her above the rank of ordinary run-of-the-mill mammal.

To declare something "ordinary" was my mother's kiss of death, an immutable judgment that was pitiless and permanent. Franco-American and Chef Boyardee spaghetti sauce, brands favored by my friends, were ordinary. Baloney sandwiches were ordinary. So were the shanty Irish, and the old gray hooded sweatshirt I used to like to wear. "That's *ordinary*," she said, after she came to live with us in Wisconsin, where the absence of style is an unspoken virtue, pursing her lips to frame the word in a flat toneless voice that I found devastating.

My mother loved fringes and lace mitts and long-seamed silk stockings. She once had a hat with a pheasant feather so long it grazed the gray felt ceiling of my father's Packard whenever she turned her head.

She knew how to play the coquette. One night she went off to a dance with a mink tail wrapped around her wrist and a mink head threaded around her neck. "Heads or tails," she winked, going out the door, "I win!" She wore a dress with cougars racing across her chest to her fortieth wedding anniversary, and a long black leather coat with a white curly lamb lining that stuck out like a ruff to my father's funeral. She looked a little like Eva Gabor in that coat. Even Father Tallantino, the priest who said the Mass, noticed it. "Mama has class," he said.

More than a condemnation, *ordinary* was a stigma to my mother. It must have been the nightmare of second-generation Italian immigrants to be linked by their clothing, their furniture, or their food to *'a miseria*— the poverty that clung like fog to the little mountain villages of southern Italy from which they had so recently escaped. "They don't even have a pot to piss in!" This was a phrase I heard a lot growing up. Pots were important. Furniture was important. Mink coats were important. *Deve fare una bella figura.* You had to make a good impression, cut a handsome figure, keep up appearances. This was the inflexible rubric the immigrants brought with them from the old country. They took pride in ownership. Furnishing a home was more than an obligation incurred by marriage; it was a social virtue. If you could point to Italian marquetry furniture in your bedroom, a satin bedspread overlaid with Brussels lace like my mother had, a crystal cellerette in the living room that looked like it was auctioned out of a Claudette Colbert movie, if you walked on oriental rugs and had an oil painting hanging above your mantel, these things all had the power to lift the stigma. They gave evidence of taste, education, and good breeding. They made it clear that the contagion of *'a miseria* was not heritable, had not pursued them across the Atlantic Ocean.

And so it was that my mother formed her attachment to things, rather than to us. "Wood needs to be fed," she would say as she rubbed rich oils into the furniture like Magdalene anointing the feet of Jesus. "Orientals have to breathe." "Linen dances." But when my brother made it into *Who's Who,* all she could say was, "Huh. Imagine that. And he doesn't even know what's what."

There was a deep insecurity surrounding our presence in Scarsdale. We were unwelcome gatecrashers, the first Italian family to move into the Crane Berkeley, a snooty enclave in suburbia where, in contrast to the garrulous and vulgar Bronx, nobody talked to their neighbors, hung their laundry out to dry, or cluttered up the stoop to gossip. My mother was nervous about all this. She tried her best to beat the Bronx out of us, to clean up our diction and curb our brawling tendencies, but she herself could be heard all over the neighborhood whenever she called me home to supper, "Jeeea-neeeee," her harridan screech rising in a steep crescendo until it reached a pitch that was as shrill as a siren. I learned a lot from that call. No matter how far Dominick, my little boy, strayed, he could always hear me call him home, and so could the neighbors, and I could always hear my mother's voice crowing inside my own. So indelible was the voiceprint in the track I laid down that a parrot that lived in the house next door to us continued calling Dominick home long after we had moved away.

All the while we lived in the house on Taunton Road East a pall hung over us. When I was fourteen, my father lost his business and went bankrupt. For a year or more all he did was sit heavily in his carved mahogany armchair in the living room smoking and brooding while creditors knocked on the door and his alcoholic brother, for some mysterious reason that went forever unexplained, repeatedly threatened to kill us. Depressed as he was, my father was forbearing with his brother. Family ties were sacred. But my mother cracked under the strain. One night she picked up a pitchfork in the garage and headed for the car, intending to drive to Pelham Manor where my uncle lived like a lord to put an end to his harassment once and for all.

These were the years when my mother failed my father most profoundly. She blamed him for all of our misfortunes, heaping hot coals on his head to fan the flames of his mortification. That was when I hated her the most. She left a hole in the place that should have been occupied by a loving wife, and I felt compelled to fill it.

One summer night, I found my father sitting alone in the dark on the patio. "Jeannie," he said to me in his gravest tone, his voice shaping the darkness, "I'm leaving your mother." "Then I'm going with you," I vowed, swearing my allegiance without a second thought. Meanwhile, my mother was creeping across the Karastan carpet in the living room like a hunted animal. Eavesdropping at the window, down on all fours again in that posture I loathed, she was spying on us. To me she had always been abject, but seeing her sink like this to the level of a common snoop, I found her utterly contemptible.

The next morning my father was still with us. He got up, put on his clothes, and went off to work as usual. The crisis had passed over us like the angel of death. But I was disappointed. Everything went on as before.

My parents left New York in their seventies after the three of us had left home and started families of our own. They drove all the way across the country to their new retirement home in Sun City, Arizona, dragging their precious household cargo with them in a moving van. I took Giancarlo with me to visit them while I was going through my first divorce and found them more miserable than ever. Trapped in the house all day like prisoners in a cell, they did nothing but squabble. My mother busied herself dusting the house and baking ceramic frogs in her pottery class; my father, having nothing better to do, climbed up on the roof to hose it down for an hour every morning, and joined the Critical Issues Club.

Sealed off from the heat, the house seemed like a bank vault. My father had always built the stout houses we lived in to last a millennium. In Scarsdale, our house was like a fortress with a twenty-foot retaining wall. Now he went about muttering, knocking on the drywall and pulling the pressed sawdust drawers out of their sockets, while he grumbled that he was living in a paper house. At night, my parents slept underneath the marquetry crucifix in their same Italian marquetry bed while tumbleweed rolled up against the white wall of the Del Webb house and the howling of coyotes came through a crack in the bedroom window.

My father called me very early one morning after I went back to Kentucky, his voice a hoarse whisper coming over the telephone. "Jeannie, I'm leaving your mother," he said.

"Daddy," I told him, "it's too late."

My mother suffered her first stroke while my parents were still living in Arizona, and then, when she fell ill with Desert Valley Fever, my father decided it was time to go back home. So they packed everything up all over again and moved back across the country to New York one last time. Soon after they returned, my father got a diagnosis of cancer of the esophagus. He had gone home to die.

The loss of my father came as a great shock to me, made all the more devastating by the emotional withdrawal he underwent during his final days. It was a rude awakening, something my family therapist was to refer to as "the kick upstairs." My father and I had always been close. "You'll always be my baby," he had told me often enough, sometimes to my chagrin, but I had always imagined a tender deathbed scene between us. Instead, when the time came, he pushed me away. "What's the matter with you, Jeannie?" he snapped when I ventured too close. "Don't you know I have pneumonia?" On the day before he died, as I stood beside his hospital bed, he turned to my mother and asked, "Has the doctor slapped her yet?" There I was, a grown woman in my thirties with a child of my own, but in my father's mind, I hadn't even been slapped yet.

My father's death came as an even greater shock to my mother, but one from which she seemed to recover rather handily. We had to hold her down to keep her from climbing into my father's coffin at the wake, but six months later, she had joined a chorus line. During those first six months of widowhood, it slowly dawned on her that she was free for the first time in her life. My father had tried to discourage her from getting her driver's license, claiming that women are constitutionally incapable of driving. She had even sheered off a whole block of parked cars while she was learning. Now she raced her blue and white Ford Fairlane all over Westchester County, gunning it in erratic bursts and spurts as she went flying around blind curves and roaring up and down the highways.

She remembered the little girl who wanted to join the circus. She remembered the tango, and the great gams she could still kick without my father's cinder block feet to weigh her down. She remembered how she had brought down the house playing Bottom in *A Midsummer's Night's Dream* back in high school, how Mrs. Gable, her mother's best friend, had laughed so hard she had to peel off her girdle in the ladies' room. So she joined a local theater group and got picked to play the Widow McFarlane in a reading of Edgar Lee Master's *Spoon River Anthology*. And even though she nodded off during the performance and had to be nudged awake, she still managed to deliver her lines right on cue. My mother was a trooper.

When Halloween came around that year, she shook the mothballs out of her black wool academic gown, dressed up in a mask and a black peaked hat with long grisly locks, and went about town trick-or-treating. Somebody snapped her photograph while she was still in costume, and it turned up in the window of the local drugstore. It was a magnificent full-length likeness in which she appeared relaxed and smiling, holding a basket and leaning against a tree as if she had just emerged from the Black Forest. There was nothing wicked or even mischievous in her smile; it wasn't a leer or a grin; it was almost sweet, in fact, a resigned sort of half-smile that seemed to say, yes, this is who I am.

Playing the witch was a role my mother was to return to again and again each Halloween. One year she became so identified with her costume that she refused to give it up. She wore it into the second week in November and shocked everyone by showing up for a luncheon at the Westchester Country Club in full witch's regalia. My sister was mortified, but I rejoiced. Mom had cut loose.

What neither of us suspected at the time was that these were the telltale signs of mania. What followed was a cycle of depression so severe it ended in a suicide attempt. The first inkling that something was awry came when she started selling off her precious possessions. She drove long distances to out-of-the-way antique dealers and consignment shops, trading off an alabaster sculpture or a treasured lamp for twenty-five dollars. She became obsessed with money, convinced she had fallen prey to ruthless con men who were taking her to the cleaners and the poorhouse. Worse, she blamed herself. She knew nothing about money, of course. My father had always played the Master of Mystery, handling the family finances. He didn't believe in buying insurance, and she was bewildered dealing with brokers, trying to make sense of a labyrinth of stocks and bonds. She became suspicious and paranoid, haunted by the specter of penury and a future in which she imagined herself living out her days as a bag lady on the street. It was a delusion we couldn't shake, no matter how much contradictory evidence we presented.

It was while she was in this distressed state of mind that my mother came to visit me in Wisconsin. I was living in Madison by this time, working as a broadcast journalist for public radio and trying my best to raise two sons as a single mother. My mother hadn't been sleeping. She became disoriented while she was staying with us. She took to walking around in circles in the living room, shaking her head and wringing her hands while she mumbled nonsense. She reminded me of a lame horse who had wandered away from its carousel and had gotten hopelessly lost. I was frightened. I took her to the university hospital to be evaluated by a team of medical experts who prescribed sleeping pills to allay her insomnia and advised me to send her back home. I followed their advice. That was Memorial Day weekend. My sister called on Monday, Memorial Day, to say she had found my mother passed out in her condo, having swallowed the whole bottle of Dalmane. "Eliminate the burden," she had written in her journal on the preceding day, while seated at her French writing desk with its chased silver inkwell and ostrich feather quill. And then she added the single word "Reprehensible."

She was hospitalized for three months. The depression never lifted. She was allergic to lithium, refused psychotherapy, wanted nothing to do with electroshock treatments, and was finally discharged into my sister's keeping at the end of summer, as depressed as ever. The downward spiral continued. Most days she never bothered to get dressed, refused to take her medicine, and spent most of her time in bed. She was locked in a power struggle with my sister, who was at her wit's end. When I visited, my mother sat on the staircase in her nightgown and threw her legs up in the air, howling and rolling her eyes like a wounded animal. She was mad as a coot.

On the morning of the Friday after Thanksgiving, George, my sister's husband, an elegant man in his early fifties, got up, showered and shaved as usual, ate his customary breakfast of toast and soft-boiled eggs, and strode out of the house on his long legs. On his way downtown, he stopped at his favorite coffee shop for a second cup of coffee and headed out the door, his newspaper tucked under his arm, shoulder to shoulder with a friend who was telling him a joke. Once outside, he suddenly stopped laughing, dropped to the sidewalk, and turned blue, dead of a massive heart attack. My sister was given the news by her brother-in-law an hour later when she stopped at the family bakery to pick up a loaf of bread.

This was a genuine crisis. I saw what needed to be done. At bottom, I knew my mother was a scrapper. I figured I could rely on her survivor's instincts, so I hatched a bold plan and made a leap of faith. I flew to New York and brought my mother back to Wisconsin, moving her into the second bedroom in our tiny eight-hundred-square-foot ranch house. Giancarlo moved into the basement, and Dominick, who was still quite young, moved in with me. It was hardly an ideal situation for rehab, but somehow, over the course of the next six months, my kids adapted to living under the same roof with their strict grandmother, and my mother slowly improved, as I slowly regressed.

She found fault with everything. She grumbled over my housekeeping and claimed that the neighbors shunned us because it was so bad. "Anybody who walks past this house looks straight ahead," she declared. "They can't even bring themselves to look at it, it's such a disgrace." She scrubbed the kitchen sink until it morphed from gray to white. She polished the chrome, and tackled the grimy windows I had never touched. The house began to sparkle. She criticized my parenting. I was too lenient. "You let that child run wild." "That child" was Dominick, my younger son, an exuberant free spirit she was determined to tame. Their clashes were titanic. Once, after going out to see the movie *Moonstruck* with a few friends, I called to check in. "Mom! Mom! Come home!" Giancarlo, my fifteen-year-old, pleaded into the telephone. "Nana and Dominick have really gotten into it! The pot is boiling, and they're throwing the pasta at each other!"

She boxed with Wizzy, our cat, another free spirit, and laughed when he stood up on his hind feet, hissing and spitting as he stretched out his claws. Dominick loved to draw and paint. I suggested she buy him an easel for a present. "An easel!" she exclaimed. "I shudder to think what that child would do with an easel." Without thinking, I shot back, "Boy, it's a good thing I didn't have *you* for a mother."

I took to hiding out with Giancarlo in his room in the basement just to escape from the sound of her carping. I sat on his bed and refused to answer when she called down the stairs in that same siren voice of hers, "Jeanniieeee?" There I was, sixteen all over again. One morning I woke up and caught a glimpse of my mother just as she was emerging from her room across the hall in her flowered, shorty nightgown. I noticed she had Dominick's Viking helmet clapped onto her head. The helmet had slipped sideways so the horns were cockeyed. *Ah*, I thought to myself, *she must be getting better.*

She began making incremental gains. She went out to lunch at the Copper Top with a Sicilian woman who had once run a famous speak-easy. I introduced her to a broker who called her the Admiral and took her out to supper clubs as he sorted through her tangled finances. She kept her appointments with her doctor, a woman internist from New York who wore smart brown alligator pumps, spoke in my mother's own New Yorker's accent, and, best of all, agreed to treat her depression without involving a psychiatrist.

About this time a wise old friend of mine, a psychologist who was keeping close tabs on our family, took me aside. "It's time to move Mama into her own apartment," he advised. I listened carefully. I talked it over with my mother. Reluctantly, she agreed to the move. We started touring retirement centers. Now it was Mom who went backward.

I recorded one of her rambling monologues:

> Where do I fit?
> Where do I fit?
> A terrible misfit.
> A terrible misfit.
> Bunch of rich bitches.
> Miserable hole in the wall.
> She can't take me either.
> This is just too much for her.
> I'm too much.
> I'm too much.
> Where am I going to be any good?
> No place.
> No place.
> Not any good.
> What happens next?
> I don't know.
> I can't figure it out.
> What do I think?
> I can't think.

One morning she climbed into bed with me. "Are you scared, Mom?"
"Yes, I'm scared."

"What are you scared of?"

"Taxes." A pause. And then, "Forgive me for being so weak."

And so my mother became the only Italian American resident living at Oakwood Village besides Joe Dimaggio's sister-in-law, who had changed her name. Oakwood was only fifteen minutes away from us by car; it had a good reputation, and there were venerable cathedral oak trees all over the grounds. Nevertheless, the thought of placing my dyed-in-the-wool New Yorker mother in a Lutheran retirement home in Wisconsin made me uneasy. In truth, I felt like a traitor.

"Oak would, if he could," my mother quipped after she had met some of her new male neighbors. She moved into the Towers, Oak-wood's independent living facility, on a day in June, wearing a black mask that said, "Best witches to you." I worried about that. "It's June, Mom. People are going to think you're crazy." "Shh," she said. "I don't want anybody to be frightened. I'm hiding from the whole situation."

It wasn't long before she called to announce in an excited voice that she had a date with a man who had asked her to dinner. But then she called back to report that he had stood her up. She made friends with a man on her floor who was over a hundred and had a habit of reciting the whole of *The Rhyme of the Ancient Mariner* whenever anyone stopped him in the hall. He called her his little Rosy. "I go to bed with Arthur Itis," she told anybody who would listen. "I sleep with Ben Gay. I get up with a jerk." "I've had three strokes but I haven't struck out yet." "I'm in-destructible." She tucked a little stuffed bear into the back pocket of her slacks and paraded around asking, "How do you like my bear behind?"

There were mishaps. Struggling with her walker, she got stuck in the elevator doors and ended up in the hospital. Another time, she got an electric shock from a lamp with faulty wiring that threw her to the floor and made her white hair stand straight on end. After that, she ran around for a week telling everybody, "I'm a shocking old lady. I'm all charged up."

To make herself feel more at home in her "miserable little hole in the wall," she pasted cartoons and poems and pictures of animals all over her galley kitchen. She bonded with a pet cockatoo we bought for her birthday. Blinky's cage hung right over the dining room table, and she didn't seem to mind when he kicked seeds all over the floor and the table. After her outsized furniture arrived from New York, the little apartment seemed choked and claustrophobic, but I liked it. It was a treat to eat her dinners at the old oak table and lounge on the carved mahogany couch that still had the same silk tassels I had played with as a child. Something of the old order had reasserted itself.

All in all, my mother made a remarkable adjustment to living in a Lutheran community, among the "bunch of rich bitches and farmers' wives" she had so feared. Soon after settling in, she joined a Bible study group, something Roman Catholics aren't famous for, and when I picked her up after one of the meetings, she asked, much to my amazement, "Who ever gave the pope the idea he could tell us what to do?" Because she had always wanted to teach young children, she began volunteering as a teacher's aide in Dominick's second-grade classroom, where the children adopted her as Grandma Rose. Feeling useful again was strong medicine, and she was faithful to her new job, showing up every Tuesday morning for three years at Blessed Sacrament School until she could no longer drag her walker through the ice and snow. She began reading to the blind once a week at Hebron, Oakwood's nursing home, where she made friends with a woman named Helen. One day, Helen squeezed my mother's hand so hard it felt like a death grip, and then she died right on the spot with no one but my mother by her bedside. My mother was upset for weeks after that. "Don't you ever put me in Hebron," she warned. "Don't you put me in Hebron."

☙

Oh, those poor people living in Nebraska! What they suffered! They didn't even have a house to live in. They had nothing but a miserable hole in the ground. Imagine that!" My mother had been reading *My Antonia* in her literature class. The two of us were cruising through the back roads of Dane County on a typical Saturday in early summer, the rolling cornfields and the bright chartreuse of newly planted alfalfa rows stretching out on both sides of the road as far as the eye could see. This was what my mother called "God's country." Displaced from her own urban landscape, she knew about America's immigrant past only from her own experience growing up in New York City in the welter of Irish and Italians, Germans and Jews, who came through Ellis Island to settle in Manhattan. Only then, through her reading, was she learning about the pioneer history of the American heartland. She was intent as she told me about the plight of this poor Bohemian family struggling to survive their first brutal winter in Nebraska with nothing but a mud dugout for shelter. I was surprised at her level of interest. This was, after all, the same mother who had never once taken me to a library as a child, the same mother who had never once, that I could recall, sat down to read a single book, who had even clucked in disapproval over the "storybooks" I devoured as a girl that kept me from the mundane tasks of family life. Italian girls of my mother's generation were actively discouraged from intellectual pursuits. Now in her eighties, my mother was discovering Willa Cather and Tillie Olsen for the first time, and it was she who introduced them to me.

In Tillie Olsen's heart-wrenching short story "I Stand Here Ironing," a working-class mother ruminates over her struggles to raise a child alone, lamenting over the daughter whose gifts will never come to fruition. The story ends with her bitter truth: "My wisdom came too late. . . . So all that is in her will not bloom—but in how many does it?"

My grandmother used to stand in her kitchen pummeling the ironing board so hard the whole scaffolding would shake, and I can never forget standing eye-level at my mother's ironing board watching her blue eyes go icy as she threatened to scald me in one of her white-hot rages. I thought about my mother's unlived life. I thought about my own life, pressed between responsibilities for an aging mother and two young sons, the mistakes I had made raising my sons; my mother's mistakes raising me. I read on.

I discovered a perfect description of the final years of my parents' marriage in Tillie Olsen's story "Tell Me a Riddle," the narrative of an old woman dying of cancer. It begins, "For forty-seven years they had been married. How deep back the stubborn, gnarled roots of the quarrel reached, no one could say—but only now, when tending to the needs of others no longer shackled them together, the roots swelled up visible, split the earth between them, and the tearing shook even to the children, long since grown."

Reading on, I recognized my mother in Tillie Olsen's protagonist, now living in a little apartment, having found "tranquility from having the house no longer an enemy, for it stayed clean. . . . Being able at last to live within, and not move to the rhythms of others." In cultivating her mind, was my mother learning at last how to live within? Here we were, mother and daughter, for the first time in our lives actually engaged in a conversation about the ideas found in books. Reading Olsen together, I discovered that the two of us took delight in the same sense of irony, the same clean truth told without sentiment, the same peppered repartee that reminded us both of her famous sparring matches with my father. I looked at her in amazement, as if I were seeing her for the first time.

And so we met, my mother and I, in the land of story, finding common ground in the circle of wagons around the same campfire. Language became the thing that entwined us, the tongue we shared. And my mother, I came to realize, was herself a great storyteller. On our weekend excursions that took us through the plowed fields and sun-drenched prairies of Wisconsin, she lost her inhibitions, forgot we were mother and daughter, and wrapped me in a skein of stories. She told me about her uncle Dominick and their special bond, raised in the same household with only a handful of years between them. "When my uncle entered medical school," she said with pride, "he used to take me to all the dances. My mother wouldn't let me take off my long woolen underwear, so I had to wear it underneath my dress, and once I danced all night and worked up such a sweat, I caught pneumonia."

"He told me I had to protect him from all the man-hungry nurses. Ooh, those nurses! They were just like wolves! All they wanted was to get their claws into him. But he was too smart for them. Once he asked my mother if he could marry me . . ." Her voice trailed off and she hesitated, thinking perhaps she had gone too far. I was aghast. Marriage between first cousins was not all that uncommon in Italian families — dispensations were easy to get from the bishop's chancery — but between an uncle and a niece? This smacked to me of real incest.

"What did Nanny say?" I asked, incredulous. "Oh, she wouldn't hear of it, of course." My mother's face got long and grave as she looked up at me with her sapphire eyes gone pale. "I had no idea he had that kind of feeling for me," she said, looking far away. "I didn't feel that way about him." But she was tentative as she said this, and I was not at all convinced. "Then, when I married Steve," she went on, "my uncle got so discouraged with the whole thing, he just gave up and married that witch, Jenny P."

Another Jenny, my great aunt was the only Sicilian ever allowed into our southern Italian family. In marrying her, Uncle Dominick breached the most fundamental law of the clan. Sicilians were not to be trusted. Jenny, it was always assumed, had won this prince of the realm by trickery and connivance. For someone coming from an immigrant community, my great uncle with his medical degree and his prospects was considered quite a catch. Everybody said Jenny didn't deserve him. But she reaped his spoils as he established his medical practice in Manhattan and became a renowned surgeon.

We used to visit Aunt Jenny and Uncle Dominick in their Fifth Avenue apartment on Sunday afternoons, where a doorman in uniform wearing white gloves would greet us solemnly, tip his cap, and usher us into the foyer. We trooped into the elevator where the bellman, also in white gloves, slid the metal mesh of the elevator door shut with a click and rode us up to the fifth floor. Uncle Dominick had a quality of gravitas. He was a tall man who had to stoop from his height to greet us. He was kind and soft-spoken, and to me he always seemed a little bit sad. I liked him a lot. He was my godfather, and that meant that every Christmas he always gave me two gold charms for my bracelet, one for my December birthday and one for Christmas. The year I turned five, he presented me with a brand new Royal portable typewriter, almost as if he knew I would become a writer. How I loved that typewriter. It served me like a faithful friend for over fifty years; I took it to college with me, wrote all of my term papers on it and, later, two books of poetry. When I was faced with a custody hearing during my divorce in Kentucky, and my father told me, "Show your teeth!" I thought of my typewriter.

Whenever there was anything seriously wrong with us, my mother used to take us downtown to Uncle Dominick's office on Fifty-Eighth Street to be examined. This always happened with my father's benediction. "Take her to see your uncle," he would say. But then, when I was twelve years old, it was my mother who fell ill. She had a hysterectomy, and when complications set in, she couldn't seem to recover. She kept hemorrhaging and went back and forth to the hospital by ambulance several times.

"When I was in New York City Hospital, trying to die," she started the story one afternoon, "my uncle came into the room to check up on me. He knew what kind of shape I was in. He had wanted to perform the operation, but the hospital wouldn't permit it, knowing he was my uncle. He looked at the chart and crossed out a lot of things and wrote some things down, and changed the orders all around. Then he changed all the tubing and when he was finished, he turned to walk out of the room, and just as he was leaving he put his hand behind his back like this, and waved to me backhanded, as if he was waving good-bye. He went out through the door and disappeared around the corner, and just then I heard this big thud in the hall.

"Overnight, I started to get better. When the nurses came in the next morning, they were amazed. I was on my way back to the land of the living. They had really thought I was a goner. It wasn't until a whole month later, after I got home from the hospital, that I found out what happened. Right after my uncle left the room, he had a massive coronary and fell down in the hall. He died right there. That was the thud I heard. Nobody dared tell me my uncle had died. I missed the wake and the funeral and everything. Jenny blamed me, but I didn't even know what was going on. They hid it from me. Poor man. He died of a broken heart. He was only fifty-three years old. He was just so disappointed in everybody."

I was wide-eyed. Coming from my mother, this story entered me like liquid gold. I tried to imagine my uncle dealing with the powers on the other side, exchanging his life force for hers, the energy passing between them like a transfusion from one side to the other in the middle of the night. She was the only woman he had ever truly loved. He had finally found a way to deliver the love that had been denied.

"Did Daddy know how Uncle Dominick felt about you?" I asked. "Oh, my uncle didn't like it at all when I started seeing Steve," she told me. "He raised all sorts of objections. One night while my uncle was still going to night school, Steve waited for him outside NYU. When he left the building, they had a fight right there in the alley, and Steve knocked him out cold."

Now that the floodgates were open, there was no stopping her. The story took on its own momentum, revelation following on revelation, and it all came pouring out, regardless of propriety. She suspected my father's fidelity. "I could never pin anything on him," she confided, "but he wrapped himself around a lot of skirts." Again, I was shocked. She went on, "He used to keep a gun in the house. Once I got so mad, I went and got my hands on that gun and I tried to shoot him with it. But I couldn't do it. My hand shook so bad, I dropped the gun." She reports this cleanly, without a tinge of remorse. We are driving through the Wisconsin countryside, the air is pungent with the smell of earth that has been newly plowed and spread with fresh manure. I look over at her. She is staring straight ahead. "I'd have liked to kill your husband too," she confesses. "That son of a gun. He doesn't deserve to live. If I got my hands on a gun, I'd shoot him right now if I had half a chance."

The hairs on the back of my neck prickled and sprang up as I took in the full import of what my mother had just said. My face and neck flushed hot as a chill ran down my spine. By this time in my life I knew a thing or two about murderous rage. I had been through two divorces, two custody fights, one of which lasted so long it ran right into the next. I remember the triggers, the nerves stretched taut as tightrope wires, the whump at the back of the brain, the primitive urge to pick up a shovel and bury it deep in somebody's skull. The same mercurial quicksilver rush of blood that flowed through my mother's veins flowed through mine. I stepped on the gas, gunning the motor as the cattle stood and stared, drooling as the car went whizzing by. We were outlaws on the road together, my mother and I.

At Oakwood, she got mean and started throwing her weight around, brandishing her cane, her walker, and her wit like weapons. She chewed out the maintenance man. She made a scene at the bank, where she berated one of the tellers, calling her an asshole and a jackass and bragging that she knew how to swear in five languages. A member of the staff called me to complain and ended the telephone conversation with the vague threat of eviction. Mother was intimidating the other residents. She spoiled a bus trip to a Swiss village. She spent over three hundred dollars at the Trash and Treasure Fair. This meant more ratty mink coats and crummy vacuum cleaners and straw placemats and note cards with puppies and ducks and maybe even another sofa, all of which would be unloaded on me. I cringed. And yet, in spite of my embarrassment, I was still proud of her. She would not go gentle into that good night.

During her second Christmas at Oakwood, in a misguided attempt to impress her neighbors, she decided to throw a big bash, using my birthday as an excuse. She signed out the party room, ordered a slew of food from the Kitchen Hearth along with two huge identical birthday cakes and issued a general invitation to everyone living in the Towers. "That'll show 'em," she swaggered. "I bet they've never seen the likes of this at Oakwood." The evening of the party, she attired herself in a slinky zippered midnight blue jumpsuit and hung a long Moroccan chain around her neck with two bobbing silver balls. The guests straggled in one or two at a time, a sedate gaggle of geriatric Lutherans, most of them hobbling behind their walkers and clawed canes. They looked around with vague interest at the table laden with food, nibbled on this or that, ate a polite piece of cake, and took their leave, mumbling platitudes, their faces showing a mixture of indifference and bewilderment. "It was a nice party." "Thank you, Rose." This was just as it should have been considering the fact that the hostess, who had red splotches on both her cheeks and was glassy-eyed, disgraced herself midway through her soiree by getting tanked on the champagne punch and then wetting her pants, bringing the festivities to an abrupt close.

She had a raging fever, as it turned out, and with the boys gone, I spent the whole of Christmas week sleeping on her couch, nursing her through a nasty case of shingles, something her memory, blessedly, blotted out. But then, as soon as she recovered, her depression set in again.

At last, the light dawned. I recognized the pattern. She was going up and down like a yo-yo. I called my sister. "Rosemary," I said, "I think Mommy might be manic-depressive." My sister agreed. "She's been that way since Daddy died." My brother snorted. "She's been that way all her life." I consulted with her doctor. I talked with the staff and bargained for a reprieve. We changed her medications. After that, I stayed on permanent hyper-alert, waiting and watching for the signals to change. The train went roaring down the tracks, or else, inert, it stayed stalled in the station and missed all the stops. When her engine began to rev, we learned how to damp her down; when she went down, we revved her up, further scrambling an already ravaged brain.

❧

As Mrs. Indestructible was getting dressed for church one Sunday morning, struggling to squeeze into a perky red knit suit, her latest bargain from the Resale Shop, her hip suddenly snapped, and she collapsed on the floor in a heap. During the extended surgery that followed she almost certainly suffered another stroke, her fourth, which further impaired her judgment and made it doubtful that she would ever be able to recover her balance. After her discharge from the hospital she was moved into Hebron, Oakwood's nursing home, where she began an intensive regimen of physical therapy.

This was the move we had both dreaded. "Don't you put me in Hebron! Don't you ever put me in Hebron." My mother's dire warnings came back to haunt me. All that she had gained in the move from New York was now seriously compromised. Hoping against hope, I kept her apartment rented in the Towers and arranged to have her beloved bird, Blinky, moved into the PT room to cheer her on, but his bleat was so shrill he soon had to be removed. After six months of therapy and a bill that ran up to almost twenty thousand dollars, we finally gave up. All the king's horses and all the king's men couldn't put Rosy back together again. Sadly, I relinquished her apartment and moved her precious furniture into storage, keeping only the marquetry nightstand and one small red velvet chair she had always favored to brighten her new half-room. Over the years these things got horribly abused, knocked around, and gouged in her corner that was always crammed with clumsy orthopedic devices. Little by little, the pieces of marquetry loosened and fell out of the nightstand; the tufts in the pretty red velvet faded over time, and flattened out.

Most octogenarian women who suffer a hip fracture and are moved into a nursing home die within the year. But Miss Health Girl had an iron constitution and a will to match. "Remember, Mom," I would remind her whenever her spirits would flag, "you're made out of number two." She lived in the same half-room at Hebron for ten long years, out-lasting eight roommates. Some of them became her friends, others just stiffened into hostile silence, and a few were already too far gone by the time they arrived for talk of any kind. In every case, the oxygen tanks would eventually roll in and drone on for a few days before another white corpse would be rolled away, the closet emptied, the walls and the bed stripped bare. My mother's bed was next to the window. I could see the toll this drumbeat of the dead and the dying took on her, how she suffered and visibly withdrew, turning toward the window during these vigils, becoming despondent. "Another notch on your belt," I would say, trying to cheer her up. But she never laughed at that joke.

I took it as a very bad sign when my mother stopped complaining. In matters that directly affected her quality of life, like bad food or a steady procession of terminal roommates, she refused to speak up on her own behalf, fearing some dire consequence as a result. External powers were once again in charge of her life. In the past, it had been her mother and her husband who had laid down the rules. Now it was head nurses, chaplains, psychiatrists, dieticians, and activities directors who were making the decisions, granting permissions, keeping track of the charts and the records and the bulging file folder that was held together with rubber bands and opened up at every care conference, and she was at the mercy of their governance. Even more importantly, her fate, day by day, was now quite literally in the hands, sometimes rough, sometimes merciful, of those ever-rotating nurse's aides, overworked and underpaid, whose job it was to carry out her care plan. They came bustling in and out of her room at all hours of the day and night, getting her up, putting her down, propping, moving, feeding, washing, brushing, dressing and undressing, yanking down her pants to seat her on the toilet, and hauling them up again.

And so it fell to me to complain when something was amiss, to malign the staff as she would have done, to scream when her hearing aides and her eyeglasses and her dentures were lost time after time, to call foul whenever I found her strapped in her wheelchair against federal regulations, or left alone for hours at a time to stare at a blank television screen that no one had bothered to turn on. Now it was my turn to be a classic loudmouth from New York.

"What's happened to the leopard outfit I just bought her? And her new blue slacks?" Her laundry was habitually lost or ruined.

"Why have you chopped off all her beautiful hair? She looks like Harpo Marx." It was painful to greet her in mismatched hand-me-downs, she who had always been so fastidious, her hair hacked off and flattened to her head or frizzed like a clown.

"Look at how much weight she's gaining! Stop feeding her potato chips!" She gained forty pounds on an institutional diet in those first few years, sitting in a wheelchair all day. I was afraid she'd get so fat she'd lose her mobility altogether. She'd become a prisoner, and I'd be forced to give up the pleasure of our outings. Sitting across the table from a succession of dieticians, I went over every item in her meal plan, string bean by carrot; I brought food from home that sat mostly forgotten in the staff refrigerator; and the steady weight gain continued. She went on stuffing herself like a stevedore whenever she had the chance. Then, without any warning, she suddenly went into reverse, clamping her mouth shut and refusing food altogether. Even then, in my relentless ingenuity, I found a way to keep her alive a whole year by providing endless cartons of frozen custard and insisting that she be fed on milkshakes three times a day.

I developed a ferocious tenacity. Knowing it was a losing battle only made me fight all the harder; I kept changing tactics like a guerrilla as she kept losing ground. "Can she have wine with her meals?" "Can her bird come to visit?" "Can we put an aquarium in her room?" Obsessed with fighting the hydra that bedeviled us, I never let up. Meanwhile, my mother was developing an altogether different coping strategy. Faced with progressive immobility, the advance of crippling disease, and the grim reality of spending the rest of her life in a nursing home, she reverted to a fresh campaign of sabotage.

Hey! Hey! Somebody help!" You could hear her yelling all the way down the hall. The aides would come running. "Rose, you can't call out like that! You have to learn to use your buzzer." She never did. Not once. She never so much as glanced at the thing where it lay within easy reach, draped over her bed like a mouse with a long tail. A last hurrah, a rebel yell, my mother's voice was her chief weapon against the powerful pressures of institutional conformity. She always screeched like a banshee, using that siren wail of hers to startle and command attention. She howled hideously when they hosed her down in the shower once a week like an elephant. She made wisecracks and dirty jokes. She called out at assemblies and in church. She once disrupted the Sunday service, astonishing everybody by announcing broadly in the middle of the sermon, "I need a beer!" And even after she lost the power of speech she continued to vocalize like a parrot, repeating over and over again in a strange high-pitched yip, "Yeah! Yeah! Yeah!" She made everybody know Rose was still there.

Humor was her other weapon. My midmorning talk show on public radio was a great favorite among the village elders. One day, she was approached by one of her old neighbors from the Towers, a woman who knew her only by her first name. "Rose, do you listen to Jean Feraca?" she asked. "You should listen to Jean Feraca." Drawing herself up in her wheelchair, my mother at her most haughty retorted, "Jean Feraca listens to me."

For most of the years she lived in Hebron she became a notorious wag and a cutup, something of a cross between Long John Silver and the Wife of Bath. In care conferences, which, as she declined, became ritualized exercises in humiliation, she deliberately subverted the agenda, making outrageous wisecracks at every turn, embarrassing the chaplain with her flirting, and announcing, "I'm a juicy gal!" whenever the subject of her incontinence came up for public discussion. Every care conference began with exactly the same question. The head nurse would turn to her and ask in a flat Midwestern twang, "Mrs. Feraca, if we come into your room and find that you've stopped breathing, do you want us to do something?" "Of course I do!" she always shot back, regardless of her own health-care directives. I was proud of her for that, too. She always managed to rescue the situation and bring some real humanity into those painful sessions.

The built-in filters that had once ensured discretion and propriety had begun to strip away, mysteriously disassembled by her new brain chemistry. What emerged in the place of the prude and the strict disciplinarian and the obsessive-compulsive housekeeper who had raised me was a vamp and a renegade, a sexual being who was bawdy and naughty and pure iconoclast. Here she was, pushing ninety, a woman who was known to wail, "I want a man!" when asked, "Mrs. Feraca, what can I get you?"

She was losing the power of speech, but whatever sentences she managed to summon up packed a wallop. "Rosemary! You have boobies!" she announced to my sister at our family reunion. "I used to have boobies. Now I have flapjacks." Not to leave me out, she looked up at me in my green velour top studded with rhinestones to say, with an appraising eye, "Your boobies are well appointed." That was at the Café Romeo. It was the only thing she said all during lunch. There were other aspects of my anatomy that she appraised. "Coo-coo is ready," she suddenly announced one day while I was busy with her laundry. "Ready for what?" I asked. She thought for a second. "For a kiss." I told her I was dating a nice man. She weighed in on my prospects, offering this tart little piece of advice: "If you want to use that thing, Jeannie," she said, "you better put it on ice."

The nurses aides who worked at Hebron came to seek her out, knowing on a dark day they could always count on Rose, the Rakish Crone, for a salty remark or an off-color joke. My mother had appetites. It was that lust for life that I latched onto, finding in it the energy I needed to keep me going. Hadn't she rallied a dozen times against the odds? Hadn't she outlived her own suicide? And here she was, living among strangers, bringing laughter into a charnel house.

On her ninetieth birthday her attendants gussied her up in a red and white striped sailor's dress, put a crooked smear of red lipstick on her mouth to match the big red beads around her neck, and stuck a purple plumed cowboy hat on her head before sending her off to a family picnic by the lake. Giancarlo, her handsome grandson, greeted her as she descended on the lift from the truck. "Nana, you're ninety years old today. How do you feel about being so old?" She thought a moment, then summed it all up, "That's a lot of hot dogs down the bowl."

Sometimes, just like Dominick, who was forever getting into trouble in middle school, my mother, too, got hauled onto the carpet for being "disruptive" and "inappropriate." The activities director asked me to come to see her one afternoon. "Rose is becoming a problem," she began, with my mother seated right beside her in her wheelchair like a kid in the principal's office. "We can't seem to get her to stop laughing and calling out during presentations. She interrupts the speakers and upsets the other residents." I was alarmed, but my mother was completely oblivious. "Mom, Mom!" I yelled, trying to penetrate her deafness. "Do you understand what Susan is saying? If you don't stop laughing and calling out, you're going to have to stay in your room and not be allowed to go to any more activities." My mother looked at me long and hard while we waited. I couldn't be sure whether or not she had comprehended. Finally, still staring at my face, she asked, "Why didn't we ever get your nose fixed?"

Hello?" I picked up the phone one morning to hear my mother's high-pitched croak coming out of the receiver. "Bring me my hat, my cape, and my broom!" It was Halloween, and once again it was time for her to get dressed up as a witch. Dominick, who always loved costumes, helped me revamp her aging academic gown and freshen her old hat with its long gray grisly locks. Each October we would go in search of something novel, a spider ring, or a black bug to attach to her cheek, some little detail to add to the mask and broom that were kept in her closet year-round. The cackle, which grew richer and more bloodcurdling with each passing year, she herself supplied. I watched her work herself up into it, drawing her twisted wizened torso as high as she could in her chair, and throwing her head back, so it sailed like a murder of crows down the whole length of the dining room, startling the gray heads nodding over their coffee cups. She kept it up all day long. The kids who came trick-or-treating in the afternoon peered into her room only to shrink back and run the other way, terrified by that screech and that shriveled claw stretching out to greet them. She was altogether too real. By the end of the afternoon hers was the only basket still brimming with candy.

One Halloween she ended up on television, featured on the last segment of the Channel 15 evening news: "Children wore their Halloween costumes to the Oakwood Village retirement home today where they found plenty of goodies and appreciative residents." The anchor's lead was followed by footage of children in ears and whiskers picking up their treats from little old ladies. "Not all of the trick-or-treaters were children," he continued, and suddenly there she was, filling up the screen, my mother in all her witchy glory, masked, hatted, and bewigged, speaking into a reporter's microphone. "And what are you dressed up as today?" asked the reporter. "The Witch of the East," said my mother in her shrill falsetto. "Is that the good one or the bad one?" "That's the bad one," she croaked. "Heh, heh, heh."

I harbored a certain horror of the day I would no longer be able to take my mother on outings. I kept her on the move, making the rounds of the zoo, the lake, the parks, and the public gardens when weather permitted, even the circus when it came to town—she had always loved the circus—and our customary dinner on Sunday. Her legs swelled up big and fat, stiff with edema. They were dead weights, like gigantic provolone you sometimes see hanging from the ceiling in vintage Italian delicatessens. Getting her in and out of the car was always an ordeal. I would tug and haul at those two huge waxy cheeses, grunting as I straddled her big Buddha belly. "Come on, Mom," I would scold, "you have to help!" Instead, she would throw her head back and burst into peels of laughter at this ant of a daughter of hers trying to lug her around, and she would be as much help as a sack of sugar.

Perversely, as she continued to lose mobility, our outings became more ambitious. We flew to Fort Lauderdale together for a birthday party when a favorite uncle turned eighty. We flew to Disney World for a family reunion. We celebrated one of her last birthdays at the home brewers beer festival, where my friend Tom, the impresario, tucked a sprig of hops under the brim of her purple cowboy hat and hung a sampler glass around her neck. We flew to New York to attend her grandson's wedding. Halfway there, sitting beside me, she got soggy in her diaper. I managed to muscle her out of her seat and down the aisle into the restroom where the two of us got stuck, squeezed into that tiny space while I tried to change her diaper. I had to stand on the toilet seat, finally, and climb right over her head to open the door and haul her out of there.

It was raining hard by the time we arrived in New York, and my nephews squabbled over how to get their grandmother down the slick grassy bank in front of my sister's house. They ended by picking her up, chair and all, and carrying her down the hill with an umbrella held over her head so she looked like a canopied relic, whooping and carrying on as she made the sign of the cross, dispensing blessings like the pope.

In the middle of the night, sharing the same room, I heard her call out in her sleep, "Railing. Railing."

"What do you want a railing for, Mom?"

"I'm going to the moon."

"What are you going to do on the moon?"

"I'll know when I get there."

*D*ementia was a word I found difficult to absorb when her doctor started using it, writing it down in my mother's chart along with his diagnosis of atypical bipolar disorder. I had come to think of my mother as bright, clever, outrageous, resourceful. Moreover, I wanted to think of myself as the daughter of the same clever mother. "My mother is demented," I would say to myself, and then to a few friends I trusted, trying to get used to it, to absorb its shock. But I couldn't shake the sense of stigma, or the image of a crooked bent hanger that kept coming to mind. Demented.

Damaged by successive strokes, her whole left side had begun to curl up, and pretty soon, no longer able to sit upright, she had to be propped in her chair, and she did, indeed, begin to resemble a crooked hanger. Added to what was already grotesque, the physical therapists gave her a bright orange stuffed carrot to clutch in her left hand to keep it from turning into a claw. It was a ridiculous prop, and it made her look like a scared rabbit.

Seeing how I struggled, the staff psychiatrist advised me to read a book called *The 36-Hour Day*. I didn't read it. I didn't really want to know the truth of my mother's condition or to be forced to contemplate what lay ahead. By this time her smile had vanished, she had lost her laughter, her ability to think, to eat, to frame sentences and speak, but as long as she continued to recognize me, I kept telling myself, "Well, at least she doesn't have Alzheimer's."

Language had bonded us, and I clung to every shred of it that was left, choosing to focus on what remained rather than on what had been lost. One day when I visited, she looked up at me quizzically and said,

"You look just like my daughter." Another time, I came in wearing a trench coat and a fedora in unconscious imitation of my father. "There he is!" she hailed me, suddenly coming alive in the lineup of fuzzy-haired heaps asleep or falling out of their chairs. To be taken for a man didn't bother me at all. I understood it as a compliment, a sign I had redeemed myself in her eyes as the once misguided daughter who had turned into a trusted son and could now be counted on to protect and defend her.

When I finally read *The 36-Hour Day* and discovered that my mother was suffering from something called multi-infarct dementia, a condition closely related to Alzheimer's, and that it was fatal, the truth hit me so hard I cancelled all my appointments and didn't leave the house for three days. I had been so focused on her bipolar disorder, it never occurred to me she could be struggling with something even worse. Multi-infarct dementia triggers little strokes that slowly eat away the brain until it becomes impossible even to swallow, and then starvation closes in, but very slowly. It's a form of living death. As the chief witness to my mother's long, slow, agonizing decline, what I found most unbearable was the way it slowly robbed her of her spirit. After all we had been through together, to have to watch the fight drain out of her like sand from a sack was heartbreaking.

I walked into my mother's room one afternoon and found her aide, a huge black man who claimed to be an exiled prince from Zimbabwe, cleaning up a mess of big fat yellow turds that had been strewn all over the floor from the bed to the bathroom. My mother used to say, *"A la scuallia d'neve si vedono gli strunz."* At the end of winter, the turds show up. Applied to her years at Hebron, it sums up the whole cruel and inexorable advance of the disease that little by little, bit by bit, robbed her of every human trait by which we knew her. All the roles she had carried off: the Clown, the Wicked Witch, the Rakish Crone, and the Grand Dame, all went the way of the great legs, the panache, the peeling laughter, the acid tongue, and the hawk eye. In the end, a fixed, impassive solemnity was all that was left of her, not just mute but sphinx-like. In the place of what had been my mother was something that resembled a stone monument that had buried her alive.

I found her in her room one day, seated in her wheel chair. There was an eerie, absent quality about her as if she no longer owned or even occupied her own body. She was neat as a pin, and perfectly still, staring off into space. She was dressed in a long, elegant, dark-blue skirt with a delicate pattern of pink flowers that I remembered picking out with my sister the previous summer. Her hair had been carefully parted and combed flat against her head. One hand was at rest in her lap, the other was curled up against her chest. Someone had applied lipstick to her mouth, and the pink stood out starkly against the porcelain pallor of her skin. She might have been a figure in a painting called "Repose." Her naked feet had been wrapped in surgical dressings, and they protruded from underneath the dark hem of her skirt. They looked like the feet of an icon. I might have been praying before a statue in church as I sat there.

Call it an essence, or a soul. Something had come to occupy the place of what had been my mother's personality. Slowly I began to discern in her a strange power that was beginning to emerge from her huge enfeeblement. As the real-life woman receded, something larger than life began to come forth, something almost archetypal that I could perceive in this enormous doll with her gorgeous arresting blue eyes that stared and blinked when you sat her up, a doll that wet and had to be cleaned and diapered and dressed and fed and carried about and put to bed. She reminded me of a baby doll I had played with as a very young child, a Betsy Wetsy, my very first doll. The doll had seemed huge to me at the time as I toddled her around, and I marveled at how those hours of innocent play so long ago had prepared me now to help my mother to die.

In the time that remained, I became like one of the Spanish men in Almodóvar's strange movie *Talk to Her*, utterly devoted to a woman who was comatose. I, too, had been ushered by accident into the offices of an unconditional love, at once austere as well as lush. No longer did it matter one whit how difficult she had been, however good or bad a mother, what she had done or failed to do, what she had withheld. The whole question of desserts was easily forgotten and put aside. It never even entered my mind. No measure for measure this time, no quid pro quo; what mattered now was matter itself, her matter, my matter, my mother. What mattered was that she was still on earth, that this body of hers, out of which my own substance had been fetched, was still here, still in my keeping, so I could still touch it, so that it could still be cherished. A strange reverence for her very flesh took hold of me. I kissed her cheek, rejoicing that it was still pink and round, that it was still there to be kissed. I stroked her hand, marveling at the transparency of the skin, as soft as old berries, at the candelabrum of veins that showed through. I marveled at how this mother of mine, who had been so unloved and unlovable for so much of her life, by some mysterious and profound process had become so unutterably precious.

I'm stupid," she had once said in a rare instance of self-awareness. So she knew. That made it much worse, of course. Her enormous vulnerability completely disarmed me. Pushing her in her Trojan horse wheelchair—and she was a load—I remembered how she had pushed me in my wicker stroller. I remembered the roll of the rubber wheels, the bumps over curbs and cracks in the sidewalk, the way my three-year-old fingers had tried to touch the sunlight coming through the slats in the wicker mesh. Now she herself was as frail as wicker, as full of holes as that old stroller. She frightened me.

There were times when I grew weary of it all, the wasting, the monkey face, the grim puckered seam that was her mouth with its perpetual frown, the hauling her around, the failed outings and the rejections. I was forever offering what she refused.

"What's the matter, Mother? Don't you like my soup?"

"It's boring."

"I want to tell you about Dominick's scholarship."

"Baloney. Don't pick your nose."

"I met a nice man. He's Jewish."

"I hate Jews."

"It's such a beautiful spring day. How would you like it if I pushed you down the street?"

"Shove it up your ass."

I arranged for her outings in all our old haunts—the zoo, the terrace, the gardens—but my heart wasn't in it anymore. It just wasn't any fun.

Still, I kept going through the motions. Pushing her in her wheelchair by Lake Mendota one perfect summer afternoon, past the scudding sailboats and the bobbing ducks, past the dogs with their wet underbellies flopped in the shade and their tongues hanging out, past the coeds lounging on the terrace, past the ice-cream cones licked by children who had their whole lives ribboning out before them, I felt that we were the only dark blot on this otherwise sunny scene. I caught myself imagining what might happen if the brakes slipped, and I lost control, and the wheelchair rolled out to the end of the pier, and my mother fell in.

"Do you like it here?"

"No," she croaked.

"Do you want a milkshake?"

"No."

"Do you want a punch in the nose?"

The old black belly laugh came rumbling up from the bottom of the barrel, shaking her whole frame and taking us both by surprise. Her tongue, rolling around in the cave of her mouth, lobbed sideways, showing the dark vein running down its underside.

☙

Mother?" This is not what I want to call you, broken bird, juju, mojo, clot of sticks and hair and bone. I rehearse in my mind driving over to Hebron to empty out your room, readying it for the next resident as I nurture a tidy, manageable grief, saying a few words of appreciation to the staff, who will remember you only as Rose, this pathetic owl clutching that ridiculous carrot that's supposed to keep you from curling up.

I remembered Giancarlo's pet hamster, Alfresca, how she lay panting on her side on the bottom of her cage. "I think she's dying," Giancarlo had said. That was a quiet decent death, deserving of the decent burial we gave her. Not like this thing that goes on and on, this mouth full of rotting teeth that hardly remembers to open and close let alone eat, that can't even suck on a straw it's so weak, this eye that rolls up but refuses to close, this indecent, obscene malingering. *Oh, how you mock me, Mother! What is it you're trying to teach me exactly? Is this a test? Is it my love for you you're trying your best to outlast?*

Everything sagged. The flesh hung from her arms, tiered and ruffled. Her heavy shoes, the stubbed toes, the puffed-out ankle in tight white hose I kept lifting, lifting, back into place on the metal plate a hundred times as the heavy leg kept falling down to the ground. Everything fell. You said you were indestructible. "Heads or tails, I can't lose." *Where is your style now, huh, Mom? Where is your sting? How could this have happened? Who was it who did this to you?*

We were all alone on the street in the middle of the afternoon when the rubber slipped off the rim of the wheel. One of the spokes buried itself in the hub. What to do now? You were halfway out of your chair, slanting toward the pavement. The street was completely empty. There was no one around. No one at all to call on for help. I struggled with it. *Oh, God, I've never been any good at this.* I fumbled and somehow managed to free the spoke, and the rubber found its way back around the wheel. Now we were on our way again, rolling toward home. It was the day after Halloween. The sky was cerulean, the maple leaves, all gold, sang in the light like sauterne. A ghost floated from somebody's porch. I stopped to point it out to you. "Look, Mom? Look up! See the leaves? See the ghost?" But you were not much interested in the ghost, or the leaves, or the light. You looked up at me instead, and there was a softness in your eyes. You reached out to take my hand in yours, your funny fin of a hand that felt like doeskin over bone in mine, and you touched it lightly to your cheek, as if to say, "My dear, you're all the gold I've got."

❧

On the day before Easter, I drove over to Hebron. The weather was mild, so I wheeled my mother outside into a little walled-in garden. It had been newly built, and there was a stiff, mortuary feel about it with its empty paths and rows of boxwood newly planted in the white gravel. We might have been alone together in a cemetery. My mother sat enthroned in her high-backed chair in the thin sunlight, mute and unsmiling as usual.

"Mom," I shouted at her, no longer expecting any answer. "Today is Saturday, the day before Easter. Tomorrow is Easter Sunday." She looked at me dry-eyed and said, much to my surprise, in a voice as flat as dirt, "A lot of good it does me."

I was stung, astonished that she had actually heard and understood me, but also hurt by what I took to be a reproach. In the past, we had always celebrated holidays as a family, but this year I had plans to spend the day with my new husband. "The kids are with their father this year," I began, hastily cobbling together my defense. "Rosemary couldn't make the trip, and Stephen . . ." I hesitated, took a deep breath, and pointed toward heaven. "Stephen is up there . . ." My brother had died within the year. She gave me one of her measured looks and said in the same flat voice, "The only one."

"The only one." Once uttered, those three words in all their bald truth shone between us like eggs in the washed light. What they conveyed was the full import of everything my mother had so stoically endured without so much as a single complaint—the loneliness, the misery, the boredom, the abandonment. She had delivered the message as dryly as the bottom line in a lading bill. I was devastated. Against the brawling clan into which she had been born, all she had left was me, a dot coming at the end of a sentence too long to be remembered. Never had I felt more inadequate, or more responsible for the shrinkage of her life, the blankness and desolation of this last place into which she had been led, an exile that could only end with death.

❧

I threw a party for my mother a few months before she died. I had the idea that it might compensate in some small way for the story she had told me about the original insult that had tainted her whole life—how her father had dismissed the band before they were allowed to play when she was born. What was required now, I thought, was a suitable sendoff with lots of fanfare while she was still alive.

I signed out the party room and hired the Ethnic Connection, a trio of village elders who played a lively repertoire of vintage ethnic music, Jewish, Italian, and Scandinavian, depending on the venue. Lots of people came, some of my mother's old friends, some of mine. My sister came from New York. Giancarlo, my son home on holiday, came all the way from Istanbul. Even my friend Tom, the impresario of the beer festival, added to the sense of festivity by showing up in his signature white-tailed tuxedo jacket painted with Holstein spots.

There were testimonials and tributes in my mother's honor; some guests recited poems, others sang songs. Giancarlo serenaded his grand-mother in true Neapolitan style, belting out in Italian an over-the-top rendition of "Come Back to Sorrento." When the band went Latin, An-gela Paratore, whose sister had been my mother's first friend, sprang to her feet in spite of her eighty-odd years and dazzled us all with a slithery tango she had learned from a cast-off lover. That got just about every-body up and dancing, and pretty soon, what with the food and the wine, we kicked up quite a ruckus, the like of which had seldom been heard in Hebron's sober halls.

My mother in her wheelchair was propped right in front of the band with a speaker placed at her feet in the hope that she might pick up the vibrations from the music. Lo and behold, somebody noticed her right foot had started moving up and down in rhythm with the music. "Look at her foot! Look at her foot! Would you just look at that?" A buzz swept through the room, and we all marveled at the way she kept it up, tap-ping out the beat with her foot.

The party began to wind down after that. As guests began to take their leave, on impulse, my friend Jung Ja plucked a pink peony out of one of the flower vases and leaned it up against my mother's chest. Somebody else added a daisy, then another peony, a third contributed a branch of bridal wreath, and so it went until all the bouquets in the room had been ravaged and my mother looked like the dowager queen of the May, completely buried in pink and white blossoms.

❧

Word came right in the middle of one of my morning talk shows that my mother was dying. As soon as I could, I rushed over to Hebron and hardly left her side over the course of the next several days. Seeing how she labored and groaned with every breath, I knelt close beside her and held her hand. "Mom, you can go now," I told her, just as the hospice nurses had schooled me. "Everything is in order. We're all happy and safe here. There's plenty of money. You don't have to worry about anything anymore. I'm happily married. Everything's okay. Daddy and Nanny and Uncle Sonny, Aunt Tootsie and Uncle Dominick, and Stephen, too, they're all on the other side. They're waiting for you. You don't have to work so hard at this. You can just let go now." It was a message I was to repeat several times. But my mother didn't let go. She hung on. For some reason I couldn't fathom, she was deeply attached to her life. The vigil had only just begun.

I brought flowers and lit candles and played Enrico Caruso tapes, and Rosa Mystica and Andrea Bocelli, hoping there was a chance she might hear through her headphones and be comforted. When I got sick of hearing the same tapes over and over, I sang to her myself, songs and prayers from the old days, hymns we used to sing together in church, Stephen Foster songs, "I Dream of Jeannie," "Too-ra-loo-ra-loo-ra," whatever I could think of, trying not to break down when my voice cracked and the tears came.

Her feet turned purple overnight, the color of dark merlot, and I watched with horror as the stain seeped slowly upward, claiming her ankles. Would she look like a beet before this was over? I stayed with her for long hours at a time, hardly moving from my station at her feet while others came and went, chaplains, nurses, aides bustling in and out to change her linen every half hour as her body kept purging itself, voiding blood and feces. A close friend arrived to keep me company; my husband showed up; we drew up chairs around the bed, but they made so much noise talking and joking together, I threw them both out, unable to bear their indifference. A woman was sent from hospice to give my mother a bath. She was a little woman, not much taller than the bed itself, and as I watched her expert movements, rolling my mother over and moving her body around the bed, performing her task with such ritual intention and respect, the feeling of hushed reverence in the room deepened.

It was late July, just a few weeks before my mother's birthday. The room was sealed against the summer heat, but, mysteriously, fat black flies kept hatching out on the windowsill beside her head, buzzing against the windowpane. I kept swiping at them, fanning them away from her head. And still, the threshing and the churning went on, the groans followed by the cries, and still the flies kept hatching out.

What could I do? How could I help? I ran cold water over a washcloth and applied it to her forehead. I stroked her brow. I crooned to her. My baby. My sweetheart. My beautiful mama, look how your eyes are still so blue, your cheeks so pink, how beautiful you are, my mama, *O sanctissima, O piissima, Dulcis Virg-o Mar-i-i-a, Mater amata, in-te-mer-a-a-ta, o-o-ra-a, o-o-ra, pro no-o-bis, pray for us,* Oh Mother of God, hear us, have mercy on us, Mother of Sorrows, pray for us, Mother of the Clean Sheets, Mother of the Bloody Stools, Mother of All Cries and Groans, hear us, have mercy on us, Seat of Wisdom, pray for us, Mystical Rose. More Andrea Bocelli, more Enrico Caruso, more strokes, more cool compresses, watching the purple darken like heartwood as the blood pooled in her feet. Was I keeping her alive? Had the bond between us become incorporeal? Was I feeding on her dying like a succubus? Or was she feeding on me?

I began to breathe with her, entering into her rhythm, in and out, in and out, until we became entrained, my mother and I, and the two of us got stuck in that love canal, tied together by an invisible umbilicus as I labored to deliver her. But she was too powerful for me, and I felt myself begin to slide and go under, caught in the dragnet of her undertow. Even when I left the room, I went on breathing her same breath, groaning her groans, so seduced was I, so much at one with her in that liminal space. There was nothing to hang onto standing on that slippery slope. I felt the need to resist, and yet I couldn't resist. I had fallen under her spell.

In all this time my mother gave no sign she knew me. Then one morning I entered her room and found everything changed. It was as if a storm had blown through overnight; all her agitation had vanished, leaving clarity in its place and a deep calm. She was sitting up in bed looking at the ceiling. There was a shine on her cheeks and brow like rosy snow on silver, a lightness about her whole being. She was intent, with a rapt expression on her face as her eyes went tracking back and forth along the ceiling. She seemed to be listening to angelic messengers only she could see and hear. Then, without any warning, she suddenly turned and looked directly at me, locking my eyes on hers.

With a shock, I felt the full force of her intelligence summoned up in that long electric look as she held my gaze, and something passed between us across a great divide. The whole treasure of her unlived life consigned came pouring into me, riding in on a swollen ice-blue stream. It was a full force affront. Beyond mother or daughter, I felt her soul pass into mine the way two rivers converge, blue flowing into brown. Knowing in that moment I was receiving everything she had ever withheld, I felt compelled to send my essence right back across that same divide, only this time I didn't care if I went under. All that mattered was the setting out itself, hapless, and at the same time sure. Hopping crazily from one ice floe to another, zigzagging across that surging current, I felt myself held up, willy-nilly, by the same force that would have swept me under, and she was that force, my mother, that blue river that was melting under me, with freedom on the other side.

Even after all that it wasn't over. A whole week went by, and nothing changed. She was thriving on the morphine. How creepy, I thought, this clinging to a dying animal. Could there be something even worse beyond the grave to make her hang on like this? Or was she groaning simply because it was so hard to get out?

My husband, who makes wine, called it a stuck fermentation. The hospice nurses finally had to tell me to quit. You're keeping her alive, they said. Go away for a few days. You have to break the pattern. Finally, I told her, "Mom, it's time. You're exhausted. We're all exhausted. You have to shuffle off to Buffalo."

I was sitting in an air-conditioned movie theater on a hot Friday night watching, of all things, a documentary about Hank Greenburg, the Jewish baseball star from the Bronx, during what turned out to be my mother's final hours. It was shortly after midnight by the time I stopped to check in at Hebron on my way home. I found a hospice nurse in her room, crouching low beside her bed. "Is this it?" "This is it." I hesitated a minute, and then, on impulse, I rushed home to grab a candle and a bunch of white roses I was keeping on hand, and in the time it took me to get back, the nurse had administered a hefty dose of morphine, and my mother was dead. I had missed it, and I wasn't sorry. I had been waiting to receive from her the mothering she herself had been denied, and she had delivered. What she needed in her last hour was for me to disappear. The tie had finally been broken. It was August 5, exactly one week before her ninety-fourth birthday.

◌

My mother's body was flown by cargo freight to New York for the funeral that was held on her birthday at St. Patrick's Church in Armonk, my sister's parish. In a deviation from the usual impersonal Catholic funeral, my sister and I both delivered eulogies before a congregation that included my mother's grandchildren and great-grandchildren and a smattering of her oldest friends. Rosemary talked about charity, the example my parents had set, my mother's volunteer work. I told my mother's jokes, which made even the Irish priest laugh out loud and wonder what I had left out. Following the Mass, the funeral cortege wound its way south down the Bronx River Parkway to Woodlawn Cemetery for the interment in the family mausoleum.

Woodlawn is a very special place. A last preserve of the Bronx River Valley, it's not only beautiful in its green Gilded Age splendor, but also truly democratic. You can find brothers who fought against each other in the Civil War lying peaceably side by side in Woodlawn, Jews buried right along with Christians, heroes and scoundrels, blacks mixed up with whites. Madame C. J. Walker, Harlem's first black millionairess, is buried in Woodlawn, as are George M. Cohan and King Oliver, the jazz trumpeter. Elizabeth Cady Stanton, the stern suffragette, lies not too far from Lotta Crabtree, the showgirl who was showered with gold dust by the miners she entertained in the barrooms of California. Between them, my mother would be in good company.

Woodlawn is the only cemetery in America where an Italian immigrant like my grandfather, who was one of the forgotten builders of New York City, could end up sharing the same earth with somebody as famous as Mayor Fiorello La Guardia. My father and his brothers acquired the neoclassic shrine they were so proud of to honor their father in the same way they acquired their furniture—from a family that went belly-up during the Depression. They had Saverio's body exhumed from its temporary tomb and sealed into a zinc-lined copper coffin. After the body had been interred, they made sure that the family name—FERACA—was carved in bold letters over the granite lintel so that there could be no doubt about the identity of the new occupants. As a final touch, they installed the bronze bust of Saverio that had been cast from his death mask inside the mausoleum in front of the stained glass window. Only after it had begun to corrode and turn green when the roof started to leak and the latch on the door grew rusty was it removed.

By the time my mother died, there were only two crypts in the mausoleum that were still unoccupied. One was on the top left, the other on the bottom right. A conundrum. My sister and I deliberated. If we put my mother on the bottom right, that meant she'd be down on the floor (and hadn't she spent enough time in her life down on the floor?) and right underneath her mother-in-law, whom she had always hated. But if we put her up on the top left, she'd be right next to our Uncle Jimmy, the brother-in-law she had once set out to stick with a pitchfork during the vendetta. In the end, we opted for the floor. That way she'd be on the same side with her husband, but not too close. Death had arranged for a little breathing room between them.

And so we left her there in the House of the Dead, a rose pressed between two stone slabs in the heavy book of history. In her purple knit dress inside her palomino coffin, wrapped in her shroud of Brussels lace, she looks very beautiful. Her face is rouged and veiled, with one perfect Ionic curl pressed into each temple. Her silver-white hair floats around her head, the same unchanging cloud day in and day out. Her powdered hands entwine like roots.

Mother, are you still deaf? Can you hear the mourning doves through all that stone? Does the sun ever shine through the tree in the stained glass window? Do you listen when the rain swells the stream that runs under the bridge and down the hill? Eighteen lions guard your tomb. Your river runs through me.

3

Get Thee to a Winery

the mystery of love

> When my son was three years old he liked to crawl into my bed in the early morning and talk about the problems of life. One morning he said abruptly, "You know there are two Gods." I was surprised and asked him, "What are their names?" He replied, "One is called Jesus and he makes people, and the other is called Bacchus and he makes wine."
>
> Freeman Dyson, *Infinite in All Directions*

"Can I have guests?"

"Yes."

"Are there any rules?"

"We don't want you to swim alone."

That was it—the only restriction to be imposed on the month of Sundays I was about to spend in a Benedictine monastery. I could hardly believe my good fortune. Out of the monastery's time-honored tradition of hospitality, I had been granted a five-week writer's retreat in which I planned to write a poem for the Dane County Cultural Affairs Commission and to work on a book about women monastics. As of the first of July, the Retreat Cottage at the north end of the property would be all mine for one entire month. Watching my name go down in the monastery ledger, I felt a sweep of anticipation, imagining the long mid-summer days in which I would write undisturbed in my little cottage, liberated at last from a punishing work schedule.

St. Benedict believed that a monastery should be as self-contained as possible, with its own farm and orchard, vegetable garden, and vine-yard, so that monks would have no need to go elsewhere. The Sisters of St. Benedict founded their center on the "Holy Hill" in Wisconsin over-looking Lake Mendota and the skyline of Madison, 130 acres of land, ninety of them native upland prairie. Evidence that it had once been a working farm was everywhere. When I wasn't working at my desk, I imagined being free to roam the monastery grounds, exploring its gar-dens and wooded glens, its Lost Lake and lacy meadows studded with birdhouses, with nothing to inhibit my ramblings but the single admoni-tion: "We don't want you to swim alone."

It wasn't even much of a rule as rules go. Had it come from one of the nuns rather than the staff member who wrote down my name and handed me the keys, I would surely have taken it to heart. But I knew that Sister Mary David, the prioress, actually wanted me to swim in the pool that was located right across from the cottage. As one of only two nuns who remained at that time out of a once thriving community, there could be no higher authority. "There's a pool right over there," she had said, her gray eyes gleaming. "You'll get some good exercise while you're here."

Mary David believed in exercising the body as well as the soul. She was a dedicated outdoorswoman who had grown up on a farm in the Midwest learning to hunt and fish. In summer, her face took on the ruddy glow of someone who might have been driving a tractor or riding a horse. In fact, there was a rumor going around that as a young novice she had once jumped onto the back of one of the monastery's saddle horses and galloped off in a fit of pique. Mary David was a force to be reckoned with. When developers gobbled up the land surrounding St. Ben's to build a gated community with a golf course and then began encroaching on the little remnant community, it was Mary David who held them off. She and Sister Joanna battled regularly with the local bishop, who disapproved of their liberal innovations, allowing lay people to deliver the sermons at Sunday Assembly and substituting language such as "Holy One, our only home" for "Our Father, who art in heaven." In fact, it was precisely because of their courage and steadfast commitment to the spirit of ecumenism that I, a twice-divorced Catholic, felt so much at home at St. Ben's. I knew I didn't have to hide out or dissemble where Christians of other denominations, gay couples, and ex-clergy were all made welcome as full-fledged members of the same community.

The Retreat Cottage was nestled into a corner of the woods at the far end of a dirt lane. With its chocolate brown shingles and brown door it was easy to overlook, a dark plum shrouded under the shifting shade of a canopy of oak trees. In midsummer, there were ferns unfurling in the shade on both sides of the front door, a screened-in porch at the back of the little house, and a deck to one side. I looked it over and knew at once it was perfect. Nothing would disturb me here except for the occasional squall of a blue jay, or a squirrel, or a chipmunk darting across the front step. Visitors to the monastery seldom ventured that far along the dirt road that led past the sisters' cemetery and up the ridge to the end of the orchard. There were deer in the woods that kept to themselves, and the rising moon, glimpsed through the leafy branches of the trees on clear nights, would be shy, reluctant to intrude.

Even the pool was undisturbed. Nobody ever swam there, as far as I could tell, except for rare visits by the night watchman's wife. Otherwise, day after day, its aquamarine eye stayed clear as glass. From time to time, the night watchman would appear, usually at dusk, to stand in the shadows by the water's edge, holding a long rake in his hand as he trolled for stray leaves and the occasional tiny bloated body of a drowned frog.

"You can make love in the monastery!" JungJa sang out in the middle of one of our conversations soon after I had moved in. "You can make very good love." JungJa was the night watchman's wife, a pretty Korean dancer who had the distracting habit of swiveling her hips around in her chair during morning prayers while she rolled her head around on her long neck. She and her husband Doug lived happily together in their one-room basement apartment in Benedict House where they were sometimes spied on during their lovemaking by stray visitors, something that bothered Jung Ja not a wit. Jung Ja had studied to become a United Church of Christ minister and was used to dispensing advice. "Play. Play with Alan," she coaxed. "Have fun. This working out of salvation, it's very heavy."

Lovemaking was the last thing on my mind the Sunday I packed up my Taurus and drove north the short distance to County M, where I turned into the long winding drive that led to St. Ben's. Alan was the man I was running away from, although, if I'd had any sense, I would have been trying to catch up with him. Alan is a research scientist who teaches biochemistry at the university. We met one stifling August night when he showed up at the Writer's Center to listen to me read my poetry. When the reading was over he stood up to ask a question and introduced himself as a scientist. "What the hell are you doing here?" I asked him. So much was I a captive of C. P. Snow's notion of the "two cultures" that I couldn't imagine why a scientist would want to come to a poetry reading.

A whole year went by before we began meeting once a week to practice Italian together. Alan was married at that time, but he separated from his wife during the course of that year and filed for a divorce, which had just become final. This new freedom on his part had induced in me a classic case of the jitters. Things would not stay the same between us. In the back of my mind, I was harboring a notion that it might still be possible for me to reverse the whole course of my life and put myself back on track. This seemed to me the perfect time to run away to a monastery. Besides, as a writer, I had come with a purpose.

I was worried about my poetry commission. The Dane County Cultural Affairs Commission had named me to be the lead poet in an annual series of public poems that was intended to reflect the landscape of Dane County. My poem would be the first to be published at the end of the year in *Isthmus*, Madison's local weekly newspaper. By this time in my writing career, I had published two books of poetry and won a number of awards. But what bothered me about this assignment was that I had never been considered a nature poet per se, and unlike the rugged landscape of the Hudson River Valley where I had grown up in New York, or the hills of Rome where I had lived, I had no real feeling of connection to the tamed fields and tilled farmlands of what constituted most of Dane County. I was a city girl. Even the storied prairies, so glorified in the annals and eclogues of the Midwest, left me relatively unmoved. Moreover, I had been promised the sum of five hundred dollars for this commission, an outsized honorarium by any standard. Could I write a poem worth five hundred dollars? Could anybody? I had never before been offered a commission, nor had I ever written a poem "for the occasion." In fact, I had never written anything that hadn't been prompted by my own imagination. Now, here I was, under a deadline. How would I begin? What if I failed? The whole assignment made me nervous. So nervous, in fact, that I had decided to take a leave of absence from my job to give myself the time I thought I needed.

Even more pressing than my commission was the anxiety I felt in contemplating the possibility of marrying for a third time. Behind me lay a dark and bloody trail left by two divorces and two custody fights waged at times simultaneously over the course of three separate battle states. My ordeal began when I filed for divorce while still living in Kentucky, a name that happens to mean "The Dark and Bloody Ground," and lost custody of my two-year-old son when the judge declared me "intelligent, ambitious, and therefore unfit," a decision that was subsequently overturned on appeal by the Kentucky Supreme Court, but not before Giancarlo had turned four and was living in New York, where I was visiting him every two weeks. There were no reciprocal state agreements in those days, and when the New York court refused to honor the Kentucky Supreme Court's ruling without holding a hearing of its own, the chaos began in earnest: court room dramas, kidnappings, ambushes, grand jury testimony, a lot of ugly stuff that landed the three of us back in Kentucky, where I was trapped once again, at the mercy of the same vindictive circuit court judge who was determined to hold me a hostage of the court.

Under duress, I remarried and conceived a second child just at the time the judge finally allowed us to move to the state border so that I could take a job at WGUC in Cincinnati. The job paid only $11,700 a year, a challenge for a family of four, but it was my first full-time job in public radio and the start of a real career. I was devastated when, just a few weeks after Dominick was born, I returned from maternity leave to discover a pink slip in my mailbox. We were dogged by poverty during those years. Living as we did on the Kentucky side of the Ohio River, forbidden to move out of state, I sometimes felt like Eliza in *Uncle Tom's Cabin,* who stood on the shore of the river swollen with ice floes "contemplating this unfavorable aspect of things." My husband struggled to hold down a job while I patched together a meager living by teaching part-time and freelancing for National Public Radio. So pinched was I at that time in my life, so much a creature of scarcity, that I remember with shame that I once begrudged a friend a smear of peanut butter from a jar I was hoarding, afraid I might not have enough left to feed my kids. The judge finally relented after another three years had elapsed, granting us permission to move to Wisconsin, where I had been offered the job of humanities coordinator at Wisconsin Public Radio. But I had escaped the bludgeoning of the Kentucky court system only to face double jeopardy in Wisconsin. Within a year, my ex-husband followed me north to renew his custody fight in a brand new legal venue just at the time that I had commenced divorce proceedings from my second husband. So there I was, embroiled in two custody fights with two husbands at the same time. Years later, when everything had been settled, both my exes were still living in Madison a mere stone's throw from each other. "You go through men like a knife goes through butter," a colleague once told me. Another one said, "When it comes to men, your IQ goes down to forty." My own son was in the habit of cautioning his mother's suitors against making a fatal mistake.

My sorry history began at a graduation party at the end of eighth grade at Immaculate Heart of Mary School when I won the paper plate contest with a boy I'll call Stanley Richendorf, the only kid in the class who had been left back twice. That summer, Stanley phoned to ask me to a matinee of *Tarzan and the Lost Safari.* I remember sitting next to Stanley in the cavernous dark of Loew's Theater on a Saturday afternoon, bored almost to tears. Stanley phoned again the following fall when we were both enrolled in same-sex Catholic high schools, this time to invite me to his Harvest Dance. I was excited. My mother took me shopping, and we picked out a dress that had a white taffeta skirt with red felt cutouts and a red velveteen top. The top was cut slightly off the shoulder, which meant that my mother had to buy me my first strapless bra. On the night of the dance, Stanley and I were doing a vigorous Lindy in the middle of a crowded gymnasium when my bra began to creep its way slowly down my chest. Desperate, I tried yanking it up every time my back was turned when Stanley spun me out on the end of his arm, hoping he wouldn't notice. By the time we left the dance floor, a most peculiar bulge had settled around my middle, clearly exposing my flatiron chest. Stanley never called again after that night, to my relief. But it wasn't just a bra that had settled. It was my fate.

Over the years that followed, my adventures with the opposite sex followed a similar pattern of disaster. I was always mismatched, paired off with either lost boys or outlaws, or a combination of both. Even in graduate school at Berkeley I misfired, falling hopelessly in love with a classy guy who, unbeknownst to me, was the heir to the Huntington fortune and who ended up marrying my roommate, a buxom bisexual blonde who suffered from agoraphobia. Heartbroken, I left graduate school in midterm and flew home to New York to hang out for a whole year with a sixteen-year-old who loved cars, was mildly retarded, and had a crush on me. Years later, when his wife left him, Johnnie Labriola ended his own heartbreak by closing himself up in his garage and switching on the ignition in his car. He was such a sweet boy.

I'm not entirely sure why things went so badly for me. I could blame it on my Catholic upbringing and the all-girls schools that left me naive, pathologically shy, and terrified of the opposite sex. It could have been my acne, my big nose, or the fact that I wore glasses and was brainy and introverted, or the fact that my father, trying to be helpful, once said, "Don't worry, Jeannie, looks aren't everything." Maybe it was growing up in the shadow of a big sister who resembled Gina Lollobrigida, attracted men like bees, and never had a moment of self-doubt in her life. Or maybe it was just a lethal combination of lousy judgment and bad luck. Whatever it was, having arrived in midlife after bouts of therapy, there were still plenty of reasons for me to wonder whether I really was cut out for marriage.

Sister Turibius, my seventh-grade teacher, used to say, "College is the graveyard of vocations." By the time I graduated from Manhattanville College in the mid-1960s, just one year before the student body erupted, I had staged so many scenes against the nuns and their autocratic rule that they threw me out of the honor society, and I left with a grudge against all things Catholic. No wonder my parents were worried about my flying off to graduate school in Berkeley. They looked so stoic as they waved good-bye. My father's tie was flapping in the breeze as they stood on the tarmac beside my grandmother, who never cried, but had tears streaming down her face as I waved back from the window of a DC-6, about to take off for San Francisco. As a virgin arriving at UC–Berkeley in the fall of 1965, just one year after Mario Savio had blown up the campus, I was woefully unprepared for the social challenges I was about to face, but that didn't stop me. On a Sunday afternoon before classes had even begun, I chanced to meet one of the founders of the Hell's Angels who was playing bongo drums on campus and went roaring off with him into the Berkeley hills on the back of his Harley. That was how the wild years began.

Nevertheless, in spite of many escapades and heartbreaks, or maybe because of them, my interest in the religious life never altogether disappeared. I remembered with a pang the ardor I had felt as a young girl contemplating a life of devotion and service, and sometimes caught myself wondering whether my disastrous marriages weren't the consequence of having denied my true calling. I had not yet learned that I did, in fact, have a vocation, but not to the religious life. It wasn't until I became a public radio producer and undertook to retell the lives of the saints that it dawned on me that there are different ways to be "in the world and yet not of it."

Despite their pathologies, the stories of the saints and virgin martyrs had genuinely inspired me in my youth and had given me an enduring template of courage and heroism I longed to live up to. It was thrilling, for example, to learn that Perpetua, a young Roman matron who was one of the earliest martyrs, had actually stood in the arena and guided with her own hand the horns of the wild cow that gored her to death. But as an adult I had to acknowledge that these stories, so replete with tales of torture, imprisonment, and self-mutilation, had caused me to attach an unhealthy value to suffering and made me vulnerable to abuse. "The primary virtues of a Christian woman are obedience, compunction, and self-abnegation," Sister Turibius had instructed me, and I had dutifully copied the sentence down on the flyleaf of My Daily Missal. Now, here I was in my twenties, reading *The Feminine Mystique* and *Our Bodies/Our Selves* and taking self-assertion lessons from the feminists. What I needed was a new set of role models better suited to the demands of living in the second half of the twentieth century. Rather than reject the stories I had grown up with, I chose to reframe them.

The series of docudramas I produced for National Public Radio was called *Women of Spirit,* a feminist retelling of the lives of the saints. In showcasing the stories of extraordinary women in the history of monasticism such as Hildegard von Bingen, Catherine of Siena, and Julian of Norwich, the series revealed a lineage of powerful female leadership inside the Catholic Church and showed how the institution of monasticism had operated as a liberating force for women. Here were the role models for whom I had been searching: Hildegard, a visionary who became one of the most influential women of her age; Catherine, a disputatious mystic who persuaded the pope to return to Rome and was named Patroness of Italy and a doctor of the church; Julian, an anchoress who gave up the right even to her own name to become a theologian and the first woman ever to write a book in the English language.

Women of Spirit won a number of awards and became a project from which I personally benefited in countless ways. More than anything else, it represented for me an exercise in integration. I had been given an either/or model of spirituality: choose the life of the spirit and renounce the world. But here were women of prodigious worldly influence, power, and authority whose very efficacy as teachers, reformers, counselors, and artists derived from the depth and quality of their inner lives. "Marvelous and splendid is the place where the Lord now dwells which is principally, as shown to me, in the human soul. He has taken there His resting place and His honorable city." Those were Julian's words, the last words to be heard in "Love Was His Meaning," the final program in *Women of Spirit.* Blended in behind Julian's voice were sounds of the city of Norwich: roosters crowing, babies crying, a cart rolling over cobblestones, the cries of street vendors. The combination of Julian's image of the human soul as the city of God mixed with the real sounds of medieval city life gave me a lasting insight, that the real monastery is the world itself, and the new monastics are at work in the world, building "His honorable city."

Still, I wanted a chance to try out the real thing. Considering my age, my two divorces, and the fact that the second of the two boys I was raising was still at home, the whole question seemed more than a little absurd. And yet, I reasoned, it might still be possible for me to become an oblate or a tertiary, like Catherine of Siena who lived at home with her family and traveled at will. I remembered those saints' stories about widows who had entered the convent late in life after raising a family. This was my last chance to give it a try. I was strongly attracted to the idea of monastic life, but then, I was also attracted to Alan.

Everything about our relationship represented a breach with my past. Here was a man who was anything but an outlaw or a lost boy, a man who was at home in the world in a way that I would never be. He loved the difficult work of science at which he excelled; he was disciplined, ambitious, and on the move. He was born in Brooklyn, New York, into an extended clan of Sephardic Jews but raised in Latin America, first in Bogotá and then in Caracas in a house his father named "Penelope." He had inherited a complex of cultures as a member of an intricate and far-flung network of relatives and friends with whom I could see he maintained close ties. On the day I watched him go off to his uncle Joe's funeral in New York dressed in a black overcoat, a black fedora, and black leather gloves, the sight of him stirred something atavistic in me. I saw him in a long line of patriarchs: men of substance and character who had survived the Spanish Expulsion and centuries of displacements by adhering to a code that had been carefully handed down and preserved through generations. In his Jewishness, I recognized a certain kinship between us, a Mediterranean bond of blood memory that had drawn us together; more than an affinity between two people, it was an affinity of tribes.

Maybe that was why he seemed to know instinctively how to please me. On Valentine's Day, instead of flowers, he showed up at my door bearing a basketful of essentials: excellent extra-virgin olive oil, a bottle of real balsamic vinegar, a chunk of gritty parmigiano, gifts that undergirded our Mediterranean bond. He brought goodness in many forms into my life. I had been living out of a sense of abiding scarcity when we first met. Alan taught me how to live in the spirit of abundance. I used to call him my reverse priest. On Ash Wednesday of that year, inspired by his habit of leaving big tips, I declared a Reverse Lent, and vowed that instead of giving something up, this year I would give, to myself as well as to others.

There was something of the Edwardian gentleman about him; he had refined tastes; he was a lover of classical music. He was mild mannered, self-possessed, and reasonable to the core. Younger by more than a decade than I, he yet reminded me of my father. Had the scales of justice been hung from his shoulders, they would have been perfectly balanced. When he smiled, his whole face cracked with laugh lines, but there was a quality about him of essential sobriety. It was as if he had been born a grown-up. In fact, his mother called him *El hombre sin infancia*, the man without a childhood, because even as a young boy, he was reading the newspaper and advising his father about stocks. I found that when I was with him, as volatile as I am by nature, it felt unnatural to be angry or irritable in his presence. He mollified me. He made me feel safe, and yet I could tell that he was consciously nurturing in me the same qualities that were contributing to his own success.

We had an unusual courtship. For one thing, it advanced at the pace of a Victorian novel. The pattern we established, meeting once a week to practice Italian together, lasted the better part of a year. I used to stand on the corner that we had designated Il Nostro Angolo, watching for Alan to come swinging down University Avenue carrying his big Italian dictionary under his arm. That dictionary got a lot of use that year.

Halting as they were, there was something magical about those conversations that tended to spiral around a theme and end on a note of transcendence, almost like a poem. Each one became memorable in a different way, imbued with the flavor of whatever ethnic food we happened to be sampling that day. One Monday in early October, shortly after we had begun meeting, we were seated outdoors at an Afghan restaurant on State Street. It was one of those perfect fall days. *"Questi sono gli ultimi giorni,"* I announced, unfolding my napkin as I glanced up at the break-your-heart blue sky. "These are the last beautiful days." Little did I know that I had just intoned a theme that was to fly back and forth between us like a shuttlecock: *ultimi giorni*, the last days. It was a classic theme among the Sephardic poets of medieval Spain such as Moses Ibn Ezra, who wrote with prescience in the eleventh century, "Ah, rosy days . . . The rosy days are numbered, numbered all . . . Tell thou their number, then, in cups of wine!"

As I dug into my salad, Alan began to talk about his older brother, Maurice, who had died three years earlier in a bicycle accident, killed instantly when he was struck by a drunken driver. This sudden drastic loss of an older brother had occasioned a big crisis in Alan's life. He was still grieving, still examining his own life, obsessed with a search for "authenticity," a word that we dubbed "the *A* word" when it kept recurring in our conversations. Tit for tat, I matched Alan's story of loss with one of my own, how my father on his deathbed had looked at me and then turned to my mother to ask, "Has the doctor slapped her yet?"

"Blue Mondays" were never blue after that, and what had started out as a weekly lunch date quickly morphed into something deeper that neither one of us was eager to define. It wasn't long before Alan began to drop hints alluding to his unhappy marriage. Veteran that I was, I could hear the chill winds of divorce beginning to blow through his words. I knew that he would need a good friend by his side to help him through the coming storm. I signed up.

Alan has one hand that is always red. Not a constant red, but one that changes, depending on the weather. Indoors, or in the heat, it's a shiny, livid red, but in the cold it takes on a grayish, chalky coloration. It was on a cold Monday in January, over steaming bowls of Thai noodle soup, that I first noticed this hand. I was watching Alan's spoon carrying the hot soup from his bowl to his mouth when I caught myself fantasizing about the other hand, the left hand. How would it feel, I wondered, to be touched by such a hand? A hand that glows? The color, as it turns out, comes from a port-wine stain Alan's had from birth that affects not just his hand, but his whole arm, extending like a map up along his left shoulder blade and across his chest, covering his heart. It looks like a kind of heraldry. And here's the joke: this birthmark is caused by an excess of capillaries just under the surface of the skin that release heat, so instead of being hot, his red hand is actually cool, while his white hand is hot! He's perfectly balanced. And this says a lot about a man who, as it happens, has been making wine, both red and white, for most of his adult life.

Alan's first forays into winemaking began while he was still a graduate student in San Diego when two of his buddies bought a five-acre
vineyard and invited him to join them in making cabernet. One year,
after spending eighteen hours stemming and stomping in the hot California sun with hundreds of bees swarming all around them, Alan held
up a camera and shot a picture of himself while he was still ankle-deep
in a vat of cabernet. He looks like a wild man in that photograph with
his long, curly blue-black hair flying all around his head and his thick
eyebrows that met above a pair of crinkly, raisin-dark eyes. He is grinning ecstatically; his strong white teeth are studded with black grapes
while rivulets of sticky red juice trickle from his beard and run down his
hairy chest and legs, disappearing into the vat. He looks more than a
little bit deranged in that picture, and a lot like Bacchus.

By the time I met him, winemaking had become an integral part of
Alan's life, a yearly ritual practiced the way old-school Catholics observe
the feast days and the liturgical seasons. The grapes are shipped from
California each year, arriving frozen around Christmas in five-gallon
buckets to be hauled down into the cellar where the whites whisper and
hiss in deep barrels, and the reds ferment on their skins for a week or
more before being pressed, filling up the house with their fragrance
all through the holidays. I remember the heart-stopping thump I felt
the first time I saw Alan up to his armpits in one of those great barrels,
swirling the mash and looking half-mad with the pleasure of it. He
stopped when he saw me standing there in the cellar door; he grinned
and lifted his arm out of the barrel for me to see it coated and dripping
with what looked like thick blood.

I learned quite a bit about wine during our year of Italian conversation. That whole year, in fact, was a series of wine epiphanies, beginning
with my first taste of sauterne at the Opera House, a cozy after-hours
wine bar where we went after Alan's appearance on *Hot Nights*, a radio
series I was hosting that summer. If champagne is like drinking stars,
sauterne is like swallowing summer, a ribbon of shimmering gold that
ripples on the tongue as it unfolds. Truly the wine of the Last Days, it
tastes of honey and apricots, a late harvest sweetness that might be cloy-
ing were it not for the "noble rot," the fungus that sweeps in with the autumn mists, attacks and withers the grapes, and makes the wine taste
vaguely necrotic.

"Wine ages in the bottle, taking on depth and complexity," Alan explained to me one Monday over burritos. "It just keeps getting better until at some mysterious point it reaches its peak and starts going into decline. If the bottle isn't opened before then, the wine is spoiled, and it can't be drunk."

To me, this news was disconcerting. "But how do you know when the peak has arrived?" I asked.

"You don't. There's just no way of knowing that with any certainty. It's one of the things I love about it. Its evanescence. Wine is a limited thing, like life. It's made to be appreciated at the right moment. Wine itself fades out and goes over the hill, just as we do."

But I didn't love it. Having reached a certain peak age myself, I took it as a metaphor for my own status as a late bloomer. Had I already peaked, gone over the edge? Would I keep? Was I was in decline and didn't even know it?

"But remember the noble rot!" Alan said, laughing at my all-too-obvious distress. "There are some wines, very rare and delectable wines like sauterne, that only reach their peak after long extended periods of aging. Michael Broadbent, a famous wine connoisseur, once opened a bottle of Thomas Jefferson's d'Yquem from 1784 and found that it was still drinkable! So stop worrying!"

My birthday happened to fall on a Monday that year. Over sushi in our favorite Japanese restaurant, Alan gave me a card with a quote from Aristotle that said, "What is a friend? A single soul dwelling in two bodies." It was signed, *"Felice compleanno, con molto affetto, A."* Next, he pulled from his backpack three little gifts: the first was a bar of very dark Valrhona chocolate, the second, a dusty-silver half-bottle of sauterne, and last, a little framed picture of some strange lumpy stuff that looked like it was straight out of a biochemistry textbook. "What's this?" I asked, holding it up. "It's a picture of the noble rot," he explained. "That's what botrycized grapes look like before they're picked to make into sauterne." Two months later we were sitting in the same Japanese restaurant on Valentine's Day, again over sushi. Alan was shy. "I really shouldn't be saying this," he said, " but I would love to take you to the wine country."

And so it was that three months later, there we were, crossing the Golden Gate Bridge on the first morning of our trip through the

California wine country, heading north through Sausalito on our way to Napa Valley. Magic comes easily to a sun-drenched place where beauty abounds and the bacchic rites of conviviality, euphoria, and sensual pleasure are all as carefully tended as the vines. Alan had planned this trip with so much forethought. We had landed in the Valley of Love and Delight. The very air we breathed was a heady stuff, laced with the mixed pungencies of eucalyptus, lavender, and rosemary. It was a pilgrimage we were on, and we were pilgrims making stops at Alan's favorite shrines along the Silverado Trail: Pine Ridge, Silver Oak, Carneros, posing to have our picture taken before the great doors, one Greek, another Romanesque, another thickly framed in honeysuckle.

The wineries all looked like monasteries, set in the midst of terraced hillsides rimmed with flowerbeds, stone walls, and olive groves, their scrupulously tended fields closely stitched with grapevines, each perfect row punctuated by a rosebush. And the tasting rooms were all like chapels where worshipers were gathered. Behind a bar of polished wood gleaming like an altar rail, there were servers who stood ready to pour their libations into rows of sparkling glasses lined up before each taster. The tastings always proceeded in the same unvarying sequence beginning with the delicate whites: Semillon followed by a sauvignon blanc, followed by chardonnay; and then, descending like a diver through a sea of ever-deeper reds: pinot noir, merlot, zinfandel, cabernet. I learned how to taste without swallowing on that first morning, spitting into the elegant spittoon that sat on top of every bar, itself a symbol of abundance.

Leaving Silver Oak Winery, I was drawn by the scent of a huge open red rose that was growing by the wall, its labial petals blackened at the edges into crisp scallops, its spread-apart heart all plush crimson and scarlet, giving off the most intoxicating perfume as the air heated up the day. We had begun tasting at Roche, then made our way through the cavernous dark of the underground caves at Pine Ridge in the afternoon, where we passed the great solemn casks that hold the wine while it ages, stopping to watch a steward test the barrel wine with a siphon called a wine thief. Later that day we stopped at TraVigne, an Italian taverna encrusted with ivy where poppies and snapdragons grew wild among the vines, and fat-bottomed cheeses and salamis hung over an open wood-burning oven, their comic shapes reminding me of my aunts and uncles. We ate fried smelt, fusilli with rabbit and pancetta, raviolini stuffed with smoked chicken, roasted peppers and polenta, finishing it all off with rum raisin gelato and espresso. In the courtyard, I delighted in a surprise fountain made out of wrought iron where water pours eternally over the side of a little table from an overturned pitcher. A bird is perched on the handle of the pitcher, and the table is set for one with bread, wine, a cork, an unfolded napkin, and a hat that rests on the back of the chair, all part of the same sculpture.

The next day, we picnicked on mangoes and French bread at Vichon with Robin, Peter, and James, a few of Alan's old friends who drove up from San Francisco to meet us. There's a photograph in our scrapbook that shows all of us sitting around a table under the trees, with sunbeams glancing off the brims of the men's straw hats, which looks like a prototype for a French impressionist painting. Under the photograph in our scrapbook I pasted a note card with lines I found in a poem by Judah al-Harizi, another Sephardic poet:

> Here under leafy bowers
> Where coolest shades descend,
> Crowned with a wreath of flowers
> Here will we drink, my friend.

We arrived by sunset in Sonoma, where we sipped cabernet while soaking in a hot tub, and in the morning climbed up into the sprawling arms of a 250-year-old live oak tree that overlooks the Valley of the Moon. At Kenwood, where they were pouring twelve wines that morning, I sampled a special reserve ruby red zinfandel from old vines. "It tastes like prosciutto!" I said in surprise—spicy, peppery, hammy, so delicious. Two miles down the road, Alan spotted the old growth vineyard at the top of a ridge. It was high noon when we parked the car on a dirt lane and walked out into the deserted vineyard. The vines, which are dry-farmed, were well over a century old with roots that went down twenty or thirty feet. They had just been head-pruned and were gnarled and twisted, some of them just blackened stumps sending out green shoots that looked like signals of distress. Alan's hand and arm were glowing in the noonday sun, his beard glistening blue-black, his face ecstatic above his black T-shirt, and he, too, had that spicy, meaty smell I love. "Have you ever been kissed in a vineyard?" he asked. The sound of our kiss was echoed by the calls of red-winged blackbirds perched on telegraph lines and circling overhead. "I have a new rule," I said. "From now on, I only kiss winemakers in old vineyards." I could see the joy rising in him like sap. "How is it that I have found you? How is it possible?" he asked, and again we kissed, mimicking and synchronizing the music of our kisses with the song of the red-winged blackbirds while, at a distance, plaintive and clear, the low bleat of a mourning dove entered the chorus, its sorrow harmonizing with the kissing of the blackbirds. I saw the tears well up in Alan's eyes.

> Wine scatters woe,
> Makes glad the life
> And brings death low.

We left Sonoma that afternoon, driving on into Anderson Valley, where all the wines tasted like green apples, and my eyes widened over a heavenly late harvest Riesling. "Don't like it too much!" Alan warned, which was how I discovered there are limits even in paradise. Climbing a mountain to Pepperwood Springs the next day, we stood on a deck and drank chardonnay from balloon glasses that magnified the rays of the sun and set the dry wood of a banister on fire. At Roederer, where they make only champagne, we both got giddy and began to play, teasing each other. "Would you ever have believed three months ago that you would be saying, 'This tastes like a classic pinot noir'?" Alan asked. "You are a real master teacher," I replied, *"un vero Maestro di Vini."* "Hmm," he mused, "I never thought of that before—*Di-vini*, as in Divine."

The joke came up again while we were homeward bound, driving down Highway 1 toward Point Reyes, and I was telling Alan about my checkered history. "Gee," Alan said, "you talk about all these relationships you stayed in for these terrible reasons. It scares me. Are you in this for the right reason?" "There's only one reason," I said. "You're only in it for the wine?" he asked. "Yeah. I'm only in it for the wine." "Oh, that's right," he said. "You're searching for di-vinity."

We spent our last night together at the Blackthorne Inn, a giant tree house made out of a single Douglas fir, where we climbed up a skinny spiral staircase into the Eagles Nest, an octagonal tower room, all glass-enclosed, to sleep under the stars. That was at the end of May, and now, here it was July, and I was hiding out in a monastery. Was it Get thee to a nunnery, or Get thee to a winery?

It took very little time for me to move into St. Benedict's the Sunday I arrived. In the spirit of monastic simplicity, I had brought only one small, battered green suitcase full of notebooks and paper, my portable Royal typewriter, now half a century old, a pound of coffee, a funnel and a box of filters, and a few changes of clothes, all carefully chosen in neutral colors—pearl gray, oyster white, sage green—to render me as inconspicuous as possible. The last thing in the world I wanted in this rarified environment was to stick out.

The cottage was clean as a whisk, and devoid of personality. I hung a pair of slacks and a couple of shirts from the few lonely hangers I found in the bedroom closet, set out my comb and brush on the shelf above the bathroom sink, and found a place for my typewriter on top of the wooden table in the middle of the living room. Exploring the rheumy basement, I found a card table tucked into a corner, which I dragged up to the porch, thinking how pleasant it would be to write surrounded by nothing but woods and birds. Then I stopped to look around at the spartan cottage with its simple furnishings and bare white walls, which would be my home for the next month. There was something unsettling about its pared-down plainness. The walls stared back at me with the blank look of an empty page, and suddenly I felt lost. Now that I was facing it head on, all that freedom I had longed for felt a bit oceanic.

That night I had a dream in which I was swimming alone in a great sea. All I could see when I lifted my head was hundreds of waves, as far as my eye could reach. Surely, I would drown. But, just then, a great wave came up, lifted me on its back, and carried me a long way until I could dimly make out a stretch of land in the distance. Closer and closer the wave carried me toward the land until it finally washed me up on the shore, setting me down on a spur of sand. I was safe.

The next morning I awoke to the clanging of the monastery bell. Right away, I remembered the dream and connected it to the gospel I had heard at Sunday Mass the previous day. It was the gospel that told of a storm that came up suddenly on the Sea of Galilee while Jesus was asleep in the boat, and the disciples were all afraid.

I hopped out of bed, washed hastily, pulled on my clothes, and was out the door and trotting down the lane in no time, anxious to give a good accounting of myself on this, my first day as a lay monastic. But "behind haste is the devil," as Carl Jung once said. The whole idea of voluntary enclosure, as I was about to discover, is to slow down and leave the racing world behind. This is precisely what gives monastic life its feeling of timeless serenity, and why so many people are drawn to it. In a monastery nobody rushes, or shouts, or laughs out loud, and even the least gestures—picking up a hymnal, replacing it on a shelf, turning to greet a neighbor—proceed in an orderly, preordained fashion, as if guided and prescribed by an invisible hand.

Back in the sixth century, it was Benedict of Nursia, an Italian monk and founder of monasticism, who himself set down the rule that still governs his monasteries today. Disgusted with the decadence of Rome, he took off for the hills and was living alone in a hillside cave near Subiaco when his solitude was shattered by a friend who found him out. The friend was charmed by Benedict's new lifestyle, and rather than return to Rome, he stayed. Word got out, and soon there were fresh arrivals. Because Benedict couldn't bring himself to send any of his friends packing, a little community began to grow up around him. Eventually, he was forced to write down his rule, thereby forming the first monastic community in the Western world. Hospitality has been at the heart of the rule of Benedict ever since, and monasteries became famous B&Bs during the Middle Ages when there were no hotels. Indeed, this 1,500-year-old tradition was the very reason I had been invited to stay. The sisters receive each guest as if he or she were Christ. When I thanked Sister Joanne for her hospitality in taking me in, she said, "We are all guests in the house of the Lord."

There's a stone fountain in the shape of a cube that stands about three feet high just outside the monastery chapel where the holy water never ceases to run, making a soothing warble. Anyone heading for the chapel is obliged to pass around it. Pausing on that first morning to dip my fingers into the water to make the sign of the cross, I immediately felt myself slow down. I had just crossed an invisible threshold. Going through the double doors into the chapel, the first thing I noticed was the palpable hush inside. It's always there, no matter how many or how few have gathered there ahead of you. Silence has a sound. You bow as you enter, as if to honor the silence, and you take your place. The silence enjoins you; it lifts and carries you the way a summer breeze sails a gauzy curtain. Instantly, I felt myself folded in, threaded into a loosely woven fabric that was breathing in and all around me. It was deeply calming and prepared me in just the right way for the recitation of the Divine Office.

Benedict himself ordained that "nothing should be preferred to the work of God," by which he meant the daily prayer life of the monastery. In chapter 43 of his rule, *Of Those Who Arrive Late at the Work of God or at Table*, he advises, "At the hour of Divine Office, as soon as the signal has been heard, dropping everything whatever was in hand, let him run at top speed. . . . Nothing therefore shall be given precedence over the Work of God." Just to follow each office, let alone take part, finding one's way among the psalms, canticles, and responses, what is chanted and what is recited, is intricate work that requires attention and a full-bodied participation. "The whole of you must go into it . . . and unless you are aware, tuned, you will make a mistake" (Rumer Godden, *In This House of Brede*).

The recitation of the psalms is at the very heart of the Divine Office. It surprised me to discover that, for all their exalted poetry, the psalms are reality-based, full of the existential knowledge that life is fleeting, harsh, and brutish. The psalmist has his feet planted firmly on the ground, and his eyes wide open, telling us flatly in Psalm 90, *Our span is seventy years, or eighty for those that are strong. . . . And most of these are emptiness and pain. / They pass swiftly, and we are gone.* Many of the psalms dwell on the theme of evanescence, reminding us, as in Psalm 62:

> Mortals are but a breath,
> nothing more than a mirage;
> set them on the scales,
> they prove lighter than mist.

Other images inspire terror, like the line from Psalm 39 that compares God to a great moth *devouring all we treasure* . . . and in Psalm 90 impute responsibility indirectly to this all-devouring God for so much human suffering: *All our days pass away in your anger . . . Give us joy to balance our affliction.*

To pray the psalms in a communal setting induces a neutralizing calm, perhaps by obliging us to confront calmly and without emotion those immutable facts about our earthly existence that we most fear. This ritual of the hours takes place three times a day, six times in some monasteries, bringing to mind the great planetary patterns of alternation where everything moves in a circle, day followed by night, light followed by darkness, winter followed by summer, and so on and so forth *ad aeternum.* The blessing of the liturgy is that it wipes out self. Benedict enjoined his monks to "Think on death everyday," not, I suspect, because he wanted them to be morbidly preoccupied with death, but because, by reducing their sense of self-importance, he sought to lighten their anxiety and bring them into the present moment, however fleeting:

> Show forth your work to your servants,
> let your glory shine on their children.
> Let the favor of God be upon us:
> give success to the work of our hands,
> give success to the work of our hands.

Chanting the psalms in the monastery chapel was a balm to me, centering my mind, washing me afresh that first morning when I entered the chapel, fearful I would be late. But Morning Prayer lasts just so long, and before I knew it, I was turning back up the dirt lane, walking past the sisters' cemetery and the apple orchard, and swinging open the screen door once again to confront a different kind of silence, this one decidedly unsettling. Again, I looked around at the blankness in my little house. Again, I felt the panic ranging at the jagged edges of all this freedom, the emptiness of the blank walls, the white page, the unbroken quiet, my own lapsed practice with nothing to mask it but the faint droning of insects.

I'll just read for a while, I said to myself.

Break the ice.

There were a few books leaning against each other on the shelf of a little bookcase on the porch. One of them was a faded red and had *The*

Rule for Oblates printed in gold on its spine. Perfect. Part of my reason for coming here, after all, I reminded myself as I settled into a chair, was to resolve once and for all the question that had never really altogether died in me since my convent school days. Did I have a religious vocation? In choosing to marry, had I strayed from my true path? Was all the suffering I had caused, to myself as well as others, the result of that original betrayal? I picked up the book and began to read: *Listen carefully, my child, to my instructions, and attend to them with the ear of your heart. This is advice from one who loves you; welcome it and faithfully put it into practice. The labor of obedience will bring you back to God from whom you had drifted through the sloth of disobedience. This message of mine is for you, then, if you are ready to give up your own will, once and for all, and armed with the strong and noble weapons of obedience to do battle for Jesus, the Christ.*

Again, the clanging of the great bell. Again, the hurried walk down along the dirt road, across the wide lawn, and down the hill to reach the chapel. Again, the chanting back and forth across the aisle, the balm of the psalms. When it was over, I filed out the door behind the others, deposited my hymnal on the shelf where it belonged, and dutifully followed the sisters into the refectory to sit down to lunch. I had spent the whole morning studying the rule like a good girl and had managed to show up on time for Prayers at Noon.

"I spent the whole morning reading the rule of Benedict," I announced, trying to suppress the hint of pride in my voice.

"Oh, you didn't do that all morning, did you?" Mary David skewered me with one raised eyebrow.

"Well, yes, I did," I confessed, somewhat abashed. "And so I intend to spend the rest of the day!"

"Oh, don't do that," she quickly admonished. "Read for half an hour, forty-five minutes at most. Then do something else. Go for a walk."

It turned out to be the perfect prescription for a writer, to give leisure its due along with study, work, and prayer. The genius of Benedict's rule lies in its balance. Most of us think nothing of doubling up on work, skimp on leisure, and pray not at all. But daily life in a monastery is not unlike the great bell itself that swings out and swings back again, hallowing the morning hours equally against the hallowing of the after-noon, so that the whole day is punctuated, plotted out, and seeded by the predictable rhythms of the call to prayer.

By the end of three days I had settled into a comfortable routine, and for the first time in my rebellious life, I began to experience some-thing of the peace that comes from living by a rule simply by obeying the summons of the bell, walking back and forth along the dirt road from the cottage to the chapel three times a day. Between the calls to prayer, I spent the hours just the way I had imagined: working at my desk or taking long rambles along the trails and across the sunny mead-ows, stopping in the middle of the day to watch swallows swooping overhead or stooping to gather wildflowers, delighting like a child in my big bouquets of Queen Anne's lace, bergamot, honeysuckle, milkweed, and deadly nightshade, all of it exquisitely inconsequential. These I bore back to my little house in triumph to make it more my own.

The emptiness in the house distressed me. I tried filling it first with ferns, then weeds, then big bunches of wildflowers. Nothing lasted very long. In the morning I would find the ferns withered, the flowers drooped on their stems, and a fine dusting of pollen scattered over the tabletop. *Our life is over like a sigh.*

Returning from a walk one afternoon, I found a little basket of rasp-berries perched on my doorstep—a gift from Jung Ja, and an invitation to play. Living the monastic life, I had discovered fairly quickly that there was just so much solitude I could take. By the end of the day I was itching for some company. Doug and Jung Ja had reached out to me, and I was especially grateful for the evening hours I spent in their com-pany. They took me with them on their walks together, and the three of us swung from the branches of a great willow tree one evening while the sun was sinking behind the lake. We went berry picking together; Doug and Jung Ja pointed out the choicest spots where red raspberries and mulberries were sprinkled along the orchard road and hidden in the hedges of the sisters' cemetery. It was Jung Ja, especially, who brought the child out in me, dropping to her hands and knees in the orchard one morning after prayers, leading me through the long slippery grass that grew under the apple trees where the two of us crawled about on all fours, growling and pretending to be tigers.

Besides being the night watchman, Doug was an artist by day. I used to spot him on the grounds from time to time looking like Van Gogh in his big, broad-brimmed straw hat as he sat painting seated in his canvas folding chair. One evening, knowing how I longed for color on the white-washed walls of my little house, Doug brought me one of his paintings on loan, setting it down on the floor against the back of the living room wall. Instantly, the wall came alive. It was a painting of an adder lily, speckled like a trout. It had fleshy freckled green leaves and roots that seemed to writhe and slither in a slippery bog. So unlike its pristine sister, the lily of Easter, this was a lily of longing and desire. It had a butter churn for a calyx and sharp teeth that made it look hungry, eager, avid. It seemed altogether more animal than plantlike, and it spoke of that Darwinian urge that over time can push a fish to walk on land, or a frog to climb a tree. The three of us stood together contemplating this painting that seemed decidedly out of place in its monastic setting. Finally, Jung Ja broke the silence. "This is you," she said.

The Fourth of July dawned hot and clear, a perfect summer day, shattering my peace with an unnatural quiet. Prayers had been suspended for the holiday, so even the monastery bell lacked its usual authority, having nothing at all to call us to. By ten in the morning, the sun had mounted the sky like a god, the pine needles were softening in the heat, and the leaves on the oak trees were slick as glass. By noon, everything had flattened out like a dog on its belly.

I was restless, unable to settle into anything. I was expecting a visit from Alan, but I had no idea when he might arrive. I kept pacing back and forth from the porch to the pool, straining for the sound his tires might make crunching gravel on the dirt road. All day long I waited without a sign. Near the end of my patience, his car finally hove into view, nosing its way slowly up the road. He pulled into the cul-de-sac and got out of the car. He was wearing dark sunglasses and his purple T-shirt from Chateau Sauverain, and he had one hand upraised, holding a bottle of wine. The bottle gleamed, catching a ray from the late afternoon sun. "I found a 1983 Botrytis Semillon," he fairly sang, having no idea how strange those words might sound to someone who'd been chanting psalms for three days.

"What took you so long?" I burst out. "I've been waiting here all day. Why didn't you call? I wanted to give you a tour, show you around before it got too dark."

He was hot. Before anything else, he wanted to jump into the pool. He stripped down to his purple bikini and dove in. Aroused out of its habitual torpor, the water suddenly surged into life, sending shock waves out to the edges of the pool. I stood at one end watching him swim laps, seeing how his black curls unscrolled down along the back of his neck and flattened out each time his body broke the surface. When he'd had enough and was standing in front of me drying himself off, I noticed how the blue-black hairs in his moustache gleamed like dragonflies in the sunlight.

I showed him around the cottage and was hankering to take him on a proper tour of the monastery while it was still light, but Alan had other ideas. He had come prepared to spread a lavish picnic supper for the two of us, including wine, of course, but in his haste he had forgotten to bring along a set of wine glasses. I tried to convince him that there were no such luxuries to be found in my simple abode, but he was not to be deterred. He strode into the galley kitchen on his long legs and set about ransacking all the cabinets, dismayed when he came up empty-handed. "Well, there have to be wine glasses somewhere in this place," he grumbled.

Drinking wine from a mug constitutes a kind of sacrilege to a wine lover. Wine must be swirled and sniffed in a proper glass in order for it to release its full bouquet. This was one of the lessons I had learned while we were swirling and sniffing our way through the wine country. Nevertheless, it was lovely to sit on the deck at the end of the day sipping the late harvest wine from our monkish mugs and nibbling on pâté.

The dirt road was ruddy in the glow of the setting sun, and we, too, were a little flush by the time we set out under a sky that was sliced by swallows, passing along the orchard where the apples and pears were just beginning to redden and swell. "Maybe we'll find some wine glasses in the refectory," I said, to encourage him.

"What's a refectory?"

"It's the place where we eat."

"You call it a refectory?"

"Yes. The place where we eat is called a refectory and the place where we pray is called an oratory. It's from Latin. You know, as in oratorio."

Reaching the end of the lane where it veers to the left, we dipped down inside the shade of the sisters' cemetery, and suddenly it was dusk. I pointed out the sprinkling of headstones and the mulberry trees where, earlier that day, I had gathered a few berries as a surprise. Mulberries do not grow in Venezuela, where Alan grew up. He sampled a few, pronouncing them delicious. "Hmm. They taste like vanilla," he said. Taking leave of the cemetery, we made our way across the clearing and down the hill to the monastery, where I punched in the code, pushed open the heavy door, and led the way down the hall to the fountain, still trickling in the dark, and through the double doors into the deserted chapel.

"This is where we come three times a day to say our prayers," I whispered, as he stood beside me in the doorway. "We sit on both sides facing one another and chant the psalms back and forth," I explained, ushering him into the side altar where the tabernacle is kept.

"This is called the tabernacle," I explained, pointing out the carved wooden box in the center of the altar. "It's where the Blessed Sacrament is kept. See that red lamp beside the altar where the flame is lit? That's to signify that the Blessed Sacrament is inside."

"What's that?" he asked.

"The Blessed Sacrament is the host that the priest blesses during the Mass. The chalice is kept in there too. Catholics believe that the priest transforms the bread and wine into the body and blood of Christ during the part of the Mass that's called the consecration."

"Well, that's probably where they keep the wine glasses!" he said, taking a few strides toward the altar.

"No, No! You can't do that!" I laughed, stretching out my hand to hold him back. Surprised, he stopped in his tracks and turned around to look at me.

"Why not?"

"Because only the priest can go in there. Otherwise, it's considered a sacrilege. These things are sacred objects. They're set aside to be used only for ritual purposes. You can't just go in there and take them out any old time you want."

It was dark by the time we got back to the cottage when Alan started pulling things out of grocery sacks, one after another, beginning with a spray of luscious red-ripe tomatoes still clinging to the vine, then a crown of roasted garlic followed by a small round loaf of sesame bread. He was like a magician pulling rabbits out of a hat, orchestrating his carefully chosen delicacies two or three at a time. The words from Psalm 68 came back to me: *O God, I watched the procession as you marched into your house / Singers at the head, musicians at the rear / between them, women striking tambourines.*

At the table in the living room he poured what was left of the Semillon. Next, he opened a Gewürztraminer he matched with salmon cakes, and in between, to cleanse our palettes, he served pink slabs of watermelon on shiny black plates, which left two green-striped smiles grinning back at us. While I relaxed, enjoying his attentions, Alan went back and forth, carrying black lacquered bowls in pairs from the kitchen.

And so it went, a fresh surprise arriving with each little course, one following after another until, at last, he carried in the strawberries, saved for the finish. I watched as he stirred with diligence, his red hand steadying the bowl while his right hand went slowly round and round, and as I watched I began to grow just a little bit impatient at this ceremony that had gone on so long, this priest so composed, so even-handed, too classy to disgrace a novice. I wanted action. I set down my wine, opened my mouth, and almost before I knew it, the fatal words flew out: "How long before we take off our clothes?"

Later that night we watched eight separate sets of fireworks from our perch on the crest of the ridge—a silent panorama of Catherine's wheels and Roman candles exploding all around the distant horizon as we stood holding thick gray blankets over our heads to protect ourselves from the mosquitoes. Traipsing back down the hill in the dark after the last rocket had sputtered out, following in Alan's footsteps, I couldn't help but notice how much he looked like a monk in a cowl.

We slept together to our own Fourth of July "Rhythm and Boom," celebrating independence in two different countries, America and Venezuela, back to back. *Come, O Fount of every blessing. . . . Teach me some melodious sonnet / sung by flaming tongues above. . . . Praise the mount, I'm fixed upon it, mount of God's unfailing love.*

The next morning, Alan was gone in a spurt of gravel. I stood alone in the middle of the road, contemplating the little dust devil he had left hovering in midair, listening to the crunch of his tires growing fainter on the gravel road. When it disappeared altogether, I looked around. Too late. I had missed Morning Prayers. It was noon before I could bring myself to resume my life of measure, heeding the bell that called us to chapel, "thinking on death every day."

Jesus and Bacchus . . . Jesus and Bacchus . . . what am I doing? In the wake of Alan's visit, I was troubled. Walking back and forth along the dirt road that day, I pondered . . . *Why do we spoon out God in ladlefuls when we could be swimming in his pool? It's deep enough, Lord knows. Does a wine thief wound the barrel? Why do we go about hungering and thirsting? Didn't Jesus himself feed the multitude? Didn't he change water into wine? Does it matter, in the end, which vat we dip from, the red or the white? Who says the* via negativa *is the only way to God? What if, when we die, like Kabir says, we simply end up in an apartment in the City of Death? What if it's the way the Jews say it is, and somebody asks us then, did you drink deeply of the fruits of the earth while you were alive, or did you only go about weeping? Rumi was drunk on God. Emily Dickinson called herself "the little tippler." If it's rapture we're after, why not drink now? Why not be drunk by noon?*

Back in the cottage, I sat down at my desk and began to write . . . *Three days after I settled in at the monastery, Bacchus paid me a visit in late afternoon . . .*

I spent the rest of the week working furiously on my new poem. At last I was on to something. It was exciting to watch it take shape on the page. After all, here I was sitting right in the middle of some of the most coveted and best-preserved land in all of Dane County. By now I knew it fairly well. I had walked its many trails, I had picked its fruits and flowers at varying stages, I had sung in its meadows. And it was here, in this very place, that I had been opened to the mystery of love. Surely, writing about that would satisfy my commission.

The next Sunday, I left the monastery long enough to pay my half-deaf mother a visit in her nursing home. "I'm writing a poem about the Greek god of wine!" I yelled, pantomiming to make my meaning plain. "Oh, he had to be Greek," she shot back. "He couldn't be Jewish?" I never could understand how she managed to be so sharp in spite of her dementia.

The following week, I arranged for a meeting with Mary David, hoping she might help me sort out my confusion. Sitting across from her in one of the rooms in the Conference Center, I began to lay it all out. "I'm dating a man who's a scientist. He loves good food, he makes wine, he wants to travel all over the world." Her eyes widened; without waiting to hear another word, Mary David suddenly leapt up from her chair, and her hands flew up. "Marry him!" she cried. "But he's Jewish, and he doesn't believe in God," I protested, astonished. "How can I marry a man who has no interest in religion and doesn't even believe in God?" "He may not believe in God," she answered firmly, "but God believes in him."

The remainder of my time in the monastery passed by without incident. When my month in the Retreat Cottage had elapsed, I moved into Benedict House for another week, but it was never the same. The institutional setting didn't suit me. I found it cold and unwelcoming. I had trouble sleeping. I missed the little house in the woods that had become my hermitage. On the morning of my last day, I went in search of Jung Ja, and together we walked in the meadow gathering gargantuan bouquets of bergamot, prairie clover, chicory, and Queen Anne's lace to welcome Jung Ja's mother, who was about to arrive for a visit from Korea. The two of us lay down side by side in the middle of the path and sang a little song while the swallows and the deerflies flitted all around us. Late that afternoon at the close of Evening Prayer, knowing it was my last liturgy, Mary David embraced me and kissed me on the cheek, calling me "Monk," to which Jung Ja added, a bit impishly, "Monk in the world."

Bacchus at St. Benedict" became something of a cause célèbre after it was published that December. Some people who were expecting a very different kind of end-of-year poem, one that rhymed at the very least, didn't know what to make of it. They attacked it as "technically weak," labeled it "offensive and disgusting," "self-indulgent blasphemy," and a waste of taxpayers' money. Even the editor of the newspaper seemed to feel the need to apologize for having to live up to his promise to publish it. One woman thought I had gone to the monastery to seduce a priest.

"I am appalled to think that after spending two weeks in a religious setting," she wrote, "all you could think of was to seduce a this [*sic*] Bacchus." None of this really bothered me. I knew I had written a very good poem, perhaps my best. Besides, transgression is the very stuff of poetry. It wasn't until I learned that on account of it Sister Mary David and Sister Joanne had both been hauled onto the carpet by the local bishop that I felt bad. I hated to think that I had repaid their hospitality with treachery. They were so often in trouble with the bishop. "And what about *this?*" he had demanded, holding up his copy of "Bacchus at St. Benedict" while he waited for an answer. After a moment, Mary David just shrugged her shoulders and said, "Have you ever tried to control Jean Feraca?"

The year after I left St. Benedict's, Alan took me to France, where we visited Châteauneuf-du-Pape and I saw for myself the papal vineyards where the Cistercian monks, such zealous and dedicated vintners, were said to have actually tasted the soil to test for acidity before planting their medieval vines. No wonder it took seventy years and the passionate urgings of a Catherine of Siena to persuade the pope to return to the Vatican. The red wine that the monks developed to perfection had its sacred uses in the Mass, the central Christian ritual that is rooted in the rites of Dionysius. The influence of the Greeks had spread to Palestine and throughout the Middle East by the time Jesus entered public life. Cana, in fact, the town where Jesus performed his first public miracle, changing water into wine at a wedding feast, was known as a center of Dionysian worship. *Jesus and Bacchus . . . Jesus and Bacchus . . .* There really was something to it after all, this collision of Greek and Christian gods who, like roots of the vine, were more closely intertwined the deeper you went. My poem seemed to have known what I had only intuited. Jesus had to die on the cross in order to be resurrected; Bacchus, in the Greek myth, is torn limb from limb, his body parts scattered, in order for him to rise again. "Unless a seed falls into the ground and dies, it cannot bear fruit." So, too, the grapes must be pressed in order to become wine.

Jesus said, "I come to bring you life, that you may have it more abundantly." But very few Christians live in that spirit of abundance. They get stuck in the Crucifixion, unlike Julian of Norwich, who meditated so deeply on the cross that she penetrated Jesus's suffering right through to his joy. This was my challenge: could I live the rest of my life in the spirit of the Resurrection?

By the time we were married, wine had become the subtext of our lives together. Given the links between wine and worship that are woven throughout Jewish and Christian rites, it was natural that we would choose wine as our wedding motif. Perusing Alan's copy of Hugh Johnson's *Vintage: The Story of Wine,* we came across a photograph of a Roman mosaic that showed the masks of comedy and tragedy from the theater of Dionysius depicted as a satyr and a maenad. Instantly, we recognized ourselves. In fact, the resemblance was downright startling: Alan at his most mirthful really did look like a satyr; I, in my habitual drop-dead amazement at the world, looked very much like the open-mouthed maenad. We reproduced the image on our wedding invitation and glued it onto the wine bottles of our wedding cuvee. "May the wine that you drink today, and that is made yearly in your home," said the rabbi, blessing a cup of Alan's 1992 merlot, "be a symbol of renewal."

And so it is. As I write this, just a few days before Christmas, the grapes that will ferment in the basement throughout the holidays, suffusing the house with their fragrance, are about to arrive from the Russian River Valley.

"Happily ever after," which is how this story ends, turned out to be a lot more interesting than I ever suspected. It wasn't easy for me to choose happiness, or even to recognize it as a choice. Alan helped. He asked very direct questions. "Are you capable of happiness? Can you bear loads and loads and loads of unconditional love?" He had put me to the test. I had to think about it. I checked the box marked Yes.

The tower room made out of a single Douglas fir where we spent our last night on the California coast reminded me of the wedding bed Odysseus, at the end of all his wanderings, built for Penelope out of a single oak tree. Our wedding bed, which has our huppah for a canopy and two little bunches of grapes dangling from its fringes, is made out of water. I never swim alone.

4

Why I Wore
Aunt Tootsie's Nightgown

everything most precious

Everyone remembers how unseasonably cold it was the day Alan and I were married. It was Saturday, the sixth of June. Dark-barred clouds threatened rain all day as the temperature kept dropping precipitously. We had worried for weeks about mosquitoes spoiling our garden party, but instead, the flaps of the white tent that had been set up in our friends' backyard had to be rolled down, and heaters were rushed in to warm the air inside. Susanne, my maid of honor, kept insisting that I wear her long underwear under my thin silk gown. Another friend, overhearing the two of us fuss, offered the loan of her rabbit-skin cape. But I steadfastly refused to cover up, and in my heightened state, I never felt the cold at all.

We had planned for the ceremony to take place in late afternoon under a huppah, the canopy required by Jewish law. The huppah was moored in a thicket of ferns near an old apple tree. It had been fashioned out of my mother's antique piano shawl, which, with its foot-long silk fringes tossing wildly in the wind, looked a lot like a tallis, a Jewish prayer shawl. Vaulted on tall bamboo poles, with fat, lustrous clusters of green and purple grapes dangling from the fringes of all four corners, the huppah lent an element of the exotic to this otherwise altogether familiar Midwestern setting. It was as if some remnant from our primitive ancestral past had somehow thrust itself into the middle of our friends' backyard. Just as the ceremony was about to begin, the sun broke through the clouds, sending its rays streaming through the huppah, fringing the rabbi's face. "Jean and Alan," Rabbi Brahms intoned, beaming at us as we met together under the huppah and joined hands, "as you have arrived, so has the sun."

I was a twice-divorced Italian Catholic marrying a Sephardic Jew. Alan had grown up in Venezuela in a family that had practiced its Judaism nominally, but I, in spite of my lapses, have been a true believer all my life. Rabbi Brahms had graciously consented to marry us without requiring my conversion because I was beyond childbearing, but also, I like to think, because Alan and I were so well suited to one another. But there were other obstacles to be considered. Centuries of enmity stretched between our two tribes. Queen Isabella and King Ferdinand, the fanatic Catholic monarchs who ended Muslim rule in Spain, passed an edict in 1492 that forced the expulsion of the Spanish Jews and sent them into exile. Over the span of the next six hundred years, my husband's family had wandered from their ancestral homeland in Spain, to Italy, to Syria, to Egypt, to Haiti, to Colombia, finally settling in New York City, where Alan's father, growing up in Brooklyn during the 1920s, had been beat up by gangs of Italian boys whenever he dared cross into enemy territory.

As a Catholic schoolgirl, I had knelt with the congregation every Sunday morning during "Prayers after Mass" at St. Margaret's Church on Riverdale Avenue to pray for the conversion of the Jews. My grandfather, who was one of the immigrants who helped build New York, forged close personal and business ties with Jews, and yet, at home, the words "kike" and "scheister" regularly circulated in our family vernacular along with "nigger," "mick," and "guinea." And as if the burden of all this history wasn't heavy enough, there was yet another abyss that yawned between us. Alan is a biochemist; I am a poet. He relies on reason; I rely on intuition. With our widely divergent worldviews, we are the perfect embodiment of the "two cultures" that C. P. Snow famously described. As Rabbi Brahms declared, "Your union is two worlds coming together. . . . It tells us in the books that the worlds of science and poetry do not mix . . . that one is interested in discipline and the other in art, that the two should not be joining hands under a canopy and yet the two of you have crossed the great divide."

But just as poetry is about the reconciliation of opposites, so are weddings. In the old Jewish tradition, the rabbis looked upon the union of two such disparate natures of male and female as a miracle as great as splitting the Sea of Reeds. The marriage of Poetry and Science would have to be that much more miraculous, a living metaphor. In order to bring about a new beginning, and a new covenant, we needed each of our families to be present along with our closest friends.

Some sixty of them were gathered in that chilly backyard, seated on folding chairs waiting for the ceremony to begin. Many had traveled long distances, coming from both coasts; Susanne had come all the way from Australia. My mother, deaf and all but mute at ninety-two, was seated in a wheelchair in the front row while everybody wondered nervously how she might respond to the spectacle of her youngest daughter standing under a huppah to be married to a Jew. Nothing that represented such a rupture with the past had happened in our family since my brother had gotten married on a Sioux Indian reservation to a woman who was part Chippewa. But Jo-Anne, my sister-in-law, had gone to mission schools run by Jesuits and was thoroughly Catholic.

At the front of the house, I stood arm-in-arm with my brother, listening for the first notes of the flute. As the first plaintive strains of the Sephardic love song we had chosen for the processional reached us, Stephen began steering me down the front steps, around the side of the house, and through an arbor hung with roses while the cantor sang in Ladino, *"La prima vez que te vidi / De tuz ojos me'namori,"* which means "The first time I saw you, I fell in love with your eyes."

Emerging in the garden, we set out across a wide sweep of lawn heading for the huppah, where Alan was standing beside the rabbi, watching me intently as he wondered just who was this creature floating toward him looking like some exotic bird. With a veil and a spray of feathers in my hair and a white plume bobbling on my shoulder, I must really have looked like a bird, my little train trailing in the grass behind me like a white peacock's feathers. A murmur lifted over the heads of the crowd like a vapor as I passed between them. I was wearing my aunt Tootsie's wedding nightgown, vintage 1931.

The first time I was married, I cried all the way to the church. My father, walking me down the aisle of St. John and St. Mary's Roman Catholic Church in Chappaqua, New York, was grim as an undertaker. I was twenty-five. It was the last day in November, also cold and overcast. I wore a formal gown made out of stiff brocade, Mennonite-plain with a high neck, long sleeves that came to a point, and a train heavy as a dragnet. The priest who said the nuptial Mass offered us a sip of the consecrated wine from his chalice, a once-in-a-lifetime privilege reserved in those days only for a bride and groom on the occasion of their sacred nuptials. Unfortunately, the blessing it was meant to carry never took, and after seven years, the marriage ended badly.

The second time around, I was a September bride. The wedding took place in a farmhouse next to an old cemetery on a shady dead-end street in the town of Versailles, Kentucky, where I was then living. A friend of ours who happened to be in possession of a mail-order minister's license performed the ceremony in a black suit and a Roman collar he had borrowed for the occasion. I wore a simple ivory gown with my mother's piano shawl tossed around my bare shoulders, the very same shawl that was destined to morph into a huppah twenty years later. In what might be called an excess of vigor, my father threw an old shoe at the back of our Pinto and yelled, "Good luck!" as we headed out of town. But that didn't stick either. We disappeared in a champagne stupor only to get hopelessly lost in a thick Kentucky fog late that night and end up in a ditch, a mishap that proved prophetic.

For a long time after my second divorce, I had a recurring wedding dream in which I was always alone. There was never even a hint of a bridegroom in these dreams as I walked down the aisle time after time. There were years when the very sight of a wedding gown in a window would send involuntary shudders down my spine. Whenever I tried to summon the word "wedding," "funeral" would roll off my tongue instead. "I went to my nephew's funeral," I would say, aghast at the mistake and all that it implied.

I doubt I would have found the nerve to marry for a third time had it not been for the brides of Palermo. Alan and I had spent a week in Sicily the autumn before we were married. Strolling the ancient sepulchral streets of Palermo by twilight on the Saturday evening we arrived, we kept getting ambushed by brides. In one church after another, where the candles were lit and the marble seemed to be melting down the rococo walls, we hovered with the guests in the pews, waiting for the bride who would suddenly appear in the dark of the nave like an apparition. All eyes would turn to devour each of these fabulous many-tiered confections nibbled by worshipful children, while somewhere off in the shadows a groom would be lurking with his head down and his hands folded, keeping a proprietary distance.

A bride in Sicily is never just a bride. She is beauty incarnate, a stand-in for the very goddess. In church, the brides comport themselves as virgins, chaste and demure, but afterward, in places such as Palermo's Piazza della Vergogna—"Shame Square"—where they go to be photographed, they cast off their veils and revel in their true nature, vamping among the naked statuary, inclining their white arms around the shoulders of a Neptune or a Bacchus. Alan almost proposed to me in Sicily. And it was the sight of those voluptuous daughters of Aphrodite, I'm sure, that first implanted in me the idea of wearing a nightgown to my wedding.

Actually, to tell the truth, I had worn a nightgown in public on two prior occasions. The first time, in a scene straight out of a Victorian melodrama, my first husband stormed out of the house in the middle of a blizzard carrying our sleeping infant in his arms while I tottered after him in my bedroom slippers, the hem of my nightgown trailing in the snow under a hastily thrown on overcoat. That was a shameful episode.

The second occasion was more calculated. In a desperate attempt to lure men into our lives, my friend Susanne and I, both of us love-starved at the time, concocted a ritual that centered on a treasure trove of heirloom nightgowns I had acquired from my mother's wedding trousseau. These were fantastic diaphanous creations in shades of vanilla, apricot, and peach that in spite of their age, and probably due to disuse, had survived intact. They had been hand-made by my aunt Tootsie, a gifted seamstress who, had she been born into a different age, might have been a famous couturier. Tootsie had stitched them out of the finest imported chiffon, and had trimmed them with silk rosettes and French lace. I had played with these nightgowns as a child, and here we were all over again, two big best friends playing dress-up.

Susanne was living in Evanston just outside of Chicago at the time, a block away from Lake Michigan. On a pre-designated Saturday morning in June, the two of us met in Susanne's third-floor alcove. Casting off our jeans and our T-shirts, we each perfumed our earlobes with pure Egyptian jasmine, rouged our nipples, and lifted the fragile stuff of the nightgowns over our heads, giggling all the while. Thus fully regaled, we traipsed downstairs past Harry, Susy's bemused landlord, and out of the house into the street where we sailed straight for the beach, clad in nothing but see-through chiffon and yards of lace. Fortunately for us, the street at midmorning was all but deserted. With us we carried a bottle of good dark beer and two copies of *Inanna: Queen of Heaven and Earth,* an ancient Sumerian myth and the oldest love story on earth. Arriving at the edge of Lake Michigan, we lifted our beribboned skirts thigh-high and waded into the chilly water to offer our libations to the goddess, pouring out the beer while we each prayed to Inanna to send us a lover. Then we searched along the beach for a suitable perch in the rock wall, and there, like sirens festooned over the rocks, we sat in the sun reciting aloud by turns the whole of "The Courtship of Inanna and Dumuzi" to the rich delight of a few teenage boys who happened by to catch a snatch of our drift on the lake breeze:

> Who will plow my vulva?
> Who will station the ox there
> Who will plow my vulva?

I dare not vouch for the efficacy of such rituals, but I have to say that it wasn't long before Susanne went sailing off to Vanuatu with her new-found Dumuzi, a lover she met "down under" while traveling in Australia, while I, well, here I was, much to my amazement, preparing to become a bride for the third time.

To marry an alpha male, I needed the sweetness of my aunt Tootsie, even though that sweetness was the very thing I most feared. I needed to cast off completely the residue of the tough fedora and trench coat that had carried me through the breadwinner years while I was struggling to support myself and my two sons.

My aunt Tootsie—her real name was Marguerite—was that rare thing in our family, a deeply feminine woman. Here I was surrounded by harpies and viragoes, but Tootsie was like the milk the milkman delivered at dawn in glass bottles, dewy and fresh, to the aluminum box that was waiting on the back doorstep. In spite of the lingering illness that afflicted her for most of her life, Tootsie never complained. In the famous pairings of women in literature, like Beth and Jo in *Little Women,* or Scarlet and Melanie in *Gone with the Wind,* there is one who is plucky and tough. That's the one who survives. The other, like Beth, sickens and dies. My mother was the tough one. Aunt Tootsie, the sickly one, seemed to melt away, smiling all the while, until there was simply nothing left of her except the taste of what she left behind, like a piece of Christmas candy in the mouth. It was as if she died of her very sweetness.

The cancer that struck early and robbed Tootsie of her breasts took her life at the age of thirty-eight. I was seven when she died. At the wake, my head barely came to the edge of the coffin as I peered in to see my lovely aunt laid out in her wedding gown. She looked just like Snow White draped in all that sumptuous satin that had to be folded back on itself many times over to fit into the coffin. My aunt Tootsie's wedding gown had become her shroud.

I wept for a week. In my seven-year-old mind, marriage became intricately tied up with martyrdom. I knew a lot about martyrs from the saints' stories the nuns told us in school, like the story of St. Agnes, who had also lost her breasts at a tender age. Tootsie reminded me of St. Agnes, the lamb who had been led to the slaughter. Better fierce than fair, I told myself. Better Joan of Arc than Snow White.

But there was something ravishing about my aunt Tootsie's willingness to be vulnerable. There was power in it, a kind of power I was just beginning to recognize. Tootsie was like the fabrics she worked, pliant and yielding as they went under the steel needle. I needed that power. I needed to find in my aunt's gentle nature not weakness but the absence of the desire to fight back. I wanted that abiding openness, that readiness to receive grace.

It was while I was pondering what to wear to my wedding that the thought of my aunt's nightgown popped into my head. Of all the trousseau nightgowns I had played with as a girl, hers was the one I had always favored. It was silky and soft with a liquid luster you sometimes see in very old silver. It was cut on the bias like the evening gowns of the thirties, and had an empire waist and a pleated bodice that flattered my figure. Plus, of all the nightgowns, it was the only one that had belonged to my aunt and not to my mother. She had made it to wear on her very own wedding night. Did I dare wear it as a wedding gown? The very thought thrilled me.

I went straight to the marquetry chest and dug it out of the cedar drawer where it lay folded up in tissue paper with its long baby-blue streamers. I tried it on. Amazingly enough, it still fit.

Despite its age, it wasn't all that difficult to bring the nightgown back to life. I was fortunate to find a dressmaker who specialized in restoring vintage gowns. The day I brought it to Sara for her inspection, she turned it over carefully in her hands, admiring the mercurial quality of the silvery white silk faintly printed with creamy stephanotis. "What beautiful workmanship!" she exclaimed over my aunt's tiny stitches and pleats, the French lace trim, the little slip train with its hand-rolled hem. The first thing Sara did was cut off the faded blue streamers, an act that seemed to separate the nightgown from its past. Then she searched for a slip that would give the nightgown structure. Next she designed a chiffon swag to fall gracefully from the shoulders in back and double as a veil drawn over the head. Adding the ostrich feathers was the coup de grâce, a glamour-girl touch from the 1930s that set the whole thing off— here a splash, there a poof, and voilà!

But getting the bride ready to wear the gown was another matter. The dress carried a charge that had to be exorcised.

A pall hung over my aunt's life. She had died childless; her marriage had been brief and unhappy; she had married a DeNigris, a family in the monument business. My grandmother sneered whenever my uncle Victor's name came up. He had been unfaithful. Tootsie had gone back to live with her mother after the cancer recurred. It was as if her life had gone in reverse. She had failed to differentiate. It was this about her that

I most feared. In taking on her sweetness, would I be invoking the same fate?

For at least a year before Aunt Tootsie died, my mother wore me out, dragging me around on pilgrimages to shrines and holy watering holes all over New York City in search of the sacramentals she believed might staunch her sister's dying. Dressed in the fuchsia wool suit my aunt had made with the pleated jumper and the Eisenhower jacket, I stood on the corner of Riverdale Avenue with my mother, my hand in hers, waiting for the streetcar that would take us to the subway. In the city we visited cloistered convents where my mother talked to nuns who were invisible. We were never permitted to see their faces. Their voices came to us muffled through a wooden turnstile, and I thought they were speaking to us from heaven. The turnstile swiveled, and suddenly, appearing right before our eyes in a space that only moments before had been empty, was a glass heart-shaped flask of holy water embossed with a cross, as if by magic.

One day, we paid a special visit to the motherhouse of the Cabrini Sisters where the body of Mother Cabrini, which was said to be incorruptible, was kept on display in a glass coffin. We knelt in the middle of a big room peering through the glass at the body of the saint with its closed eyes and waxen face. Mother Cabrini was my first corpse.

If my mother was diligent in her quest to rescue her sister from an early death, my grandmother was downright fiendish. When Tootsie's cancer recurred, Nanny swooped down and plucked her daughter right out of the apartment in Jackson Heights where she was living with my uncle Victor and brought her back home to the two-story walk-up in the Bronx where she had grown up, and where she would die. Ensconced in the master bedroom, surrounded by big mirrors in wooden frames and bureaus covered with tatted linens and heavy ivory-backed combs and brushes, Tootsie sat up in bed to receive us always with that same beatific smile.

Tootsie was angelic, but my grandmother in her iron-willed determination did battle with the powers. Whenever we visited, she was busy, bustling about, cranking the hospital bed up and down, plunging in her hypodermics, ceaselessly boiling the goodness out of chickens and beef bones she had bribed from the kosher butcher to make the highly nutritious palatable dishes that kept Tootsie alive. When the cancer spread to the bone, she plumped fourteen feather pillows around the sickbed to ease her daughter's pain, laundering and ironing the linen pillowcases every day. She kept Tootsie like a spun chrysalis inside that house. It was almost as if she wanted to draw her daughter back up into her womb, acting out of the same instinct that prompts alligators to swallow their babies whole if they sense their young are in danger. As it was, Nanny managed to stretch out the thin thread of my aunt's life another ten years before it finally snapped.

Like the two fates, it was thread that bound my grandmother and my aunt together. In the days before Tootsie became bedridden, we would often find them working side by side in the small back room that came alive with the whirring and the thrumming of the shiny black Singer while my grandmother pumped the treadle and my aunt plied her needle. In their master craft, they took the greatest pleasure in working fabrics imported from France: silk organza, ethereal chiffon, and slippery satin. They somehow got hold of a mess of parachute silk during the war and set about making blouses for my sister and me. The stuff was so airy it had to be anchored by wide bands of intricate smocking and even then it escaped, ballooning out from around our bodies so that I felt airborne whenever I put on my blouse.

Nanny and Aunt Tootsie made the dresses my sister and I wore for all of our special occasions: party dresses, my sister's Little Buttercup costume, my piano recital dresses. They made our Easter outfits and our first communion clothes. They sewed up our lives, those two. On the day of my First Holy Communion, three nuns kneeling on the classroom floor like crows at my feet couldn't unravel the hoop my grandmother had sewn into the hem of my dress no matter how frantically they tried, so tiny were the stitches she had worked in with the extra thread so as not to waste one bit of it. I was destined to stick out. My grandmother's eyes gleamed in satisfaction when I brought that story home. "Jeannie," she said, "put a spool of thread, a thimble, and a needle into my coffin when I die so I can sew for the angels."

Almost fifty years had gone by since those days, and yet it was my aunt who was uppermost in my mind as I set about preparing for my wedding day. Would she go with me under the huppah? In putting on her nightgown, would I take on her sweetness and her smile? Or would I feel like a thief in filching for myself what she had been denied? Did I dare draw honey from what had turned so bitter in her mouth?

Whenever I was faced with this kind of dilemma, I would pay a visit to my friend Kay Ortmans. Kay was a very special person and one of my great teachers. A holistic health pioneer and a spiritualist who had run her own wellness center under the redwoods in Ben Lomond, California, before retiring to the Midwest to live with her son, Kay went back into active practice after appearing on my program to talk about Wellsprings, her program of integrated arts. She was in her nineties by this time, still dispensing wisdom and giving alignments that brought body, mind, and soul together. Because she was accustomed to living in two worlds, the world of the living and the world of those "on the other side" with whom she regularly communed, nothing could have been more natural in her view than for me to want to connect with this aunt of mine who was only waiting to be "twinked." So two days before my wedding, there I was facedown on a massage table, under Kay's expert hands dredging up all of my deepest feelings about my aunt and the trauma of her early death.

"She was so sweet and so gentle," I bawled into the mat. "Everything about goodness is gentle," Kay countered. "You don't have to push it. You have it too. It's your nature as well." "You really think so?" I asked, lifting my head as the tears streamed down. "Sure." Kay's voice was pure music. "That's the reason you're so drawn to her now. You're ready to drop off all that sadness." And then she added with fervor, "It's so good you have that nightgown."

The nightgown was my material link to the memory of my aunt and the beauty she represented in my life. "Do you think it's fair for me to bring her under the huppah? To use her nightgown to usher in my own happiness when she herself never had that chance?" "Of course!" Kay beamed. "I think she would be thrilled!"

In Jewish tradition, the huppah has multiple meanings, as I discovered from reading Anita Diamant's wonderfully instructive book, *The New Jewish Wedding*. It's meant to signify God's presence at the wedding and in the home being established under the canopy, bringing to mind the tent of Abraham with its flaps that were perennially open on all four sides so that visitors would always know they were welcome, hospitality being the central tenet of all Semitic peoples. Alan and I were so taken with this symbolism that we extended the huppah in our ceremony to signify openness of mind and heart as well as home.

At its most intimate, the huppah also signifies a garment and a bedcovering. In fact, there was a time when the huppah had a very specific function. "In Talmudic times," according to Anita Diamant, "the groom's father set up a royal purple tent in the courtyard of his home where the marriage would be finalized by consummation." Over time, the act of consummation became symbolic, accomplished by the groom's covering his bride with a veil or his tallis. That was how the word huppah became identified with the act of "covering" or "taking" the bride. It was said that in the very first marriage in the Garden of Eden, God created ten splendid *huppot* for Adam and Eve. And even the tabernacle built by the Israelites in the desert was described as a bridal canopy. After learning all of this, the idea of wearing a nightgown to my wedding actually made sense.

But there was yet another reason why I wanted to wear Aunt Tootsie's nightgown. It was sexy. The Sabbath comes as a bride in Jewish tradition. That's a very beautiful notion. And it is also very sexy. There is no such sanctioned place for sexuality in Catholicism, and like so many Catholics, I had suffered a sexual wound that needed to be healed.

In the hierarchy of the Church, holy orders has always been considered the highest state in life, and chastity its central virtue. Catholic schools used to operate as forcing houses for vocations. If you were said to "have a vocation," if you were "called," that meant only one thing— you were destined to become a nun or a priest, a choice that necessitated taking a vow of celibacy, and heaven help anybody who went against God's will in denying such a calling. There was a time when I suspected that the real reason I had so much trouble in marriage was that I had denied my vocation. College, I had been told, was the grave-yard of vocations. I had gone to college. I had lost my vocation.

Compared to the religious life, marriage was a rather shabby second-class choice. As a sacrament, it was officially sanctioned by the church, but nobody ever talked about marriage as a calling. We were conditioned to think of it rather as a kind of asylum for ordinary mortals who needed a refuge from the temptations of the flesh. Lust was one of the seven deadly sins and always associated with the devil. The pleasures of the flesh were strictly condemned outside of marriage and never encouraged, or even alluded to, within marriage itself. There was no record of Jesus ever having married. His mother was "Mary ever Virgin." Her marriage to Joseph was allegedly celibate. The primary purpose of marriage was for the propagation of the faith. That meant babies, and the less pleasure you took in the act of copulation, the nearer you were to heaven. The saints all triumphed over the temptations of the flesh, most of them lived celibate lives, and the only married couple Pope John Paul II ever championed for canonization was an Italian couple who lived in the first half of the twentieth century, Luigi and Maria Quattrocchi, who gave up sex after giving birth to their four children, all of whom grew up to enter the religious life.

If the Catholic Church has been consistent in its recoil from sex, Judaism has been just as consistent in asserting its holiness, as I discovered while attending a prenuptial course in Judaism for non-Jews. The rabbis considered marriage divine in origin and a holy obligation. In the Jewish tradition, a man must take a wife before he can be considered fully adult, and any man who has no wife cannot become a rabbi and is not considered a complete human being. "To rejoice his wife . . . behold how great is this positive mitzvah," wrote one rabbi. "Understand that if marital intercourse did not partake of great holiness, it would not be called 'knowing,'" wrote another in a thirteenth-century marriage guide. A husband's most unshakable duty was *onah*, his wife's sexual pleasure. He wasn't allowed to take a celibacy vow that lasted longer than one week, lest he neglect her. To this day, making love to your wife on Friday night, as I learned from my Jewish friends, is considered not just a mitzvah but a double mitzvah, and all of the Sabbath preparations—the lit candles, the flowers on the table, the telephone left off the hook, are actually designed, in part, as a form of foreplay.

Long before I met Alan, I had sniffed out this difference. As a guest at a Jewish/Italian wedding held on a Saturday afternoon at a tiny jewel box of a synagogue perched on the edge of Madison's Lake Mendota, I witnessed the charming ceremony of havdalah that marks the close of the Sabbath. The rabbi held up a spice box as he invited first the groom and then the bride to sniff its aromatic contents. Then he blessed them, saying, "May the pleasure you take in each other never fade from your marriage, like the fragrance of these spices."

On hearing those words, my Catholic jaw fell open. Right then and there I decided that if I were ever to marry again, I wanted it to be in just such a ceremony, before just such a rabbi. There was prophecy in that wish, as it turned out. Alan and I were indeed married by the very same rabbi, Rabbi Brahms, in a ceremony on a Saturday afternoon that began just as the Sabbath was drawing to a close. When the right moment arrived, Rabbi Brahms held up the spice box and said, "As Shabbat concludes, we pause for a moment to remember its beauty, its lust, its happiness, its rest . . . May the fragrance of your lives together always smell sweet."

Lust! Under the canopy! Sanctioned by God in the person of the rabbi! He had actually used that very word. At first I was stunned. Then I was sure I had imagined it. But when I went back to review the video, there it was, captured on tape. In his wisdom, and knowing about the nature of my wound, Rabbi Brahms had made sure to use the very word that, transformed from a deadly sin into something good and holy and divinely ordained, would have the greatest power to bring about my healing.

The Jewish mystics saw each wedding as the beginning of a whole new world. What was established under the huppah that day was a new order and a new covenant, one that by borrowing from ancient traditions and across cultures, we had managed to make uniquely our own. When everyone you love best on earth is gathered together in the same garden, a kind of alchemy transpires. That's the very purpose of ritual: to throw you out of ordinary time into an eternal moment. As Anita Diamant writes, "somehow, in the heart of the ritual, custom is forgotten.

Time collapses. Details like the hour, the date, the style of the bride's dress, the music—all vanish. Somehow it is the wedding of the first bride and groom, when—according to the old story—God braided Eve's hair and stood with Adam as his witness. . . . During these moments every wedding is the first and also the ultimate wedding in a four-thousand-year-old chain."

In Hebrew and then in English, Rabbi Brahms blessed the wine of the new order and the new covenant—Alan's '92 merlot—and I embarrassed myself by drinking so deeply from the *kiddish* cup that I drained it, causing the whole crowd to erupt in laughter. We shared what was left of the wine in communion with our witnesses and the closest members of our family. I stepped away from the huppah to offer the first sip to my mother, who drank it greedily, much to everyone's relief. After the exchange of vows came the kiss, and then we began walking seven circles around one another while the cantor, who had once studied opera, sang, *"O mio babbino caro"* from Puccini, in a tribute to my Italian family and my long-dead father. Susanne gave a glorious recitation by heart of a George Herbert poem that ends with the spiritually lusty lines, *"You must sit down," says Love, "and taste my meat." / So I did sit and eat.* And then, as a final symbolic act separating each of us from our pasts, Alan smashed the crystal wine glass under a red napkin at his feet with a resounding stomp, triggering a chorus of blessings, "Blessed be the bliss of lovers!" "Blessed be their bliss!" out of which soared the ecstatic ribbon of Susanne's powerful voice, crying out in a final Blakeian proclamation, "Arise, you little glancing wings and drink your bliss! Arise, for everything that lives is holy!"

In the Japanese movie *Afterlife* the ghosts of the newly dead are detained in a kind of way station where each of them is required to name and re-create the day that was their happiest on earth before they are allowed to move on. For most, this proves to be a daunting task, and one man in particular ends up having to spend many dreary hours alone in a cubicle reviewing his videotapes. Were I ever to be put to such a test, I would have no such trouble.

Almost seven years have gone by since Alan and I were married. Every night, we climb into bed to sleep under a silk canopy embroidered with flowers of rose and violet and gold. Two little grape clusters are twisted into its fringes, one on each side, to remind us of the real fruit of the vine that hung from all four of its corners on our wedding day. Beside the bed, on top of the marquetry bureau that was my mother's, stands a full-length wedding portrait of my aunt Tootsie. She looks achingly young and beautiful in this tinted photograph as she turns toward the camera smiling her radiant smile. As I look at her, I think of lines from Keats: *Thou still unravished bride of quietness / Thou foster-child of silence and slow time.* In her hands she holds a prayer book and a long crystal rosary that dangles down past her knees. In her hair she wears a wreath of orange blossoms. A long veil streams out from behind her head like a vapor trail, and swirling around from behind, her train pours out in front of her, yards and yards of cascading satin, a veritable river of dimpled cream that floods the picture frame. The little poof of ostrich feathers I wore in my hair on my wedding day rides over the top of the frame as my token. Sometimes when the window is open a subtle breeze entering the room will stir the drapes and cross over to the bureau where I will look up and catch the feathery fronds faintly curling and uncurling as they nod and wave.

5

Caves

art . . . if it be noble

I watch you harden
slowly
to stone, tied in your armchair.

Your eyes
are hollows in a wall.

I want to live inside you, the way
darkness lives
crouched
at the bottom of a lake.

When you hunt for yourself
in caves
I want to be darkness
hanging upside down inside you

In Plato's "Allegory of the Cave," human beings live all their lives in an underground den with their legs and necks chained so that they cannot move or look behind them toward the light. They can see only their own shadows, or the shadows of one another, which the fire throws on the opposite wall. It was during just such a benighted period in my life that I learned how to write poetry. Poetry brought me out of the cave and into the light.

I was in my midtwenties, having just moved from New York to join my new husband in Ann Arbor, Michigan, where he was studying to complete his Ph.D. in political science. We had met in a trattoria in Rome the previous year, and the two of us had taken advantage of every opportunity to travel together all over Europe. We had crossed the Alps on my birthday, and had celebrated Christmas in London and New Year's Eve in a French chateau. When spring arrived, we headed for Greece, played hide-and-seek in the Palace of Knossos on our way to Athens, belted down shots of slivovitz in Sofia, and made it all the way to Istanbul by Easter. Now, suddenly, here we were, holed up in a second-story apartment in a gray clapboard house on Huron Street in Ann Arbor, where I was about to experience my first winter in the Midwest. It was a bad way to start married life.

All that year while he was preparing for his oral exams, my husband hardly moved from his corner of the living room where he sat in a faded brown armchair surrounded by stacks of books, one of them spread open on a shelf suspended over his lap. He had rigged this little shelf from the ceiling to keep his arms free while he read for hours on end, but instead of liberating him, it appeared to have locked him into place. There he sat day after day, with only the intermittent whisper of a turning page to break the silence. That, and the ticking of the snow against the windowpane when winter began in earnest. This was our cave.

Watching him read was like watching someone drifting slowly out to sea. As the weeks turned into months, he and his no-color chair became one. I studied him and thought of those translucent fish that learn to see without eyes, circling around in the dark at the bottom of deep underground lakes.

The year was 1969. Women's Lib had yet to arrive, and I was trying to conform to a 1950s notion of what it meant to be a wife. Basically, I had no idea what to do with myself. I took up crewel embroidery. I enrolled in a sculpture class where I chiseled and filed and sanded down big chunks of alabaster until they were smooth as silk. I signed up for an evening sewing class and managed to make a ruffled wrap-around dress, doubting at first that anything wearable could possibly come from pieces of tissue paper fluttering out of an envelope. Had I been at all awake, I might have seen in those oddly shaped pattern pieces an image of my own scattered self. But light had not yet entered the cave. All I could see were shadows flickering on a wall. Shadow husband. Shadow wife.

I decided I needed a job. I got myself a substitute teacher's license, but my teaching career came to an abrupt halt the day I incited a riot in the school gym. I was assigned to be the music teacher that day and was leading the sixth graders in a rousing chorus of "Alouette," which, for some strange reason, seemed to excite the boys. They suddenly broke ranks, picked up their music stands, and began crashing the stands together over their heads like cymbals. Still booming "AH-LOO-ET-TAH! AH-LOO-ET-TAH!" they stormed the bleachers, stomping about and making such a colossal din it might have been a scene straight out of *Lord of the Flies.*

Finally, I did the only thing I seemed to be any good at. I went back to school. One fine September evening in the fall of 1970, I stood at the front door of a big white clapboard house with dusty black shutters, cobwebs in the windowsills, and pine needles strewn all over the porch. I rang the bell. It was the night of the first class of Donald Hall's creative writing seminar. Light was about to enter the cave.

I had always fancied myself a writer, beginning with the backward *J*s for "Jean" I used to scrawl on the blackboard standing in a corner of the kitchen while my mother cooked supper. I remembered the thrill of learning cursive in the third grade, practicing making *O*s with a fountain pen filled with Waterman's blue ink. The first story I wrote, about the day Yippee, our fox terrier, jumped into the ocean while we were at the beach in Cape Cod and disappeared chasing after a duck, won a prize and was published in *American Girl Magazine.* In high school I became editor of the school paper and began writing poetry. One day my sister found a half-blue orange rotting away in my desk drawer. "Slob! Slob! Slob who writes poetry!" she screamed, standing in the doorway of my bedroom. "That's what's going to be written on your tombstone!" It wasn't until I got to graduate school that I really learned how to write poetry, but it was a little clutch of poems that had landed me in Donald Hall's class.

Don himself would tell you there was something special about that class. Jane Kenyon was in it, the poet who would become his second wife. There were eight of us in all and a core of five who were so deadly serious about our writing that we continued to meet long after the class had officially ended. We gathered every Monday night in Don's living room, sprawled all over his sofa and floor with our papers and packs while he sat in a cone of light in the middle of the room, ensconced in his favorite reading chair.

Don was a big man who seemed intent on getting bigger. There was a kind of fuzziness about him. It wasn't that he was unkempt. Not at all. It might have been the tweed jacket he habitually wore, the fine curly hair, or the occasional haze of hangovers, for he was going through a midlife crisis at the time and was drinking a bit too much. But there was something else, something in him that insisted on more life. One night when we ended up discussing one of his poems, "Self-Portrait, as a Bear," he told us that he had always been fascinated by pregnancy and had even taken to following pregnant women around as a boy. Now in his midforties, he seemed to be deliberately taking on girth and texture. It was as if he were sprouting, and his whole house, which he so thoroughly occupied, had this same quality. A rambling four-story colonial with lots of hidden-away alcoves and niches, the house had no clear sense of boundaries or division of purpose. He and his house were everywhere at once, growing the way a garden grows, overspreading borders, undergoing alterations that could be perceived only over time, slowly changing shape, turning to seed.

Hundreds of books and magazines lay stacked on the shelves that lined every room from ceiling to floor, even into the upstairs hall. Walking from room to room always made the floorboards creak, and from time to time you could hear the whole house wheeze and groan under that immense shifting weight. Surrounding us, balanced on the shelves next to old copies of the *Paris Review,* were lithographs and rare engravings, first editions of W. B. Yeats, and "Billy Blake," as Don referred to "the greatest poet in the English language," pulling down an illustrated copy of *Songs of Innocence* for our perusal one night. I always felt a great sense of privilege and intimacy being in that house.

Week after week, the lessons accrued. He was like a grandfather handing out a set of well-worn precision tools, adding one after another as our skill level increased. My mind was open, my defenses down. I had arrived at a supremely teachable moment. The series of failures I had experienced after leaving college had humbled me. So what if I spent the entire semester revising a single poem? Hadn't Plato predicted that "the time which would be needed to acquire this new habit of sight might be very considerable"?

"Poetry happens in the minute differences," Don told us. He trained us to search for the exact word, to pay attention to the nuances of punctuation and line breaks, to study the shape of a poem, the way it looked on the page, all of it adding up to what he called "the body of the poem."

There was a physicality about it, a musculature, a beating heart, as well as a brain. It made sense to me when he told us that Theodore Roethke, a poet whom I especially admired, had often sat at his desk in the nude to compose his poems. Don was a sensualist. To him, poetry was one of the life's great pleasures, like eating, drinking, or making love. He even drawled the word, "Play-zure," lengthening the diphthong so that it lasted longer. He taught us that meaning in a poem is embodied in the sounds that the words make. We studied their subtleties the way wine connoisseurs study flavor notes, beginning with the fat plosives, *P*s and *B*s on the lips, then the *L*s on the tip of the tongue, followed by the dark, bottom-heavy *D*s deep in the cave of the mouth, and deeper still, the gutturals that growl in the back of the throat. We learned that consonants can be harsh, and vowels ecstatic, descending on a scale from *A* to *U* like notes on a flute. The wonder in all of this was unlocking the mystery of the body itself as a vibratory hut, a hive, a buzzing synagogue of sound.

When Don described Keats's voluptuous poem "To Autumn" as a four-hour siesta, I could hear the yawns and the drowsy *Z*s in the line "Thou watchest the last oozings, hours by hours." I readily grasped how a word as universal as *mother* with its humming *m* could morph into murder—mama, manna, matter, murder, Mordor (perhaps because my own mother ran the gamut)—and why Hamlet used so many sibilants to hiss out his disgust for a mother who would "hasten to incestuous sheets." There wasn't a single negative emotion, be it pain, rage, anger, or humiliation, that couldn't be harnessed and used to advantage. Even a demented king like Lear standing out in a thunderstorm could be made to seem the very equal of the elements with lines such as "Blow, winds, blow, and crack your cheeks!" "The material may be dark," as Don explained it in *The Pleasures of Poetry*, "but the shape that the words make is a pleasure to us in itself."

Don taught us to be tough, to cross out, rewrite, and rewrite. He instilled a discipline that was austere, almost monkish as we scrubbed away at our poems. "Practically no one has ever found it easy, or has ever been able to write decently on a first draft," he told us. "The attitude to cultivate from the start is that revision is a way of life." We were not to count the hours, or the drafts. The poem would speak to us from within, dictating its ultimate form. We would know when it was finished by the sound it would make, which Yeats described as "the click of the lid of a perfectly made box."

Sitting at my desk staring at what I had written, combing my way through countless drafts, I was reminded of the parable of the Zen monk who was so determined to reach satori that he meditated with a knife in one hand. It was satori or bust. We were all deadly in earnest. We sparred and wrestled, testing our teeth on one another. We called each other out, exposing pretense, pointing out clichés, denouncing sentiment. Each poem contained a secret that, once possessed, led to the next. I had a tendency to melodrama that was dealt a blow one night when Don clapped a Captain America mask over his face, stuck out his fist, and yelled the last line in my poem, *"Tomorrow I unclench the sun!"*

Beyond mechanics, we were learning to read the underside of a poem, to sort through associative logic in order to discover unconscious feelings and intentions. Did the poem ring true? Did it have closure? Had it earned the right to make that final statement? It was integrity we were testing, the poet's as well as the poem's. Beneath what was written on the page, we were learning to read ourselves, to unearth in the poem's encryption our own deep-seated dreams and fears.

All of this teaching derived from the imagists, those upstarts led by Ezra Pound, who had dared to challenge and overturn the formalism that dominated poetry during the first half of the twentieth century.

There were clear rules: Less is more. Go in fear of abstraction. No ideas but in things. Don't say *tree* when you mean *oak*. There is no such thing as a synonym: *verdant* isn't the same as *green;* a *home* is not a *domicile.*

These rules got reinforced during the year through our exposure to a steady stream of famous poets who came to the university to give readings and pay visits to our class—poets such as Galway Kinnell, Gary Snyder, and Louis Simpson. None of them challenged Donald Hall's essential teaching. It never occurred to us that there might be another doorway into poetry until Robert Bly, Don's old archrival and best friend from his Harvard days, arrived on campus and took us by storm.

Bly swooped down from his farm in northern Minnesota like a Viking on a raid. Instead of standing sedately at a podium turning pages, here was a poet who dared to dance around on the stage like a shaman in a white, fringed serape reciting poems from the Spanish surrealists by heart—Lorca, Jimenez, Machado. These he delivered in a nasal Midwestern twang that reminded me of the whine of high-tension wires in the middle of a blizzard. None of us had ever seen anything so exotic. He was mesmerizing. Rebelling against what he saw as the white bread tradition of American poetry with its picket fence complacencies, he wanted to break out of the paddock and gallop, which explained his fascination with poetry in translation, especially the Spanish surrealists. Nothing in the English canon had enough duende for him.

"Bob would write his poems out of amino acids if he could," Don told us in private, sensing a challenge. As a teacher, Don was doctor, nurse, and midwife all rolled into one. Coming from him, poetry was dark porter with a creamy head, something to be consumed in a British pub with the sun setting at three o'clock in the afternoon. Coming from Bly, it was straight vodka. It wasn't the sound of words that he cared about; it was their power to intoxicate and inflame. It was as if he was after some kind of invisible ether or irreducible essence like a philosopher's stone. Part alchemist, part con man, he was running on high octane, and we all got a contact high just from being in his presence.

When he came back to campus as poet-in-residence the following year, yapping about the Great Mother in psycho-spiritual language he had pirated from Erich Neumann, Carl Jung's disciple, I felt myself being drawn ineluctably into his sphere like an asteroid sliding into orbit. He exuded a magnetism I found impossible to resist. I was seized by a wild desire to sleep with him. I was desperate for his imprint, not realizing at the time that it was poetry itself that had temporarily deranged me.

All that semester Bly was obsessed with the archetype of the Great Mother, anticipating years before anyone else the great wave of feminism that was about to break over us. One day in class he drew a figure on the blackboard in the form of a cross that was supposed to represent the Axis of the Great Mother. The horizontal line stood for life and death, the physical plane, with the Earth Mother on one end and the Death Mother on the other end. The vertical line represented inspiration and madness, the spiritual plane with the Mother of Ecstasy on top, "but if you go too far, like Dylan Thomas," Bly explained, "you'll end up right here," he said, pointing with his chalk to the x at the bottom of the chart, the place of the Stone Mother. The vertical line was obviously where Bly wanted to take us. He had a certain disdain for mere earthiness and tended to dismiss those poets who operated primarily on the physical plane, while on the other hand, he was clearly drawn to the poetics of ecstasy and madness. He had written a major poem against the war in Vietnam called "The Teeth Mother Naked at Last," which allied him with Kali, the great Hindu goddess of destruction. He even looked a little like Kali dancing around on stage in his white serape. And Don? Don was just as clearly connected to the poetics of the body. He used to tell us, as a matter of fact, that there were only two subjects worth writing about: love and death.

As different as they were, my two great teachers, trying to separate them and their distinct influences on my psyche always felt like an act of self-violation. Could I choose father over mother, mother over father? Tear limb from limb? I could no more separate them than render body from soul. Ultimately, like the axis of the Great Mother itself, they were indivisible, these father/mother figures in my young adult life who were reshaping me in their image. I loved them both.

So what was happening to my marriage during all this time? I hardly thought about it, to tell the truth. In the absence of any real embodied relationship, metaphor had become my lover. In poetry I had discovered a powerful opiate to which I had become addicted. There was so much pleasure in the craft, the layering of sound and imagery. My poems were becoming dense and intricate. I was utterly absorbed in the fascination and challenge of making poetry out of misery. Whatever it was I was suffering at the time—anger, loneliness, frustration, depression, estrangement, the growing distance between my husband and myself—what did any of it matter? Could anything really bad ever happen to a poet? It was all material. I was Rapunzel, spinning straw into gold.

Even the vagaries of the weather in the Midwest—brutally cold in winter, sad in spring, oppressively hot in summer—could be turned to advantage. I used it to express my own seasonal discontents. "These days hang / like gray socks filling up / with snow," I wrote at the start of a poem called "January Thaw." "I am / empty inside them, hollow / as the small caves / of boots / left side by side / to stiffen in the hall"—lines that earned Don's praise for their close domestic observation. During the worst heat of summer, while my husband, who was a zealous gardener, distracted himself by tying up his tomato plants and pollinating his zucchini, I stayed indoors on the daybed all day reading *Lord of the Flies* with my feet propped up on the wall and wrote

> Everything was wet. The pitcher sweated.
> Wooden doors swelled up like thumbs.
> Saliva pooled from the tongues of the cats.
> Even the beeswax candles melted
> And keeled over. Only he
> Stayed dry as a snake, his neck blackening all summer.

The emotional neglect I was feeling was turning into a hostility that I released in poems that cut and had a slow killing effect. Later, in a poem called "Troubled Sleep," I wrote

> Nightmare fumes around my face like camphor in a sac.
> Your shoes are open graves I stumble on.
> Your socks, dead birds to gather up

Anyone reading those lines would have discerned in them the warning signs of impending disaster. Anyone, that is, but me. I was too absorbed in the pleasure of crafting them to pay much attention to their real import. This was the stuff of my art. It was a luxury to be able to

turn pain to profit, to make something shapely and beautiful from feelings that were anything but. If in the past I had lacked the confidence to
stand up for myself and make clear choices on my own behalf, at least
here "in my dark and sullen art" I was finding my voice. What matter if
my personal life was falling apart as long as the poems rang true? It was
much easier to fix my poems than to fix my life. It would be many years
before I faced up to the false exchange in that transaction, and oddly
enough, it was poetry itself that forced the encounter.

Meanwhile, my work was gaining recognition. By the time I graduated, I had won two major awards for my writing. Both my parents flew
in to attend the ceremony. We picked them up at the airport in Detroit,
where my father insisted on stopping at a liquor store to buy champagne, bragging about his daughter, the writer, to the shopkeeper. That
was a happy time. In the festive mood that prevailed, we ended up dancing to Greek music in our tiny living room after supper one night; my
father, joining in after the rest of us, pulled a white linen handkerchief
from his pocket and waved it in the air. I never saw him more exuberant.

Since he had always loved poetry and had studied it in college, I decided to take him with me the next morning to attend one of Don's university lectures. We sat side by side in one of those huge lecture rooms in
Angel Hall, my father listening with great attention to every word that
Don uttered, taking it all in. He nodded gravely at the end of class, pro-
nounced the great poet learned and erudite, and wondered whether we
might invite him to join us for Easter dinner. The invitation went out;
the great poet accepted.

That weekend the weather turned warm, and on Easter Sunday
afternoon six of us squeezed into our little porch to gather around the
table. We served platters of antipasto, homemade ravioli, roasted lamb,
and lots of wine to wash it all down. We feasted for hours, and by the
time it was over there were thirteen bottles open on the table and Don
was drunk. The great poet had to be steered home like a ship with too
much cargo in the hold. My father, who was never anything but sober,
blamed himself for serving too much wine.

*See what will naturally follow if the prisoners are released and disabused of their
error. At first, when any of them is liberated and compelled suddenly to stand up*

and turn his neck round and walk and look toward the light, he will suffer sharp pains. . . . And suppose, once more, that he is reluctantly dragged up a steep and rugged ascent, and held fast until he's forced into the presence of the sun himself, is he not likely to be pained and irritated?

In terms of Plato's "Allegory," my sight was still weak. I had started sending my poems out to editors, and much to my surprise, they were readily accepted and began to appear in reputable literary magazines. I even received a fan letter from a reader in Salt Lake City. This was heady stuff to someone who was just beginning to develop a sense of voice. It proved to me that the personal poems that had turned me inward had resonance and worth in the outside world. I began to think maybe I had arrived at the start of a real career.

Had I persisted in writing primarily for aesthetic pleasure and the rewards of recognition, I would have been like Glaucon's prisoner in the cave. "Surely I would have entered into a greater and more abject darkness even than before," a darkness akin to that which eventually engulfed Sylvia Plath and Anne Sexton, the famous suicides. But something happened to change my course, not all at once, but slowly, over time, the way sight returns to someone who has been temporarily blinded. The bandages come off, and what one sees at first may appear to be diffuse, inchoate, even upside down. It takes awhile to adjust to the pain of clear sight. The brain must make rapid alterations in what the eye perceives before the image is revealed as true. Above all, the one who is recovering must want to see.

Discovering Sylvia Plath's *Ariel,* the book Ted Hughes published posthumously that made his dead wife famous following her suicide, had a lot to do with my turnabout. I wanted to write like Sylvia Plath. I was dazzled by her brilliance, her mastery of sound and image, her sardonic wit, the bold way she broke her lines to cinch in and intensify emotions that were already overwrought. Here was a woman poet daring to write primarily out of her personal experience as an unhappy wife. That in itself made her a dangerous role model. Confessional poetry was the "in" thing in those days, a genre that had been invented by one New Englander, Robert Lowell, during the Miltown decade of the 1950s and brought to an excruciating peak by another New Englander, Sylvia

Plath, who endured a series of brutal electroshock treatments for her depression, which did her no good at all except to provoke some extraordinary poems. She was dead by the time she reached thirty, a death she rehearsed with grim ritual regularity until she finally succeeded. "Dying / Is an art, like everything else," she writes in "Lady Lazarus," "I do it exceptionally well / . . . I guess you could say I've a call." Underneath the bitterness of her sarcasm used at her own expense was a well-brought-up Smith girl who was secretly pleased with herself for having pulled off her "big striptease." "Do I terrify?" she flirts, "The nose, the eye pits, the full set of teeth?"

What disturbed me in rereading *Ariel* was the abundant evidence I found throughout the book of her having actively courted death like a lover and consciously cultivated her own already abundant self-hatred. She had fed her own sickness for the sake of her poetry. In her poem "Cut," for instance, a commonplace kitchen mishap becomes an occasion for perverse celebration: "What a thrill— / My thumb instead of an onion," the cut thumb morphing into a Redcoat, a Kamikaze, a Ku Klux Klansman in a series of dazzling slapjack metaphors until it finally settles in the last two lines into what she most wants it to be—a loathed surrogate self—"Dirty girl, / Thumb stump."

I understood exactly how it felt to be a dirty girl. I thrilled to it, this exaltation of the grotesque. I could see in myself the same latent tendencies, the same desire to hype and mythologize what might otherwise be thought of as ordinary experience, the stuff, actually, of soap opera. Was I too courting my neurotic tendencies for the sake of art? Did I really want to be another Lady Lazarus?

Dylan Thomas, another poet whose work I admired, drank eighteen whiskeys in the White Horse in Greenwich Village whereupon he collapsed and was taken to St. Vincent's Hospital, where he died later that night of a cerebral hemorrhage. Sylvia Plath put her head in the oven on a bitterly cold day in February with two small children at home in her London flat. Anne Sexton gassed herself to death in her garage. These were my role models.

It wasn't until Donald Hall published "Dylan Thomas and Public Suicide" that anyone dared to attack the cult of the poet as suicide. "No one who loves literature can deny that disease can give birth to great poems," he asserts in that essay. "In our culture an artist's self-destructiveness is counted admirable, praiseworthy, a guarantee of sincerity. . . . The poet who survives is the poet to celebrate. The human being who confronts the darkness and defeats it is the most admirable human being. . . . Death and destruction are enemies to art, to consciousness, and to the growth of consciousness. Gas and sleeping pills kill poets; drink and drugs kill poets more slowly, but on the way to killing the poet, they kill the poems."

I didn't discover Don's essay until after I had left Michigan, but reading it was a liberating experience. Right then and there I made a decision. I would not enter that snowy wood that Robert Frost had stopped to contemplate, his metaphor for suicide; like him, I would move on. Even if it meant that I would become a lesser poet, I promised myself that I would not feed my own self-destructive tendencies for the sake of my poems. Instead, I wanted to use the insights that I gained from writing for self-knowledge and self-transcendence, for the sake of that "enlarging, enhancing wisdom" that Don describes as "poetry's real wickedness and real salvation." I wanted to strive after fullness of life, just as he had done. As much as I wanted my poems to ring true, even more, I wanted my life to ring true.

Don and I developed a closeness that went beyond the bonds of student and teacher. If poetry had become my anchor, he was my lifeline. I once met him at the Algonquin Hotel in New York City when it was a fading but still famous hangout for the literati. We took a taxicab together to attend a reading across town, and on the way Don said to me, "I want you to promise me that you'll become a better poet every year of your life." I thought about it for a minute. "I promise you that I will become a better poet every year of my life," I said solemnly.

My first test came when my husband and I returned to Italy for a second year after completing our degrees. He was studying the rise of neofascism in the south, and while we traveled through Italy's poorest and most primitive provinces—Basilicata, Calabria, and Sicily—I worked on a series of poems exploring ancestral landscapes and questions of identity, which eventually formed the substance of my first book, *South from Rome: Il Mezzogiorno.*

My father's yearly recitations of his favorite poems from *The Golden Treasury* had imparted to me a strong sense of ethnic identity along with a love of poetry. Those sessions always ended in exactly the same way. After delivering the last line, he would snap the book shut and declare, like a lawyer summing up his case before a jury, "Now *that's* beautiful language. And we can understand beautiful language because this is language that comes from the heart. And *we* are people of the heart— not like these Yankee Doodles."

The Yankees Doodles were our next-door neighbors who shunned us because we were Italian, but in a wider sense what my father really meant was the whole Anglo-Saxon domination of American culture. It took me many years to untangle the twisted message encoded in those words. I set out in search of the people of the heart—my people. The funny thing was that when I got there I realized that I didn't speak their language. It wasn't Dante my father was passing on. His favorite poems, after all, a point that seems always to have eluded him, were written by Tennyson, Browning, and Wordsworth—all pure Yankee Doodle. Impelled by my father's words, I studied Italian and went in search of my roots. Geography was a great teacher. But language, which is the ultimate carrier of identity, was a much greater teacher. The home I was searching for was not to be found in my motherland so much as in my mother tongue. The English of Dickinson and Hemingway taught me to curb my Italian tendencies to melodrama. It taught me, against my inclinations, the value of understatement and restraint. It taught me that the opposite of one deeply held truth is another equal and opposing truth. Poetry, with its capacity for complexity and ambiguity, was the perfect vehicle for delivering the complex truth, the paradox of what it means to be an American with a dual identity. In a poem, it is possible to be both attached and estranged at the same time.

I loved the harshness of the south of Italy with its barren hills ribbed with rock walls. I loved the towns that looked from a distance like a handful of dice scattered over the mountaintops. I loved the twisting olive groves, the speared agave thrusting its way out of the hillsides, the outcroppings of rock needling the shore. But at other times this same landscape could also weary and repel me. Driving east through the ancient olive groves of Calabria that spring, I felt a pang of longing for the tenderness of spring in the North Atlantic States where in April the maple trees were pushing out their sticky leaves like scouts.

At the end of the road was a deeper maze. Traveling through the land of my ancestors, I was discovering how American I was.

We left Italy in June and returned to our house in Michigan only to begin packing up again, bidding good-bye to all of our friends and leaving Ann Arbor for good. We were headed for Kentucky, where my husband was about to begin his teaching career. One September day soon after we had settled into our new home in Lexington, a letter arrived in the mail addressed to me. I thought I recognized Don's handwriting on the envelope, but there was something strange about it. In the past, his letters to me had always been neatly typed on personalized stationery. But this one had been written in red ballpoint pen on a small business envelope that bore no return address. I tore open the envelope, pulled out a folded sheet of yellow legal paper, and read

Jean—

I was just rereading a lovely old letter from you—about poems and other things—from last December.

BUT I'm afraid that for now it is best if we don't have contact at all, either by letter or by meeting—and Jane thinks so too.

I'm sorry.

Don

I folded it up, slipped it back in the envelope, took it out again, unfolded it, reread it, trying to absorb the shock. The phrase "either by letter or by meeting" kept coming back to me like a bone stuck in my throat. I knew what had happened. Jane was jealous. During the year I was away while she and Don were becoming intimate, Jane had discovered our history and decided that I was a potential threat that needed to be eliminated. She had forbidden any further contact between us, "either by letter or by meeting," and Don had agreed. The closure was permanent. Don and I were not to meet again until after Jane died. A terrible void opened up in my heart. I was left to contemplate the road not taken. It was a loss made all the more palpable by the estrangement from my brother that occurred around the same time. I felt bereft and betrayed by the men I held most dear. For the first time in my life I began to contemplate having a child. It wasn't long before I became pregnant, and I delivered a son in due time whom we named Giancarlo.

Just as Giancarlo was learning to walk, an invitation arrived from our friends in Rome. They were inviting us to join them for a few weeks in August at a seaside villa in the south of Italy, in Basilicata, which happens to be the home province of my mother's family. We hesitated. Giancarlo was teething and had developed a low-grade diarrhea he couldn't seem to shake. We were worried about the possible consequences of traveling abroad with a one-year-old. My mother issued a dire warning, "Don't you take that baby to Italy! Don't you dare take him to Italy!"

Giancarlo slept peacefully all the way to Rome, curled up in a box at our feet. As soon as we arrived, we bought him his first real pair of shoes and took him to Piazza Navona, where we held his hand while he practiced taking baby steps on the ledge of one of Bernini's fountains. Everything was fine until we headed south. A commotion ensued as soon as we arrived at the villa. Nobody was expecting a baby. Out of nowhere a makeshift crib appeared with only three legs, carried ceremonially down the stairs and into our bedroom where it stood propped against the wall.

In the middle of the night we were awakened by a loud knocking. Giancarlo was crying, standing up in his three-legged crib with both hands gripping the rails, banging as hard as he could against the wall. *Knock, knock, knock.* It was like a knell from the nether world. He was burning up with fever, and before long a fine red rash had broken out all over his body. I walked him for hours that night and most of the next day, but nothing I did seemed to afford him any comfort. I was frightened. He stopped eating; his diarrhea got worse. He had never before been so sick, and here we were stranded in Basilicata, of all places, the land of *'a miseria* my great-grandparents had abandoned so long ago. There were no doctors to consult, no medical clinic nearby, not even an obvious way to get back to Rome. I was beside myself. On top of everything, it was mid-August, *fer'Agosto,* the Feast of the Assumption, when everyone in the whole country goes on vacation at the same time. We were trapped. My mother's warning came back to me. I was wracked with guilt.

Knock, knock, knock. Again, that knocking in the middle of the night. Again, the walking, the rocking, the crooning, and the crying. All day long, I walked the floors with my baby in my arms, crossing tracks with a pet duck that waddled through the house, leaving a trail of excrement on the white tile floor. And still, my baby cried. One day leached into the next; nothing changed. I was becoming unhinged. My nerves were taut and raw; I began to lose my sense of time and slip into an altered state. Here we were in this godforsaken place where it was said that "Christ had never stopped" and the Great Mother was on a rampage. The very landscape seemed to rise up against us, the skull-bald mountains all around us pressing in, massive and terrible, looming overhead like great evil-eyed aunts with darning eggs for heads. In my overwrought state, every tower on the hill turned into a tooth; every cave became a gaping mouth, and the sea with its incessant churning hissed like a serpent. I was in the grip of the Stone Mother. The words of the Memorare came back to me; I prayed, *Remember, O most gracious Virgin Mary, that never was it known that anyone who fled to thy protection, implored thy help or sought thy intercession was left unaided.* In my state of sleepless semi-delirium, I imagined that the sins of the mother were being visited on the child:

> This, the old dream to be martyred,
> the calling denied
> floats up, a kidney in a bowl
> carried to the altar, St. Agnes's breasts
> Ophelia's face . . .
>
> the procession of Virgins advances, she carries
> a candle
> she wears a white dress
>
> a thimble rolls out of my grandmother's coffin
> I am bound on the hoop sewn into my hem
>
> This is the way, each moment
> I mount
> ever higher, the life
> of the flesh
> falls away . . .
>
> *knock knock knock*

I was tapping into the primal mind. In my extreme state, anxiety combined with heat and fatigue had brought me down into the place of the unconscious. I was channeling the old gods, knocking on the door of the underworld in a language I didn't know I could speak. In my heightened state, poetry began flowing out of me like a riptide. Whenever I wasn't actively nursing my sick child, I was sitting on a stoop or a stone somewhere, writing frantically like someone possessed. It was almost as if I were taking dictation. Out it all came in a jumble, a welter of words and lines and phrases, a cacophony of voices speaking all at once. There was no point in pausing to question what was happening or trying to make sense of it; I needed only to get it down on paper before it was lost. I covered page after page, scribbling sideways in the margins when I ran out of space. At last, like a storm, it was over. I looked down at the thick sheets in my lap and realized that something had broken loose. I was writing from a much deeper place, and the poems were like markers pointing the way. They were prescient. The poems knew what the poet had yet to discover.

Meanwhile, all around us the other guests in the villa were indulging themselves, effete Italian Marxist intellectuals with nothing better to do than to lounge about on the terrace all day in their skimpy bikinis, smoking and making jokes as they nibbled on artichokes and tiny meatballs, inquiring from time to time as I glided past them like a ghost from hell, "Giancarlo, *come va?* His fever? The color of his spots?" I hated them all, their primping, their prattle, and their politics. They spoke of Marx and revolution while butter rolled around their tongues. It all seemed to me like so much mental masturbation while in the distance I could plainly see rings of fire on the hills where shepherds were burning their fields. I had never felt more like an American.

And then something really strange happened. Right in the middle of the worst of the crisis, a voice emerged in my head that I didn't recognize as my own. *I shall live out my life rejoicing*, it announced with the authority of prophecy. The voice was serene and transcendent. It came again: *There is no reason for this joy, knifing through me like a canyon.* Joy? In the midst of what I was going through? And then, this statement, even more astonishing, solving once and for all my whole riddle of identity: *There is nothing in this landscape that defines me.* At last, I was free.

When we finally managed to get back to Rome we headed directly to the American Hospital. The doctor who examined Giancarlo said that he couldn't be sure, but he thought, judging from the bumps on the baby's head, that what he had contracted was roseola. Thankfully, by this time he was all but recovered and bore no permanent signs of the ordeal. The frightful episode was over.

But for me it had only just begun. By the time we returned to Kentucky, I was a different person. I simply could not return to the old life. The poems I was working on, scribbled down in such haste in Italy, had taken me ahead of my own life's course. They were dictating a series of major life changes that simply fell into place, one after another. The first decision I made was to leave graduate school to work on a book of poems. Then, after a long period of agonized reflection, I drove to a lawyer's office on a cold blustery day in March and filed for divorce. After that, events unfolded in an unalterable sequence, creating all sorts of havoc.

"You cannot change your language without changing your life." The poet Louise Bogan said that. I had to wait several years before I found the right words for "Crossing the Great Divide," the mysterious poem that became the title poem of my book. I didn't understand it at all at first. My poems were ahead of my own experience, even my own skill. I had to learn to break some of the rules I had so painstakingly learned in order to solve some of the problems they posed. But I also had to wait to discover the courage to act. The floodgates had opened, and there was no going back. I had crossed a great divide. I had dreamed dreams and seen waking visions. In the absence of the teacher, poetry itself became the guide.

People write poetry for different reasons. Some people write because they simply have no choice; they suffer what Denise Levertov once called the blessed compulsion of art. Donald Hall writes for love, or so he says. For a long time I used poetry as a ladle to scum off the soup. I was unhappy, and here was a marvelous route of sublimation that allowed me to escape without ever having to leave home. At first it was enough just to know I had stumbled onto something I could be good at, something I could earn a living by teaching. I had no way of anticipating that writing poetry would become a way of life, a *tao*, a hinge that would connect me to my deepest source. Metaphor is a bridge to the soul. Poetry allowed me to see—darkly—into the prism of the self. It revealed truths I would have preferred to hide from—dark reaches, inaccessible feelings, unconscious intentions and desires. It taught me that I needed to transgress in order to grow.

Poetry reconnected me with my body and the life of the senses, as Don had predicted. It signaled the end of my marriage. It shaped my voice and prepared me for public life. It brought me out of the cave of self and into the light of the world. In my search for roots it led me into a wilderness of jagged joy and taught me that identity at its source goes far deeper than family of origin or inherited religion. It guided me at last into a place where I least expected to land: the Valley of Love and Delight.

6

A North American in the Amazon

labor . . . if it be worthy

It is dark in the Amazon where it is often overcast and raining, and vision is obscured by mists and downpours. The river T. S. Eliot called the "brown god" is muddy along most of its four-thousand-mile epic length, and when the silt clears in the dark-water tributaries, the river runs black. Very little light ever penetrates the gloom. In the forest, the great trees that soar over 150 feet in their race for the light are intertwined and laced with lianas and epiphytes. A tree might hoard more than a thousand epiphytes, clustered on a single branch. When the sky breaks open, illuminating the crowns, light is deflected, entering in shafts that dazzle and confuse the eye, causing it to glance over the surface of things. To reach the forest floor, the sun must zigzag and deviate, making its way through an immensity of tangled, interwoven layers. In such a miasma, one can never be sure that what one sees is real. Animals move through vapors disguised by spots and stripes, matching, melting, and blending into their shadowy element. The jungle is a shape-shifter, a place of mimicry, trickery, and camouflage where the anaconda and the jaguar may be conjured by *ayahuasca*, and where the jaguar and the shaman are said to regularly switch places. It is a place of original mystery and complexity, undifferentiated and pre-Edenic, where light is

135

never truly separated from darkness, the last place in the world where anyone should ever go looking for truth or certainty.

The week I spent in the Amazon in 1994 very nearly unpacked me. It was at the end of October, just before Halloween. I was traveling in the company of a group of pharmacologists, herbalists, and holistic health professionals bound for the Peruvian jungle to study plant medicine at an international workshop called "Pharmacy from the Rainforest." Ostensibly, my job was to document the expedition for Wisconsin Public Television. But my real motive for being on board was to investigate a medical clinic that had been built by Rotarians near the banks of the Amazon as a consequence of one of my radio programs.

I had been working as a talk show host for Wisconsin Public Radio for almost ten years when I first learned of the existence of Yanamono Clinic. It was on a foggy day in mid-February, and I was plunged into one of my classic midwinter funks, questioning the worth of my work, asking myself, *What else could I be doing with my life? Where else could I be doing it?* when I chanced across a strip of wire copy from the Associated Press. "State-of-the-art medical clinic built on the banks of the Amazon as a result of an interview conducted on Wisconsin Public Radio." I gasped. I read it again. My God! That was my interview! That was my story!

The real story, of course, was the doctor herself, Linnea Smith, a spunky, no-nonsense eccentric with a streak of wanderlust who likes to ride her motorcycle through the back roads of Wisconsin whenever she comes home. She had been working in a flower shop selling exotic houseplants at the time she decided to go back to college and get a medical degree. One winter she took a week's leave from her group practice as an internist in Sauk City, Wisconsin, to travel to the Amazon as a member of the Nature Conservancy. On the last day of her vacation at Explorama Lodge, an ecotourism center run by a Swede also from Wisconsin, she was suddenly summoned to treat a man who had just been bitten by a fer-de-lance, a smaller but deadly relative of the bushmaster, one of the most poisonous snakes common to that part of the Amazon. The man had gone numb up to his thigh by the time she was able to inject the vial of outdated antivenin serum provided by the lodge, improvising a toilet paper tube for a stethoscope to check for wheezing. That did it. The patient recovered, but the doctor was smitten. She went home and spent the year studying Spanish. By June she was back again in the Amazon, living as a guest courtesy of the lodge and establishing her new practice out of a tiny one-room dispensary with no electricity or running water, spartanly provisioned with a thatched roof, a cot, and a kerosene lantern. The news that there was a doctor ensconced at Explorama spread like contagion through the jungle. Before a few weeks had passed, she was already on call day and night, delivering babies and dispensing snakebite serum and penicillin free of charge to the Yagua Indians and the ribereños, the river people living along the banks of the Amazon. When circumstances dictated, she would paddle a canoe or travel on foot through the forest to pay a house call to a particularly sick patient. Occasionally, she had to sit down on the palm-slat floor of a jungle house to sew up a cut or perform minor surgery with curious children looking on, and chickens, dogs, and the occasional pig wandering by. "It's a little tricky to sew up machete cuts by kerosene lamp late at night," she reported to my Wisconsin Public Radio audience when she came back home for a visit.

It was statements like that, laid down with Linnea's characteristic drop-dead aplomb, that caught the attention of Jon Helstrum, an architect living in Duluth who happened to be listening to *Conversations with Jean Feraca* that morning and was quite taken with Linnea's tales of jungle medicine. He called the station and asked to speak to Linnea. Next, he got hold of his friend and fellow Rotarian Joe Leek, a retired surgeon in Duluth, and the two of them hatched a plan to go down to Peru together on a reconnoitering mission.

Cheery and energetic in spite of their long flight, with Joe sporting his golf hat, the two Rotarians disembarked at the airport in Iquitos in May 1992 and made their way through customs to find Linnea waiting to greet them. No sooner had they arrived at Explorama and been ushered into the clinic than Linnea was obliged to perform an impromptu surgery and Joe was recruited to advise and assist, pulling a curtain for privacy and holding a flashlight for Linnea as she worked to excise a huge cyst from a woman's hip while a tarantula was crawling up the clinic wall. Over the next few days Jon and Joe witnessed firsthand the conditions under which Linnea was running *la clínica*, watching as she brushed sawdust away each morning, and swept the floor and the bed clear of debris that had fallen overnight from the thatched roof, with nothing better than a small tabletop stove and a pressure cooker with which to sterilize her instruments. They were appalled. One morning Jon sat down on the bed that served as an examining table when it promptly collapsed, the wooden slats under the mattress having been chewed through by termites overnight. By the time the two of them were ready to make the trek back home, they were resolved. They would build Linnea a real clinic.

The first thing they did was raise $35,000 from three different Rotary Clubs, one of them in Thunder Bay, Canada. Jon took six months out of his practice to develop an ingenious design uniquely adapted to jungle conditions. The clinic would be thirty feet wide by sixty feet long. It would be constructed on a platform raised on stilts to protect it from flooding during high water season and set back about two hundred feet from the river, close but not too close, so that patients who were traveling long distances by foot and dugout canoe would have no more than a short walk from shore to reach it. It would feature solar panels manufactured in Germany to generate electricity and a metal clerestory roof designed for air flow when it heated up—"I'm not going to build a clinic just to have it burn down when somebody kicks over a kerosene lantern"—and, against Linnea's protestations, a flush toilet. It was the first clinic Jon had ever designed.

Rotarians have a bylaw that states that they can't just throw money at a problem; whatever form their charity takes has to be hands-on. So in February of the following year, thirty-nine stalwart Rotarians, traveling with their wives, friends, and children, flew from Duluth to Iquitos carrying lumber, saws, generators, a router, and a suitcase full of hardware and roofing nails that weighed 120 pounds. They hauled it all downriver, slogged through primordial mud, suffered through relentless heat and insects, dug a well, and managed to hammer and pound the whole thing together over the course of a month. They even built furniture for the clinic and a jungle house for Linnea. Most of them were unskilled. One woman had packed a child's hammer, but within a day's time she was driving in roof nails with the best of them. Some of the sheet metal didn't get on straight, but by the time they were finished, Yanamono Clinic was the only medical facility of its kind within a twenty-five-mile radius of dense jungle with electric lights, running water, a pharmacy, an office, a lab, and even a dental clinic for pulling rotten teeth. During its first year alone, 2,500 patients were seen at Yanamono Clinic, about 200 a month. Traveling by hammock, by foot, and by dugout, suffering from all kinds of acute illnesses and infectious diseases, they came to be treated by La Doctora, to be delivered of their babies when they couldn't do it themselves, to get birth control pills, and to be stitched up for their machete cuts and abscesses. Now that's a North American story.

And was I proud of it. Joe Leek had called me Big Mama, but I knew better. It was radio that was first cause and prime mover in this story of intrepid do-gooders, people of enterprise and good will who had improved the lives of countless Indians living in the rainforest, acting out their motto of "Service above Self." Words open the mind, as St. Teresa of Avila said; they tenderize the heart and lead to deeds.

I wanted to see for myself what state-of-the-art might look like in a place as remote as the Amazon. As the daughter of three generations of immigrant builders who had seen skyscrapers raised and whole neighborhoods added to the city of New York as a result of their labors, I was eager for tangible evidence that I was not wasting my life in ephemera, that what had begun as a series of electromagnetic impulses transmitted over hundreds of miles and received as intelligible could actually translate into the sound of sawing wood and pounding nails and roof beams being raised. Little did I know that when the opportunity arrived, it would be my descent into the maelstrom, a place where my Kantian categories of good and evil would break down along with everything else in the jungle.

One day at work I got a call from Mark Plotkin, a maverick adventurer I knew from the radio. Mark has great respect for medicinal plant knowledge among tribal peoples of the Amazon and is deeply concerned about its preservation. He had been documenting the ethnobotany of northeast Amazonian Indians for fifteen years, but it wasn't enough for him to study it at a distance. In order to learn firsthand, he took himself into the jungle, acquiring knowledge by apprenticing himself to medicine healers of great renown. His many ordeals, both harrowing and profound, are recounted in his book *Tales of a Shaman's*

Apprentice. Mark is a bit of a showman, great on the radio, and we had become friends after he had spoken on my program several times about his innovative efforts to preserve tribal tradition and plant knowledge. He knew all about Yanamono Clinic and my connection to it. "Hey," he said, over the telephone, "International Expeditions is putting together a week-long seminar at Explorama called 'Pharmacy from the Rainforest.' I'm going to be one of the presenters. Linnea will be there as well. She'll be giving guided tours of the clinic. Why don't you come along?" It was simply too tempting an invitation to turn down. Although I had no idea how I would manage to finance the trip, I was bound for the Amazon.

Stunned at my good fortune, I hung up the phone and went wandering down the hall in a bit of a daze when I happened to bump into the director of programming for Wisconsin Public Television. "James," I said, "you won't believe what just happened to me. I'm going to the Amazon with an expedition of botanists." "Can you keep a diary?" he asked as soon as he had grasped the outlines of the story. "Can you take some pictures that would correspond to what you find there?"

So that was how, instead of a tape recorder and a microphone, standard radio gear at that time, I ended up lugging to the Amazon an H-8 video camera that I didn't even know how to hold. I staggered around for the week with that clumsy camera stuck to my face, completely obsessed with "getting it," peering up at one of the last great wildernesses on earth through a tiny black-and-white picture lens that kept fogging up. But that was only one of many ironies.

Amazon. The word itself has magic in it. Say it out loud, and you can feel its muddy *m* humming and its zigzag *z* vibrating in your mouth. Amazing Zone. For weeks beforehand, I sat up in bed at night with the big green spiral-bound notebook International Expeditions had sent out in preparation for the trip. It had a picture of a toucan and the word *AMAZON* printed in capital letters on the cover. Like a child learning to read, I would trace down along those big letters with my fingertip, beginning with *A*. *A* was for alphabet, for alpha, for alligator. *A* was a mouth, a maw, full of the hot breath of jungle creatures I might apprehend but never see. The longer I contemplated it, the more I fantasized.

A was an archway leading all the way back to the beginning, to the place where the world began; it was a gate through which to pass and altogether vanish. *Abandon hope all ye who enter here.* That was what was written over the gateway to hell. *A* was for abandon. But what would I be asked to abandon? Hope? Faith? Certainty? I was going to the Amazon. *Exploradora de la Selva.* Jungle Jean. I told my brother, the anthropologist, and without thinking, he said, "Be careful, Jeannie. You know, there's a jungle out there."

There were about seventy *exploradores* who met on a Saturday afternoon at the airport in Miami: physicians, pharmacists, botanists, herbalists, and homeopaths, all decked out in their safari-hatted, jungle-zippered, and many-pocketed glory. We stood around waiting with our lumpy duffle bags and knapsacks for the plane that would transport us to Iquitos. By the time we arrived in that nether world it was too late to see much of the squalid sprawling frontier city that had once been a wealthy town fueled by rubber barons. The power flickered on and off all night at the Hotel Dorado where I passed the first of what was to be many fitful nights in the tropics, awakening the next morning to a heavily overcast sky and my first glimpse of the brown god, a muddy line on the distant horizon.

On our way out of the hotel, we passed through a cacophony of vendors who were hawking their local medicinal remedies in the lobby for our benefit, some claiming to have captured the evil genie of AIDS in their murky bottles. From there, we wended our way into the city market, itself a jungle pharmacy in its raw state where every manner of herbal, floral, animal, and mineral extract was for sale in the stalls or displayed on dirty mats or in the laps of vendors squatting in the streets. I wondered how anybody could possibly tell the quack from the real thing in such a melee.

By midafternoon we queued up at the dock and were loaded aboard our riverboat, finally on the Amazon, flowing backward in time. We churned past island after island, some several miles long, following the meandering course of this jungle-lined "river-sea," keeping a lookout for pink river dolphins and marveling at its sheer size, over two miles wide even at this distance from its mouth, as we headed some fifty miles downriver toward Explorama Lodge, our ecotourism destination and the site of Yanamono Clinic. After a journey of a few hours, we pulled into shore and landed at a dock where a band of boys was already waiting for us on top of the bank, silhouetted against the sky.

I'll never forget the momentous feeling of stepping off that boat in my rain boots into Amazonian mud for the first time, gazing up at the tall trees along the path as I started for camp. I was conscious of the clunk clunk clunk of my heavy shoulder bag full of video equipment bumping against my hip as I tromped past the baleful eyes of big-horned water buffalo. Two little boys coming in my direction stopped me in my tracks before I had gotten very far. They had black eyes and streaked faces and were munching on chunks of watermelon as they walked along, using their dirty, hole-filled T-shirts that went down to their knees for mopping up the juice. I pulled out my camera. This was my first Colombian Encounter.

"Me, Jean," I said absurdly, signaling and using a lot of body language to try and make myself understood. "Zheen. Zheen," they chorused. "What's your name?" I asked. They looked at each other in puzzlement and conferred. One of them tapped his chest with both hands. "Weel-sohn," he said. "Weel-sohn?" I asked, incredulous. "Weel-sohn," he insisted. By golly, his name must be Wilson. "Candy? Candy?" I smiled and shook my head. "Pin? Pin?" I frowned, trying to grasp his meaning. Suddenly, I understood. He was asking for a pen. Just an ordinary ballpoint pen, a thing we might throw away without a thought. Beads and trinkets in the old days. Twenty-four dollars to buy Manhattan. Now it was candy and pens. Should I give him my pen? There were plants in the jungle that surely could be milked for ink, a process that might take days. If I gave him my pen, would that make it too easy for him? Would he stop going into the forest? Would he forget which plant to look for? The big faded purple T-shirt Wilson was wearing looked like it had come from Goodwill. Was he already spoiled? I could easily have reached into my bag and pulled out a pen, but in my confusion I didn't, not wanting to corrupt this noble little savage, not wanting to contribute to the degeneration of his culture. Oh, the meanness of it. And the double standard. To this day, I often think about Wilson and the treasure I withheld from him. Me, a writer.

It didn't take long for me to start unraveling in the equatorial heat and humidity. The first thing to go was my carefully coifed and sprayed hairdo, which simply died. Makeup was the next thing to go. By day two my cotton underwear felt like wet swaddling. By day three, the layers peeling away became more subtle. Poise. Composure. Equanimity. These too began to slip. And then, belief in self, that quintessentially North American construct—that, too, began to wobble. Struggling in equatorial heat and mud up steep slippery jungle trails when you're loaded down with luggage and video gear and on the verge of heat prostration is humbling. Having to be rescued by men is humbling.

So is walking around in the shade of trees 150 feet tall. Or losing your place in the dinner line to a tapir, a beast that looks like a cross between a pig and a horse. The tapir's name was Hugo, and he was exceedingly rude, snuffling lewdly at our crotches and gobbling up the fruit he pulled down off the table with his trunk onto the floor of the veranda. I tried filming Hugo that first morning when he woke me up with his tap tap tapping as he pranced in his high heels along the boardwalk right past my door. Immediately, I grabbed up the camera and followed him out into a clearing, filming him while he grazed until he stopped to lift his head and look at me. I kept the camera rolling right through the astonishing moment when the nozzle of his trunk closed over the lens of the camera and I let out a series of whoops that somebody told me later sounded just like a woman in orgasmic extremis. No wonder I attracted a crowd.

Worse, much worse, was watching a boa constrictor uncoil one evening like a thick pile of pottery rope right in the middle of one of the dining room tables. The snake had a visible wound in its side. It looked like a knife slash. I looked on in horror as Amanda, the young woman standing beside me, reached out to touch it and began gently stroking it awake. The snake unhinged its jaw as it began to uncoil, hissing and flickering its forked tongue madly back and forth as it sensed us, striking out first in one direction, then in another. I stood absolutely transfixed, my feet nailed to the deck, my own jaw coming unhinged. Dr. José Cabanillos, a native Amazonian who had just joined the expedition as one of the presenters, happened to be passing by at that moment. Seeing my alarm, he took me by the elbow and gently steered me away from the table, saying, "You shouldn't be watching this. If you stay here, you're going to have nightmares."

Linnea broke from the group, suddenly announcing, "The stars will be out tonight. Who wants to come with me to the buffalo pasture?" We followed Linnea single-file out along the trail into the middle of the buffalo pasture, José leading the way, where we joined hands with a circle of stargazers. There were five of us in all, a little constellation of earthlings searching the spangled night sky for the Southern Cross. Everything turns upside down in the Amazon. I stood there holding hands with strangers in the dark without being able to recognize a single constellation, feeling lost, infinitesimal in all that vastness. *Well, of course you can't recognize anything, Dopey,* I said to myself. *This is the southern hemisphere, and all your stars are crossed.*

Insomnia and paranoia began to set in with my second dose of malaria medication. Unable to sleep, I took to wandering around the encampment in the middle of the night in my nightgown carrying a lantern. I was allergic to the medication I was taking, but how could I possibly have known that it was the methloquine that was working havoc with my nervous system when there was so much to be nervous about? There were tarantulas we were supposed to shake out of our shoes every morning; there was that huge winged thing, whatever it was, that flew right into my face and took a big bite out of my chest; there was Linnea trotting down to breakfast to announce that she had just showered that morning with a fer-de-lance. I grew up in the Bronx, a civilized place. I remembered how puzzled I was the summer I worked as a counselor at the Herald Tribune Fresh Air Fund Camp when the kids from the inner city stayed awake at night, terrorized by the singing of the katydids and the rattle of the frogs. Now I understood.

I had begun to have some doubts about the medical clinic I had come to investigate. Quite honestly, I was expecting something a bit flashier when, after scrambling over tree trunks and fording muddy streams, following Linnea, I had my first glimpse of Yanamono Clinic. There it was, a brave little outpost set back in a sugarcane field, now only about a hundred feet from the ever-encroaching river, the only medical facility of its kind serving anywhere between five thousand and ten thousand people. Setting aside questions of language and culture, what could one woman possibly hope to do, faced with an onslaught of tropical diseases and widespread malnutrition, against such formidable odds? "State-of-the-art" has such a nice ring to it. But wasn't it more like a firefly flickering on the edge of an immense and obliterating darkness?

There were other questions that were even more troubling. Was it really a good idea to build a Western-style medical clinic in the heart of the Amazon? Wouldn't it contribute to an already damaged culture? Destroy the local people's faith in their own healers and lead to the further loss of plant knowledge? "Those people should be left alone." That was what Carmen Jackson, my Peruvian producer, had stated outright back in Wisconsin as soon as she learned about the clinic. I couldn't forget those words that had entered my ear like a slow drip of poison. And yet, "those people," the ribereños, were mestizos said to be "in transition," people whose culture was already seriously fragmented and subject to erosion. Contact breeds contamination. They may not have had televisions in their homes, but most of them had visited the city at least once, according to Linnea. They wanted the same TVs and sunglasses and running shoes that we wanted—all the attributes of North American civilization. With the arrival of cancers and AIDS, diseases that their shamans couldn't cure, they had lost faith in the efficacy of their own medicine, and I could readily see that Linnea wasn't interested in making any compromises to accommodate the local belief system. Linnea had learned medicine from books. She was the product of a print culture. "Bring me a book, show me a picture," she said, clarifying her terms. "Explain to me what it does, how it works, what kind of a dosage to use, what side effects to expect. I would like that idea. I'm a plant person. But so far, nobody's brought me that book."

Had I gone to check out the clinic by myself, or in the company of Rotarians, my experience might have been quite a bit different. As it was, I landed willy-nilly right smack in the center of a crossroads, at the intersection of two radically opposed views of medicine that had produced two distinctly different health-care systems, one based on material science and the other on spiritualism. Whether intentional or not, the seminar had brought these two antithetical worldviews into collision. Shamans, herbalists, and native healers were demonstrating their healing practices and giving workshops on plant medicine right alongside botany and chemistry professors, pharmacologists, entomologists, and ornithologists. Many of those in attendance were alternative health-care practitioners and New Agers, individuals such as Marcus of Hollywood, a naturopath with a Beverly Hills practice, or Michael Tierra, an herbalist and acupuncturist, also from southern California, who was affiliated with something called Planetary Formulas and had specified "herbs, shamans, healers, nature, mystery, and magic" under Interests on his application. Several had arrived clutching their well-thumbed copies of *The Celestine Prophecy.* These people had also lost faith in their own system. Fed up with pill popping and the overreliance on the technological fix that has come to characterize Western medicine, they had come to the Amazon like hungry ghosts seeking something they were convinced their own culture had denied them, something they believed might be found hidden in the secret recesses of the rainforest.

On a day when Linnea was giving tours, a few of us met setting out on the path that led to the clinic. Along the way we were joined by Francisco, a *curandero* who was eager to share his knowledge of medicinal plants. Francisco had started a botanical garden for sacred plants in Iquitos and had a brother living in Los Angeles who was famous for his visionary paintings induced by *ayahuasca,* the hallucinogen used by Amazonian shamans. When we reached the river, he stopped to rescue an errant water hyacinth, cupping it in his hands and carrying it tenderly down the steep embankment to return it to its waterbed. Then, clambering back up again to meet us, he patted his stomach, explaining that water hyacinths are "good for colic." I was impressed that he would care so much about a single flower among so many of its kind.

There was a venerable old tree with a thick black trunk that grew near the path. When we came to it, Francisco stopped again. Grabbing hold of a vine that hung from one of its lofty branches, he lifted off the ground and swung all the way from one side of the tree to the other, and back again, dropping deftly at our feet as he let go. "The people who live in the river," he told us, "have much confidence in this tree." "Is it a teacher tree?" somebody asked. "Yes. Teacher tree," he said. "The people come here to dance." He skipped to show us a few steps, and whistled a tuneless song through his hands to demonstrate how the tree spirits are called. Then he went straight to the tree and scraped a bit of bark from its trunk, collecting the sap as it ran out. Michael Tierra dug into his backpack and pulled out a book that he opened to a certain page and began singing. Francisco recognized the chant and joined in. When the two of them had finished, they laughed and hugged and called each other brother.

There was one more botanical lesson in store for us that day. As we drew near the clinic, Francisco stooped down once more to pick a plant that was growing right alongside the path. It looked to me like an ordinary weed. Again, he touched his stomach. "Anti-concepción . . . no children more," he explained in his rudimentary English just as Linnea appeared. "Welcome to Yanamono Clinic," she hailed us, coming halfway out the door. "Oh, are there medicine plants that grow out there?" The irony did not escape me. Here we were following in the footsteps of so many women who had traveled this same path to get the birth control pills that Linnea freely dispensed through a government-sponsored program, walking right past the herb that would have provided the same result, had they only known how to use it. But wasn't it much easier, and probably more effective, just to take the pills from the gringa doctor? After all, nothing homegrown could possibly be as good as what comes in a package from North America. Here it was, concrete evidence of how the very existence of the clinic was contributing to the loss of plant knowledge and the erosion of local culture. This was an old story that went all the way back to the Conquest, a variant on Wilson and the pen he had begged. But did it mean, then, that it really was a bad idea to build a Western-style clinic in the heart of the Amazon? The question dogged me. I kept posing it all week to my interviewees. The most intriguing answer came from Dr. Cabanillos, the Amazonian who had joined the expedition to teach herbal medicine. He turned the question back on me. He looked straight into my camera while the tape was rolling and said, "The gringa doctor they will listen to, if she gives them the herbal medicine. But it's not the doctors or the medicine in the end that matter. It's education. It's this thing." And he reached out to touch my camera, placing his finger on its glowing red eye as if it were a fetish. "This is power."

The night following our visit to the clinic, Francisco conducted healing ceremonies for anybody who wished to volunteer. I got in line. When my turn came around, he ushered me into a room scarcely big enough to hold a cot. Lying there in the pitch dark, I was aware of much whistling and blowing of smoke and rattling of palms, presumably to chase away the evil spirits. Francisco gave me the equivalent of what my friend Kay the spiritualist would have called "the brush off" using a palm fan that made a loud swishing and rustling noise. When it was all over and he had blessed me, he looked into my eyes and said, "Tonight, you will have a revelation." I didn't. I slept fitfully all through the night expecting the revelation that never came and woke up with my eyes sealed shut. When I went down to breakfast to report my adventure, the herbalists all agreed that the yellow gunk in my eyes was from my liver. Justin, the Englishman, was the only skeptic. "Yes, well, this is all very well, isn't it," he said, "but what about your brain?"

On Thursday morning we left Explorama for Napo and the ACEER (Amazon Center for Environmental Education and Research) Center, a highly anticipated excursion that was intended to be the climax of the week. We tromped down to the river with all of our gear and got into the boats to head downstream to Explornapo Camp, or Napo for short, a remote encampment nestled deep in the jungle on the boundary of the Amazon Wildlife Reserve, an area of 250,000 acres of primary rainforest, and the site of the fabled Canopy Walkway. There was cold beer on board to swill and fresh pineapple to munch on as we floated along past blue herons and red plover. About seven miles downstream, just as we rounded a bend to join the Napo, the largest of the Peruvian tributaries, a woman who was standing near the prow shouted out, "Dolphins!" but they disappeared as quickly as they had surfaced. A long four hours later, we entered the Sucusari River, a serpentine dark-water tributary where we landed and began the steep slippery trek up to camp in sweltering heat, me huffing and puffing all the way, loaded down with all of my gear, grateful when Mark and Wayne relieved me of my bags.

It was very close in Napo. The understory was swarming with butterflies, satyrs and morphos, the air vibrating with the sound of the jungle's teeming wildlife. In my anxious state, I felt claustrophobic and found it difficult to breathe, having to compete with all of those leaves that were also breathing. There were covered walkways with thatched palm roofs and bananas dangling from the trees. On my way to the bathhouse I passed a single leaf that by my casual calculation was as big as a chaise lounge, big enough for me to lie on. The sheer scale of it all was overwhelming. So was the sense of menace. It seemed that every tree was armored; every leaf had teeth.

We were up at dawn the next morning, early birds on our way to the Canopy Walkway, hoping to catch a glimpse of something spectacular, but my camera wouldn't work due to the heavy humidity. The lens kept fogging up, and the mechanism balked. I had trouble climbing one-handed up the wiggly rope stairway, unbalanced by the video bag that was strapped across my shoulder. An hour passed, and all we had seen was a pair of birds and one flat-headed lizard that was cause for excitement only for Julio, our guide.

Back down on terra firma, we were off again on the Medicine Trail right after breakfast, this time with Mark Plotkin in the lead, making frequent stops along the way for him to point out the properties and uses of various medicine plants. When we arrived at the entrance to Don Antonio's encampment deep in the jungle, he paused before leading us down the pathway. "It's not every day," Mark said, "that you get to see a medicine man making *ayahuasca* in his ceremonial camp."

The clearing where Don Antonio had set up camp was itself a kind of clinic, being a place where sick people come to be healed, but to me it felt more like a sanctuary. Ceremonial camps are placed in remote settings far from the village in order to protect it from possible contamination by evil spirits that might be released during a ceremony. As white people entering a medicine man's sacred space, I had a distinct feeling of trespass as we filed in and arranged ourselves in a semi-circle around Don Antonio's campfire. The *ayahuasca* was already boiling in a big iron cauldron that was sitting on top of two logs on the ground. Don Antonio was absorbed in tending his fire as Mark began to speak.

"This is Don Antonio Montero, a Cocama. He's one of the paramount shamans, not a second-class healer, a full-fledged healer. You often have in these societies two levels of healers, a *curandero* who is like a GP, and a *brujo* who is the specialist. A lot of the *ayahuasca* cults that flourish in the Amazon today are not indigenous. They're mestizo—a mix of Hispanic, Amerindian, and even African. He's of the last line of a tribe of the real thing. Cocomos are a tribe once dominant in this region who have been reduced to a few scattered communities and are on their way to becoming culturally extinct."

Throughout the time it took for Mark to deliver his introduction, Don Antonio continued tending his fire. Calm, sagacious, he went about his business with the air of a man who knows what he is doing and who is fully in control. There was a certain gravitas about him, and a certain sadness as well, the sort of sadness that inevitably clings to those who know they are the last of their line. He kept adding sticks to his fire as he swatted insects and fanned his coals using a paddle and a noisy fan similar to the one Francisco had used to dispel the evil spirits. When he was satisfied with his fire, he crossed over to a wooden plank table that stood at the edge of the clearing where he began laying out all of his ingredients. The first plant he picked up to display had a pink trumpet-shaped flower that he held upside down by its stem while describing it to Mark. "This is toé," Mark told us, interpreting from the Don's Spanish. "It's related to the tobacco family, full of tropane alkaloids and God knows what else, a hallucinogen on its own, related to daturas, the one that the kids eat in Florida and end up in the emergency room. The problem with these pseudo-*ayahuasceros* in Iquitos is they take these kids on a rent-a-shaman trip—they don't know the plants, they aren't really in control, and it's a disastrous experience." And so it went, Don Antonio methodically taking up each of his plants in turn, naming them, explaining to Mark which ones were toxic, which ones benign, while right in front of us the *ayahuasca* went on cooking in the cauldron.

Ayahuasca in Quechua means "skull of an old man" or "spirit of the dead." It's a powerful hallucinogen, the agent of exchange by which the shaman makes his journey to the underworld and crosses back and forth. In the Amazon, the *ayahuasca* induces visions of the jaguar and the anaconda, the two most powerful forces in the jungle besides the *ayahuasca* itself. The shaman must do battle with all three powers in confronting and overcoming his greatest fears. That is what makes him a shaman and what constitutes his power. In learning to heal others, he must first allow himself to become sick, a sickness unto death. It's a kind of voluntary psychosis he agrees to undergo for the sake of others at great personal sacrifice. Mark told us that the regimen of diet and discipline required by the training is so psychologically and physically taxing that most of the initiates become skeletal in the process. Don Antonio held up four fingers. "There are four of them that Don Antonio knows," Mark continued, interpreting. "Out of the four, three have died and one was driven insane." Obviously, you had to be a very special person to make it to the top of the heap. No wonder Don Antonio was the last of his kind.

It is difficult to describe exactly what was happening to me while all this was being explained. Certainly, nothing in the footage I reviewed after coming home revealed anything like the real nature of my experience. It was all internal, nothing that could be captured on video. I stood there in that clearing holding my camera right over the boiling cauldron, close enough to feel the vapors wafting across my face as I listened to Mark. I was in an altered state, completely mesmerized. I couldn't quite believe that I was standing there in a jungle clearing watching a medicine man prepare his *ayahuasca* as if I were in my grandmother's kitchen in the Bronx and she was showing me how she makes her chicken soup. Mark brought over a sprig of basil for me to identify from Don Antonio's table. I sniffed it distractedly and said it was oregano. He teased me after that, saying he would have to report me to the Italian embassy. But I couldn't take my eyes off that cauldron. The longer I stared into it, the more I began to see.

I saw the layering of the jungle itself in all that had gone into that cocktail. I saw that the mind of the shaman, with all of its layers, was in there, too. Staring into that cauldron, I even understood the split in my brother's psyche that made it possible for him to be both cruel and kind at the same time, a scoffer and a believer. I saw the Amazon itself as a gigantic cauldron in which science, art, nature, and magic were all swirling together in an undifferentiated state. It was consciousness that was cooking on those logs. I saw that the jungle in its deepest meaning is a mirroring of the preconscious mind, an ancient primordial order from which we had all emerged. I understood that poetry had come out of that roiling cauldron, and religion as well, two remnants of the primitive bicameral mind from which we North Americans had severed ourselves.

We had turned our back on the world of the spirits, ignored and scorned the wisdom that shows itself in dreams and visions. The gate had locked behind us when we left Eden. We were all suffering enchantment or suffering from the lack of it. We were all looking in one form or another for *le vrai voodoo*. We North Americans, who couldn't figure out what ailed us, were hankering after what had been lost when we split in two. It wasn't just the world that split apart, it was consciousness itself. So here we were, back in the garden of good and evil, brother and sister, north and south, staring at each other across a continental divide. That was what had brought us here, to this clearing, where a white man was explaining the words of an Indian, the last of his line. And why was he telling us all of this anyway?

Mark said that in the fifteen years he had been researching shamanism he had never seen anybody open up the way Don Antonio had. Nobody in our group was likely even to remember the names of the plants he had taught us, let alone to be boiling up his own brew. Why, then, had he given us this glimpse into his secret world? Was it because he was the last of his line? Did he see, in this little clutch of white people standing around with their cameras rolling and clicking, his last chance to pass along knowledge that might otherwise be forever lost? Was it possible that we were this man's last hope for survival?

As we left the clearing, I made sure to train my camera on the bottle of *ayahuasca* that was sitting on Don Antonio's table, a bottle that held the captured genies of the jaguar and the anaconda. The jaguar is the symbol of the shaman. As we started down the path, Mark pointed to a spot where, just the day before, another group had seen the clearest paw print of a jaguar. I didn't believe him. He promised to send me a photograph to prove it, but when it arrived in the mail after I was back at work in Wisconsin, try as I might, all I could see in the photo was a pattern of leaves on the forest floor.

We had grilled piranhas for lunch that day down by the river. They were delicious, and it struck me as only fair that we were eating them when they might just as well have been eating us. In spite of the piranhas, a lot of people went swimming. I had no such inclination. One young man I observed emerging from the river had obviously gone "native," painting his face blue and decorating himself with feathers.

That night Julio took us hunting for caimans. We glided out a short distance onto the river in our dugout canoe where Julio made us turn out our flashlights and be quiet. There were no stars at all or any light from the sky. It was like being engulfed in black felt. The only species of illumination came from strange gossamer globs that kept winking on and off among the lowest branches of the great trees, far above our heads, which I finally realized were huge fireflies. We sat single file on both sides of the dugout as fish began jumping all around us. One of them thwacked Justin, the Englishman, so hard on his upper arm that he let out a yelp, imagining that the guy sitting next to him had punched him. Another one flipped in the air right beside me and landed in the bottom of the boat—a silver dollar fish, pure pearly white with a pink iridescent eye. It looked as if it might have leapt from the moon. The sky began twitching and fuming with lightning, on and off, now here, now there, in slow, spasmodic convulsions. We sat there floating on the black river in the silence for what seemed like a long time, with the sky twitching, and the fish leaping, a little gaggle of humans in a boat between two Indian guides, afloat on the Amazon in the middle of the blackest night. How small we were, how insignificant in this great cosmic scheme of things, with the ancient jungle all around us palpating with life, the fish flipping in the air, and the smoldering sky, all of it without seam or division, and us, with nothing but our own awareness to keep us from being swallowed up.

Suddenly, Julio started. He had spotted the red coal eyes of a caiman glowing on the shoreline. We glided swiftly into shore where he reached out and grabbed it in a flash, catching it in his bare hands. An instant later, there it was, sprawled on the bottom of the dugout for all of us to see. It was a baby, perhaps a foot and a half long.

We passed our second night in the ACEER, sleeping under mosquito netting on the bark floor of the raised platform camp. It was very cozy tucked between the fresh linen sheets with light from the kerosene lantern filtering through the gauzy netting and the sounds of my fellow campers sleeping on the floor just a few inches from one another. In the middle of the night the great storm finally broke. Rain fell in sweeping torrents. It was a rain unlike any I had ever before experienced, delicious and caressing, like black satin. It came in sheets, in three passes, advancing and retreating, advancing and retreating, like three visitations from a god.

The next morning, Friday, I woke up feeling too ill to go birding with the others at dawn. "You don't look so good," Lyn told me at breakfast. "You'd better lie down." So I spent the morning lazing about in a hammock, feeling weak and nauseous and shaky, sipping cola laced with various infusions and thinking maybe it was that iced gin and tonic I had guzzled guiltily the night before leaving Explorama that had given me the runs. But I wasn't the only one who had taken sick.

Someone had been poisoned. Who was it? The camp was swarming with rumors. It was Marcus of Malibu, Mr. Natural Physician of Hollywood himself who had been stricken, the Adonis whom I had last glimpsed emerging from his floral bath covered in petals. He arrived at the ACEER so weakened there was some speculation that he might have to be airlifted out. Don Antonio was summoned. It took him but a few minutes to deliver a diagnosis and confirm, in private, the wild speculations. Marcus had been bewitched. Bewitched! But by whom? It had to have been someone in our group, a sham shaman who had given him some bad stuff. Suspicion fell on Dr. Cabanillos. I remembered how, the day before, José had been all over camp looking for Marcus, carrying something in his hand. He who has the power to cure can also harm. There was black magic and witchcraft afoot in the Amazon. I was thrown into consternation. Had Marcus been poisoned out of malice or simple ineptitude? Don Antonio grumbled about these tricksters who pass themselves off as medicine men without having done the full course. Marcus blamed himself for not having followed his instructions carefully enough. The jungle is a shape-shifter. Things were not what they seemed. But if I couldn't be sure of Dr. Cabanillos, did that mean Francisco was also suspect? My own feelings about it all? Had we all been duped? Bamboozled by dueling trickster shamans? Questions flew out of the pot like phantasmagoria.

On my last day at Napo I got an offer to fly back to Explorama by piper jet, a real luxury. Late in the day, I decided to pay one last visit

to the clinic to get some additional footage. Just as things were winding down there, Jubencio, Linnea's assistant, went to the door and came
back announcing that a patient had just arrived. She was a young woman
nineteen years old who was about to deliver a baby. As soon as she was
put on the table she immediately went into seizure. Lyn, a young resident sent from Duluth to cover for Linnea during the week of the seminar, slapped a blood pressure cuff on her arm and immediately began
preparing an injection to bring her blood pressure down. The patient
was suffering from eclampsia, as it turned out, an acute condition in
which a woman becomes allergic to her own pregnancy. It is very dangerous. Everybody went into high gear, suiting up in surgical garb to
prepare for a possible Caesarian. Lyn probed the woman's vagina and
she moaned in pain. I stood there with my camera, clearly in the way,
feeling extraneous and slightly obscene, but galvanized by the drama
that was unfolding before my eyes, wanting to "get it all." The screen on
the camera was flashing red again, the dreaded signal that meant that
my last battery was about to run out. I hesitated, torn between wanting
to save whatever was left for "the good stuff," yet not wanting to lose
what was happening in that moment. "You cannot film this," Linnea
called out from across the room as if she could read my mind, "but you
can watch."

Again, I was torn, feeling an acute sense of trespass, loathe to be a
mere voyeur in this arena where others were scrambling to save a life. So
I compromised by lingering just outside the operating room, flitting
back and forth across the open door, turning the camera surreptitiously
on and off, hoping at least to capture the story on the camera's audio
track, knowing that this was exactly what I had come for, what fate and
luck had conspired to deliver with this child that might or might not be
born. As I sat there on the floor with my back to the wall outside the
door, Dr. Cabillero's words came back to me, "The gringa doctor they
will listen to, if she gives them the herbal medicine." There was no
herbal medicine to be found anywhere in that clinic. But then he had
also said, "It's not the doctors or the medicine in the end that matter. It's
education. It's this thing," and he had pointed to my camera. "This is
power." I thought about that. Did that make me a doctor as well? As a
journalist, did I, too, have the power to heal or to bring down? Was it

possible that with my camera and my tape recorder and the power of words I could supply in another form the medicine that was missing? Did radio have the power to cross the great divides and bring the world closer together? Was I willing to become that firefly flickering on the edge of a vast and obliterating wilderness?

Yes, this matters, I thought to myself, as I began packing up my gear. *This little outpost on the edge of the jungle matters. Here, life and death cross paths every day.* Only that morning, at dawn, Lyn had delivered a dead baby in a dugout down on the river. And before this day would end, she would help to deliver another baby, this one born live, suctioned out of its mother after it had crowned and she had suffered yet another seizure, causing the contractions to stop. The doctors attending this birth, Linnea, Lyn, and Jubencio, would marvel at the baby as she drew her first breath, and declare, all three, that indeed, she was beautiful.

"The snakes start to come out at dusk. It's probably a good idea for you to start back now." That was Linnea laying down another one of her drop-dead pronouncements. I finished packing up in haste and began to make my way back, hurrying along the darkening trail that had by now become somewhat familiar, passing by the riverbank, passing by the great tree that Francisco had swung from, passing the spot where Wilson and I had made friends on the day that I arrived, imagining the snakes slithering toward me from all four directions, while my bag with its camera and spent battery kept bumping against my hip, weeping as I went, weeping for all of us, for the woman in her aloneness and pain, for the baby about to be born on the banks of the Amazon, for the Rotarians, those crazy optimists who had lugged all that stuff through this eternal mud, for the glory and the pity of it all, for the fragile thread that links us to this life, and to each other, here on earth.

7

A Big Enough God

thought . . . if it be inspired

He likes clean lines. I like rococo clutter. We have tchotchke wars. Soon after we were married and I moved in and began redecorating, he imposed the Tchotchke Rules. Rule #1 (adapted from William Morris): A thing must be beautiful and/or useful before it's allowed in the house. Rule #2 (also known as the Steady State Tchotchke Rule): For every tchotchke that comes in, one must go out. He wants to keep things simple. That way he can think better, he says.

He thinks about science. Mostly, when he's at home, he sits on the porch in his big tan overstuffed armchair and thinks. My son's cubist painting of him, thinking, with his whole head a jumble of nuts and bolts and widgets, hangs right above the chair.

I like claw feet, cushions, carved furniture, candlesticks on the mantel. I want paintings on the walls, baskets and pottery above the kitchen cabinets, my mother's parrot lamps perched on both ends of the sofa. I like to shop. He hates to shop. On those rare occasions when we go in search of something for the house, his brain goes into overload; he gets sleepy and has to come home to take a nap.

When we travel together, we visit churches. I favor the ones that titillate, encrusted with forms, a saint in every niche, banks of ruby-red votive lamps swimming at their feet, and a Christ who weeps blood. This disgusts him. "How can you Catholics call yourselves monotheists and go on worshiping plaster statues?" he rails. For him, God must be abstract, an elegant theorem that explains the universe, odorless, tasteless. But he says there is no God.

For every hundred churches that we visit—in Italy, there are sometimes five within a single city block—there is only one synagogue. Tucked into the corner of an obscure courtyard or hidden away in some slanting second-story annex, the synagogue is always hard to find and, in general, not very rewarding, not much more than an unadorned meeting room. The synagogue on St. Thomas in the Virgin Islands, the oldest in the New World, is so unassuming that it still has a sand floor. Churches are invariably much more beautiful. This makes him defensive. By law, synagogues were not permitted to compete with churches. Then, too, there is the problem of graven images, which, according to Jewish law, are strictly prohibited. *You shall not make for yourself an idol.* So states the second commandment. No tchotchkes.

"The danger in symbols," he says as we walk away from the Jewish ghetto, "is that they can so easily turn into idols. I've never understood how you Christians made three gods out of one. You say you believe in the Ten Commandments and then claim that Jesus was a god and go on worshiping the Virgin Mary. It's noncompliance. You have a million gods and worship tchotchkes. There wouldn't be a junkyard in Italy big enough for all the junk you'd have to haul out of all these churches. There must have been a tchotchke entrepreneur somewhere way back who removed the second commandment from your Bible and started a tchotchke factory. Then the semitrucks started rolling, and hence, a thriving industry for two thousand years."

No lesser deities, no roadside shrines for this professed atheist. "Demigods are the worst," he snivels, by which he means the popes. What bothers him most about the popes is that they claim to speak for God. He insists that God must be ambiguous. "God cannot be named; God's name must not be spoken; God cannot be represented in any way. The concept must be limitless. To define is to limit."

"But you have a name for God. What is it?"

"Yahweh."

"There! You said it."

"That's because I don't believe in God."

This is an old argument between us. It began in the Jewish ghetto in Venice over a bowl of inky cuttlefish pasta that, in the middle of defending my religion, blackened my lips and teeth and made me look like a goth in the photograph he snapped. We had spent the morning visiting the ghetto's two synagogues, the "ghetto" being another Jewish abstraction that, except for its bronze memorial plaque depicting the deportation and murder of 205 Venetian Jews in 1943, looks like any other *piazza*. On our way to lunch we stepped into a church and were immediately confronted with a skeleton encased in a glass coffin and a particularly gory statue of Jesus, crowned with thorns, eyes rolling, blood streaming down its face. Sensing his revulsion, I tried to explain that when it comes to God, most humans need some kind of mediation, something with which to identify. Otherwise, the idea of God is just too abstract and overwhelming.

"What do you have against saints?" I asked him.

"Look at who makes them."

This was a remark that went back to our first real fight, over whether the pope has the right to name saints. It surprised us both, an argument that kept coming back like bouts of malaria. The argument was aggravated by his reading of *Hitler's Pope,* a biography of Pope Pius XII who, while he was still Cardinal Pacelli, the acting papal nuncio, made a devil's pact with Hitler, thus creating an alliance between the Vatican and Nazi Germany. "There is no God," he said. "Pacelli proves it."

One fall, he flew off to Edmonton on a business trip and called me from a costume party the next night. It happened to be Halloween. "I want to dress up like the pope," he announced over the phone, much to my astonishment. "I will issue an encyclical making it a mortal sin to declare yourself infallible." This became his favorite fantasy until it ratcheted up. "I want to be God on Judgment Day," he suddenly declared one morning after reading a bit of pope news in the *New York Times.* "I want to be sitting on my throne when the pope comes before me. 'So,' I'll say, 'you thought you were infallible . . .'"

Frankly, this obsession with popery leaves me mildly bemused. I no longer pay much attention to what the pope says or does, and consider the doctrine of infallibility downright silly, a hoax obviously invented by the Catholic Church in an attempt to render its authority unassailable. However, I do love my saints. I was regularly dosed with saints' stories while I was growing up and found them to be fortifying, sort of like spiritual castor oil. Vivid accounts of the virgin martyrs, young girls who defied patriarchal authority and who suffered the consequences nobly and with gladiatorial courage inspired me. So, too, did the accounts of the Jesuit missionaries, those so-called Black Robes who freely relinquished the comforts of European society out of love for God to travel alone through the savage uncharted wildernesses of North America. These stories introduced me to the dimension of the heroic and taught me indelible lessons about the human capacity to transcend its own limits. I felt compelled to defend the honor of my saints before the attacks of an avowed atheist and explain their formative influence on my character. But I needed ammunition. Fortunately, just about this time a new book about the saints that I really liked, called *A Tremor of Bliss,* became available. It was an anthology of essays written by contemporary writers. I chose an essay by Tobias Wolf to read to him one evening when we were dining out together. The essay, titled "Second Thoughts on Certainty," was about St. Jean de Brébeuf, a Jesuit who worked to convert the Huron Indians and was eventually martyred by their enemies, the Iroquois. Brébeuf was tied to a stake and tortured for hours. Nothing broke him, not even when the Iroquois daintily flayed his flesh and ate the strips before his very eyes. "Finally, in a fury," I read, "they cut his heart out and ate that too. By his calm fortitude, he inspired them to kill him much sooner than they'd intended." I closed the book and looked up at him. "Now do you see why such stories would have such a profound impact on a young girl?"

He was impressed. I could see I had gained some real ground. But I lost it all once Pope John Paul II began his program of wholesale canonizations, naming saints left and right as if they were breeds in a dog show, dramatically revising the standards, even doing away with the devil's advocate and the need for three proven miracles. John Paul ended up adding more saints to the Catholic roster during his single reign than in the whole history of the church. To make matters worse, he was even working on beatifying Pope Pius XII, Pacelli himself, at the time he died. It was like grade inflation. Never would I have dreamed in my wildest moments that my staunch defense of sainthood would end up being undercut by the pope himself. Now it was my turn to be disgusted. When he asked to borrow my copy of *Fracture Zone,* a history of the Balkans, I hesitated and handed it over reluctantly, only after exacting a promise that he would skip the chapter on Cardinal Stepinac, a Croat who forced the Orthodox Serbs to convert just before permitting them to be slaughtered and, you guessed it, one of the pope's chosen sons for canonization. Ah, history, you are no help.

When he was only eight years old, his brother gave him a World War II history book that he opened to the pictures taken at Auschwitz. He saw the bodies piled up like cordwood. "Oh. There can't be a God," he said.

One morning, not long after we had been married, I came downstairs to report a dream. "I saw Jesus as a Jew," I said. "He had big, sorrowful, dark eyes and a long face that looked very Semitic, and he was very sad. The reason he was so sad was because of all the suffering his people have had to endure on his account." My husband just looked at me. "Jesus *was* a Jew," was all he said. How could I not have known that?

He has long legs, like stilts, that carry him cleanly across campus, along boulevards, up mountains. I trot along beside him like a terrier, panting to keep up, or mosey along behind, sniffing at every turd he overlooks. This, too, is about God. When we go hiking in the mountains, he plunges ahead, eyes on the summit, oblivious to all else. Subject neither to fatigue nor to distraction, he heads straight for the clouds where the thunderheads gather. Being a creature of the lesser slopes, I am content to meander, loitering beside the quick streams and in the mossy hidden places, where God is a whiff, a warble, a glimmer. I am given to transport. For me, every valley is exalted. I step out into the winey air and come back reeling. "God! God! There is nothing but God!" said Shams of Tabriz, Rumi's teacher, even as his assassins were plunging in their jealous daggers. The difference between what is called *sacred* and what is called *profane* has never been completely clear to me. I love the things of this world. Meat. Wine. The simple act of sitting down to supper. The green rose of the artichoke I stuff with nuts and olives. God on low, simmering on a back burner, the ever-replenishing pot.

He is self-possessed. He stands out in the rain, completely dry under his collapsible umbrella with his two long legs folded neatly together. For him, the Messiah must never come. How else would we ever finish mapping the human genome? Find a vaccine for AIDS? A cure for diabetes? He believes in the Big Dis, as in *dis-provable,* as opposed to my Big Gaga. He is guided by a search for truth that is exacting and requires vigilance and constant recalibration. A scientist must practice suspended belief. To be robust, a hypothesis must be testable. This is how science makes progress. You often build an edifice only to demolish it, a predisposition that conditions and demands detachment.

But he, too, has his moments of transport. I saw with my own eyes how, standing in the Great Mosque of Cordoba, in Spain, surrounded by what appeared to be an infinitude of overlapping red and white striped arches ascending in all directions, he had a genuine spiritual experience, which, of course, he flat-out denied. All he said was, "I could write a really great grant here." Listening to music can also send him into transport. The music that fills our house on Sunday morning is often better than anything I've heard in church. He has a special love for vocal music—Bach's cantatas, Handel's oratorios, the great chorales. With his father, he used to sneak into New York City's cathedrals on Christmas Eve to hear them performed. And just last week, I watched him go into ecstasy during a concert of songs from Rilke's suite of poems, *Les Chansons des Roses:*

> I have such awareness of your
> being, perfect rose,
> that my will unites you
> with my heart in celebration.
>
> I breathe you in, as if you were,
> rose, all of life,
> and I feel the perfect friend
> of a perfect friend.

I saw tears in his eyes as the song was ending. He leaned over to whisper in my ear, "That reminds me of you."

Afterwards, over ice cream, we talked about the concert. "That's the reason people go to church," I said. "To have that kind of experience." "And I can have it without believing in God," he replied a bit smugly while licking his coffee ice-cream cone. "It's not a matter of belief," I countered. "It's a matter of experience. You just had an experience of God."

There was a time when we used to meet on a corner once a week to go off to lunch to practice Italian together. The corner was right outside the office building where I work, at the intersection of two busy downtown streets. Over time, it came to be known as "Il Nostro Angolo"—Our Corner. The telephone in my office used to ring on Monday morning, shortly before noon, and the conversation would go like this:

Sei pronta?	"Are you ready?"
Si. Prontissima.	"Yes, absolutely."
Fra dieci minuti?	"Can you be there in ten minutes?"
Al nostro angolo.	"I'll meet you at the corner."

We have a mutual friend who, unbeknownst to us, was operating as the mastermind behind our courtship. It was he who had instigated the Italian lessons. To underscore our sense of assignation, he scratched "Il Nostro Angolo" into the pavement on our street corner, and there it stayed, persisting all that winter in spite of ice and snow, still dimly discernible until it finally grew too faint to be deciphered. But the words showed up again on the day we were married. This time "Il Nostro Angolo" had been etched into a black marble slab that magically appeared under the huppah, the words *Il Nostro* carved along the top of the slab, and *Angolo* down along one side. Now it sits on top of the mantel in our living room as a kind of cornerstone. So much collided at that corner where the Angel of Science is still wrestling with the Angel of Art, where Judaism dukes it out with Christianity, and where God, amazingly enough, makes room for No-God.

Is my God big enough to contain his No-God, I ask myself? Do I have the courage to hold at arm's length my most cherished beliefs? Adjust, examine, discard, recalibrate? Belief, of course, is not a testable hypothesis. And yet, who wants a wimpy God? Was an old man in the sky with a long white beard any improvement over the Venus of Willendorf? God is still God, no matter how our conceits keep changing. All of our words for God are metaphors, according to Paul Tillich; we need those boats, as he put it, until we reach the shore. Even the idea of No-God is just that—only a conceit. Isn't it about time for me to discard my tchotchke-esque version of Christianity? My "smells and bells"?

Much as I love my saints in their niches, infinitely more moving was the niche I once encountered in one of the great mosques in Istanbul, a niche that was completely empty, a frame for That-Which-Cannot-Be-Framed. Bowing down before it was a man on his prayer rug, worshiping the Ineffable. That is the closest I have come so far to my husband's No-God. So, again I ask myself, is my God big enough to contain his No-God?

Jesus said, "I and the Father are one," which got him into big trouble. In the eyes of the Jews he had blasphemed by making himself equal to God. Meister Eckhart, the German mystic and theologian, goes one step further. He points the way beyond God, which got him into trouble too. "Before there were any creatures," he writes, "God was not 'God' but he was what he was . . . so therefore let us pray to God that we may be free of 'God.'" This suggests to me a way in which I might find God in my husband's No-God.

I wonder at it all. The plan whereby I would marry a man whose nonbelief would cause me to question my belief and drive it into deeper waters. *Atheist* was such a dirty word when I was growing up, and it still carries a charge, even though I know it's not what you believe that matters in the end, it's how you live your life. Now he is reading *The God Delusion*. A great test. I stifle an urge to throw him and his book out of bed. How do I find God in his No-God? It's not like Ruth in the Bible. It's not a case of withersoever he goeth, I goeth; his people shall be my people and his No-God, my God. But, I have to admit, there is a way in which his No-God has made my God bigger. It's as if we are paddling around a coral reef, pointing out its wonders to one another. "God! God!" I say, "There is nothing but God!" "Nature! Nature!" he says, "There is nothing but Nature!" And then he takes me by the hand and leads me out beyond the reef to the place where it drops off and there is nothing as far as the eye can reach, only a Great Void. I hover at the edge, contemplating this Great Void. It frightens me. No tchotchkes out there, nothing but a Voice that comes out of the deep. God, are you there? *There is no God but God. . . .* it says, and then I hear . . . *There is no God in God.*

8

Roger and Me, Too

"Il piacere e 'tutta' mio"

There is no word in English to describe the special closeness that
sometimes binds a man and a woman who are never lovers, but
more than friends. Had Roger and I met decades earlier when we were
both young and crazy, given half a chance, I would have jumped on the
back of his Harley and ridden off with him without so much as a backward glance. As it was, what grew between us was something much
subtler, something that had shading, texture, and seasoning. But because
there is no word for it, it stayed mysterious in my mind, to be brought to
light, among so many other astonishing revelations, only in the course of
my becoming Roger's memoirist.

Roger was my husband's best friend, but I loved him too. Ours is
a marriage fueled by the energy of opposites: Alan, the scientist; me,
the poet; Alan, the atheist; me, the believer. Our temperaments are also
opposed. Alan is forever climbing Mount Olympus while I am down
below, dancing with Dionysius. We circled each other warily when we
first met, careful to avoid any minefields. But Roger and I needed no such
delicate negotiations. Attraction between us was simple and spontaneous.

We were roughly the same age and had both grown up in second
generation immigrant families in twin boroughs of New York City,

165

Roger in Brooklyn, and I in the Bronx, densely ethnic neighborhoods that stamped us for life. We were old enough to remember the clatter of horses dragging their wagonloads over the cobblestones, the whine of the scissor sharpener, the rumble of trolley cars, the cries of the ragman, and the pleas of gypsies begging in the street with their sticky palms outstretched and their sickly babies slung around their necks.

Following that age-old American imperative, Roger and I "lit out for the territory" as soon as the way was clear. We boarded the same freedom train bound for the West Coast and came of age on parallel tracks during the tumultuous sixties. While I went roaring around the Berkeley Hills with one of the original Hell's Angels, Roger was getting ready to stage his own motorcycle rampages through the evergreen highways of the Pacific Northwest. We were both children of William Blake, Aldous Huxley, and Walt Whitman; we shared the same wild streak. Whatever wisdom we were destined to acquire would inevitably come from following the road of excess. But beneath these several layers was something deeper, some invisible substrate. It was as if we were standing in the same stream, miles apart, with our feet on the same contiguous bedrock. "He adored you," Kathy confided in her low, mellifluous voice when we met in Aspen to scatter Roger's ashes. Coming from a wife of thirty-some years, that was pure gift.

I suppose you might say that deep down I'm one of those Catholic school girls afflicted with a biker babe fantasy and a weakness for bad guys. Alan grew up in Latin America. The first time I met him, he was leaning against a stone wall, wearing dark sunglasses and one of his drug dealer shirts. As attached as I am to that first impression, it didn't take long to disabuse me of it. Okay, so he might have known his way around the back alleys of Caracas once upon a time, but here was a guy who lost no time in introducing me to classic movies, vintage wine, and Beethoven's late string quartets. Alan was a mensch. Roger was the badass.

Just as I was confronting my sixtieth birthday, a package arrived in the mail from San Diego. Inside the box, hidden under the crisp folds of pink tissue paper, was a silver belt with eagles that were strung on a double chain, and a skimpy sleeveless black T-shirt edged in lace. The shirt had a winged skull printed on the front, the classic Harley trademark. As I held it up, a piece of paper the size of a ticket stub fluttered out, landing in my lap. It was a tiny hand-lettered coupon. I picked it up and read, "Good for one ride on Highway 101."

I had to wait a few years before I finally got to claim that ride. It was during a visit to San Diego shortly before Roger died. I remember the unnatural crush and weight of my helmet as I hung on to Roger's broad, black-leathered back, feeling the vibrations that came shuddering up through the thick, padded seat as Roger gunned the engine and started tooling up the long, winding drive to the road. Rounding the bend, we passed right in front of Alan, who was standing there at the top, waiting to wave us on as we zoomed by. Glancing back, I noticed that he looked a little worried at the sight of his best friend riding off with his wife.

He was a big man with a nose worthy of Cyrano and a bushy moustache to match, massive shoulders, and a barrel chest so heavy it seemed to tip him slightly forward with its weight. Inert, he was like a boulder storing heat. When he walked, it was with a half-saunter, half-strut, with his chest thrust out, his head thrown back, and his butt tucked in so tight it looked almost concave. He had a habit of hooking his thumbs in his pockets and scuffing his penny loafers, which stuck out sideways, with a little half-kick. When Roger's daughter brought her boyfriend home for the first time, he took one look at Roger and said, "Kimmie, your dad walks like a gangster."

Always bigger, stronger, and smarter than his twin brother, Roger was born first, but his mother favored Neal, the baby who took after her. She made up a game she called "The Perfect Kid of the Week Club." Roger never won—not once. She often predicted that her big ox of a son would go bad and one day end up in prison, a prophecy that haunted Roger all his life, and which he only narrowly escaped.

As a teenager, he hot-wired cars and stole them for joy rides. In graduate school, he shared needles with black men just to prove he wasn't prejudiced. He played pool for money, got into barroom scrapes, and occasionally came home to Kathy with his forehead split open. He rode a Harley all his life and even named his son after his bike. Once he even picked a fight with a Swiss Guard at the Vatican and came close to kicking him in the shins. I always imagined Roger as a kind of half-man, half-bull, and was pleased with myself when I came up with a name for him. "Roger," I said, "You're the Bull in the China Shop of Life!" But he was hurt. "That's what my mother used to call me, he winced, '*You Big Lummox!*'" "I had heard and read about men who were like that," Kathy told me, "men who were fearless. He was the only one I ever knew." So when his diagnosis came up and he was finally forced to face his own mortality, we wanted to believe that if anybody could lick prostate cancer, it would be Roger.

Tough as he was, Roger had charm. "I'll be the one wearing the Panama hat and the pink carnation," he liked to say whenever we arranged a place to rendezvous. And there he'd be in front of O'Hare, looking stunning in his houndstooth jacket and blue Hawaiian shirt, his aviator sunglasses and spectator shoes, and, of course, his Panama hat. He had such a fondness for women that it made me eager to please him, and it never took much. Show up in a ruffled blouse or a flouncy skirt, and it never went unnoticed. "*Sella Bella!*" he would exclaim, drawing out the syllables in his ardent faux Italian. I took special delight in cooking for him whenever he came to town; I once prepared an osso buco so tender it slid off the bone, and rejoiced watching him dig into the marrow with a Lilliputian-sized spoon. I even indulged a fetish he had for bright red toenail polish, and took pains to apply Candy Apple Red to my toes even after Roger died and we were on our way to scatter his ashes.

If it hadn't been for Roger, Alan and I might never have gotten together. Roger was big-hearted and wise. Right away he surmised that we were exactly suited to one another. But Alan needed encouragement. I was twice divorced and almost a dozen years his senior. Dominick, my younger son, didn't help matters when he took Alan aside to whisper into his ear, "Are you sure you know what you're getting yourself into?" Being a nurturer, Roger watched this budding romance from a distance and moved it along, sometimes not so gently. Not long after we met, acting on impulse, I presented Alan with a copy of *Talk Dirty to Me* on Valentine's Day. The book had a picture of a peach with a deep pleat perched provocatively on the cover. Alan was puzzled. "What do you think that means, Roger?" That was a question Roger didn't have to ponder. "What do you think it means, you idiot?" A year later, just as matters were heating up and coming to a head between us, Alan got cold feet. "Alan," Roger threatened, "if you don't marry Jeannie, I will."

Roger always called me "Jeannie," drawing out the long "e" through his colossal nose in a way that reminded me of my father. In fact, there was a lot of Big Daddy in Roger. Sometimes when we met, out of sheer childish glee, I would run and jump into Roger's arms. With Roger, "you always felt safe, even driving down a highway on the back of his Harley at a hundred miles an hour," Kathy testified. Roger had other names for me too. He would look at me from time to time, turn to Alan, and say, "That's Some Tomayta"—also vintage Daddy. At his most avuncular he declared, "Jeannie, you're an old-fashioned girl," but when I once stood up to him, he dubbed me "Mighty Mite," and after reading my memoir, he proclaimed me "a tough broad from the Bronx."

The first time we met, Roger greeted me as Aunt Julia. He was sitting in Alan's living room. As I walked through the doorway, he rose slowly from the couch. Dressed in jeans and a pale blue denim work shirt with his hands in his hip pockets, rocking slightly back and forth on his heels and nodding with his eyes half-closed, he took my measure. "A-a-a-unt J-u-u-lia," he purred in a descending cadence after a moment or two, smiling his guru's smile and pronouncing the name as if it were a benediction. There was no mystery about the name. At Alan's urging, we had both been reading *Aunt Julia and the Scriptwriter*, a novel by Mario Vargas Llosa about a young man who falls in love with his aunt. If Roger dubbed me Aunt Julia, it was certain I had won his approval.

By the time the three of us set out for Deb and Lola's, a trendy restaurant on Madison's State Street, we were already in an altered state and flying high. There was a lot of hilarity at the table; the jokes were good and the laughter so infectious that it rippled out and spread to the surrounding tables. Then suddenly, the mood shifted. Our heads cleared. In the place of hilarity, there was clarity, and in the charged air, a certain solemnity set in. It was as if we had taken truth serum. There was something about Roger's presence that seared through the barriers that had kept Alan and me guarded with one another. Beyond the euphoria of the moment, we were both suddenly conscious of having arrived at a plateau of real happiness, perhaps for the first time in our lives. That made us bold. We turned to face one another and began, a bit absurdly, to declare our real feelings. "Have you any idea how you have transformed my life?" I asked, directing the question to Alan, but once out of my mouth, the words seemed to unfurl over the table and hover there like a banner. It was as if we were seeking Roger's imprimatur. And Roger rose to the occasion. Simply amazed at the naked truth of our ecstatic outbursts, he listened attentively and nodded from time to time, taking it all in. The table had become a kind of altar, and Roger, the impromptu priest who intuited his role perfectly. Three years would go by before Roger would pronounce the blessing at the close of our marriage ceremony, "Blessed be their bliss," but it was on that night at Deb and Lola's that our wedding really began.

We had barely settled into our hotel in Khania on the edge of the Aegean when the bad news arrived. Holding his laptop open in his arms, Alan burst into our room, crying, "Roger's going to die on my birthday! What the hell does that mean?" There we were in Crete, thousands of miles from San Diego, marooned on the island of the Minotaur, and Roger had been bullish all his life, especially in the way he battled his cancer.

We slept fitfully that night. Waking in the half-light before dawn, we dressed hastily without uttering a single word, and sped down the spiral staircase all the way to the basement, where the Internet signal was strongest. Seated side by side in the gloom outside a conference room, we braced ourselves for the worst. Alan took a deep breath, lifted the lid on his laptop, clicked open his e-mail . . . and there it was. Roger had died overnight.

They had met thirty years earlier, working in the same crowded lipoprotein lab at UC–San Diego. At twenty-one, Alan was lean and wiry, a Ph.D. student with a mass of wild, blue-black curls; Roger, ten years older, was a burly post-doc, red-headed and slightly balding. They talked incessantly about everything they cared about—science, of course, movies, books, music—in passionate conversations that lasted long into the night, but the real gorilla glue that bonded them was mischief. Growing up in Venezuela, Alan had a cultivated contempt for authority based on his tussles with the small-minded teachers who ruled his early life and the corrupt cops he still insists on calling "criminals in uniform." Roger was a complete anarchist with a wicked sense of humor who rode out the sixties like a cowboy, still wearing his vintage "Mother Fuckers" black leather jacket in 1976 when he growled up to the lab every morning on his Harley. They saw themselves as renegades and outliers and they hatched a friendship that lasted a lifetime. They got into each other's heads and loved each other like brothers. They shared every dimension of their lives, and never stopped being bad boys together.

It was Alan who was right there by Roger's side when Harley was born, watching him set the baby down on the floor to take his picture with a baseball mitt, a copy of *The Complete Works of Shakespeare*, a football, and Jim Watson's *Molecular Biology of the Gene*, the very textbook he had read over and over to teach himself biochemistry. Their careers as lipid protein biochemists developed along parallel tracks. They both secured teaching positions in universities where they set up labs. They had overlapping research interests and conferred incessantly; they followed each other's experiments and read each other's grant proposals; whenever one of them had a paper rejected or a grant turned down, the other was always there to buck him up. When Alan made a dramatic mid-career move to take up diabetes research and become a geneticist, amazingly enough, it wasn't long before Roger followed suit, so strong was his desire not to lose the conversation. They traveled widely, met at conferences, and went on backpacking trips, sometimes with their wives. When Alan's marriage fell apart, it was Roger who guided him through his divorce, eventually becoming his best man at our wedding. During the last months of Roger's life, the two best friends made time to talk together at the end of every day, using a videoconferencing system Alan set up in his office that allowed him to read Roger's expressions and see into his every mood.

The last time we saw Roger, the four of us met at our favorite rendezvous, the Furnace Creek Inn overlooking Death Valley with its breathtaking view of the Panamint Mountains, where Charles Manson had once holed up in his last hideaway. Alan and I flew from Madison to Las Vegas and drove west from there through Red Rock Canyon and the

Amargosa Desert, while from the opposite direction, Roger and Kathy were tempting fate by driving two hundred and fifty miles east from San Diego, expressly against doctor's orders. Roger had been in and out of the hospital two or three times a week for transfusions to counteract the anemia that became acute when the cancer reached his bones. He had suffered a frightening episode of bleeding from his brain just one week before setting out, and the danger was that he might bleed to death in the desert. But Roger was his own man, and after all, what did he have to lose? I made him laugh when I teased, "Roger, you can't die in Death Valley. You'd never live it down."

The sun was at its zenith in the cloudless desert sky by the time Alan and I arrived, and we waited anxiously the rest of the day for Kathy and Roger to roll in. It was mid-March; the days were still short, and dusk had fallen by the time we recognized, with a shock, the shadowy, stooped figure advancing slowly up the flagstone walkway, leaning heavily on Kathy's arm. Roger had severed his Achilles tendon and was limping badly. Suddenly, he looked like a frail old man hobbling along beside a woman who might have been mistaken for his daughter.

Hiking was out of the question, but we decided to hazard a trip to Scotty's Castle, and while Alan waited in line for a ticket to one of the tours, Kathy and I found a spot to hang out with Roger. The three of us were sitting on a rock wall and eating ice-cream bars when a blood vessel suddenly broke in Roger's leg. "See that?" Roger asked, reaching down calmly to swab at the rupture with his paper napkin. "That's a hematoma." We knew then that, despite his heroics, he couldn't survive much longer.

Cancer was Roger's labyrinth. He paced it tirelessly, exhausting first one pathway and then another in his relentless quest to escape. By the time his tumor was discovered and removed, the cancer cells had already escaped the capsule, but that only made him redouble his resolve. Whenever he struck a dead end, he would rethink his strategy, choose another path, and head off in a fresh direction. Even at the end, his brain was hemorrhaging, he was losing consciousness, but he simply refused to give in. I kept thinking of him in the middle of that prison with the walls heating up, and nothing but his raw determination to keep him alive. Kimmie and Kathy were desperate to get him out of the house and into the hospital. But even at that extreme, they heard him mutter as they ushered him out the door, "I'm a fighter. I'm gonna lick this thing."

Science wasn't just what Roger did, it was what he lived by, his tao. His modus operandi. As much as his cancer terrified him, it also fascinated him. He treated it as an intriguing problem to be solved, and turned himself into his own in vivo experiment. Acting with his oncologist as his chief collaborator, he designed and subjected himself to entire regimens of cutting-edge treatments, each one more desperate and more imaginative than the last. They all took their toll. He was losing ground, but he was extending his life at the same time.

When his doctor advised against successive bouts of chemotherapy, Roger came up with a cocktail he thought had a chance of working and talked his doctor into letting him try it. When a secondary tumor developed in his leg and was declared inoperable because of the nerve bundles and blood vessels that had wrapped around it, he persuaded another surgeon to cut it out anyway, and thus saved himself from becoming a cripple. When he learned about a promising experiment underway at UC–San Francisco's medical school that was designed to boost the immune system and kill tumor cells, he flew up to San Francisco, collared the researcher in charge, and bullied his way in even though enrollment was officially closed. These treatments were particularly grueling, involving the extraction of dendritic cells from his bloodstream to be incubated in vitro with PSA (prostate specific androgen: a protein produced by prostate cells that is elevated by cancer) and then re-injected after several days. In Roger's case, this caused an extreme allergic response. His blood pressure plummeted; he went into shock and became so sick that he was hardly able to walk, hobbling out of the hospital bent in half to flag down a taxi to the airport. With each successive treatment, the effect became more painful and more debilitating but it worked, and he persisted. In the end, Roger had become the research subject with the most successful outcome. But he was cruel to himself. Cruel and unsparing.

Cancer was the goad. It maddened him. In his bullishness, he kept charging ahead, crashing headlong through every barrier. Each treatment killed off 99 percent of the cancer cells but left a more aggressive remnant intact. His PSA went down, only to creep back up again. Once, it went all the way down to zero and stayed there for a while. Roger was elated. He discussed the possibility of writing a paper with his oncologist and publishing their results. He sent out a group e-mail declaring, "I will beat this disease!!!!!!!!!!!" "My future is so bright I have to wear sunglasses," and went into detail: "I just learned my newest paper will be published in PNAS (Proceedings of the National Academy of Sciences) without any requested revisions—a rare occurrence for me! From this research we were led to propose a new angle on enhancing the efficacy of cancer drugs. In any case, I have formulated a therapeutic regime based on my research and I started the treatments on Thursday! Who knows, maybe I will become cured and will also be able to have enough data for a paper! Best of all worlds!"

At his most Panglossian, Roger's optimism extended to every member of his family, who were all prospering according to his glowing reports: "Kathy's graphic design business is growing. . . . Kimberley has been accepted into medical school. . . . Harley has moved into his own apartment near the beach in Oceanside." He was so relentlessly upbeat that after a while we came to believe him. Even Alan, as levelheaded as he is, came home one evening and announced, "Roger has decided he's not going to die." But privately, in iChats with Alan at the end of the day, Roger would let down his guard and allow himself to weep, not for himself, but for the family he was being forced to abandon.

Meanwhile, he was consumed with preternatural energy. As death came closer, Roger speeded up. He started a biotech business, wrote two NIH grants that got funded, published a seminal scientific paper, managed his lab, and when he could no longer drive, met with students in his own home, conducting his last lab meeting just three days before he died, all while undergoing treatments, refusing pain medication, and entertaining a steady stream of house guests. "I'm going to go out swinging," he told Kathy. As soon as the message went out that Roger had suffered a brain hemorrhage, his friends started coming. They came from everywhere— from Alaska, from L.A., from Colorado—and they kept coming nonstop right up until the end. Christian Drevon, Roger's old nemesis and lab mate from his UC–San Diego days, traveled all the way from Norway. Christian was a strict teetotaling Lutheran; Roger had once tried to force beer down his throat. Franz Simon, Roger's friend from Colorado, arrived bearing a venerable old bottle of 1982 Chateau Mouton Rothschild, a noble red valued at five hundred dollars he had unearthed from his wine cellar. Roger said it had legs as long as Kathy's, and she kept the cork. Throughout it all, "He was determined to romanticize his death," as Kathy said. Her sister, Mitzi, a bereavement counselor, was amazed at the courage and grace he displayed. In the spirit of William Ernest Henley's poem "Invictus," he resolved "to be the master of his fate and go out bloody, but unbowed." He thanked whatever gods for his unconquerable soul, and sent a copy of the poem to Alan in his last waning days with the tag "This is me."

A year and a half earlier, the four of us had met at Casa del Zorro, a resort in the Anza Borrego desert, right after New Year's to celebrate what we thought would likely be Roger's last birthday, January 6. At that time of year the place was all but empty. We ordered dinner to be delivered to our suite, and halfway through a bottle of cabernet and a platter of roast lamb, Alan presented Roger with his birthday gift, an album of photographs from their many escapades together. On the cover, above the words "Roger and Me," was a photograph I had snapped of the two of them while we were vacationing in the Greek islands. There they are, the two rascals, seated side by side on a terrace overlooking a nude beach, looking like yin and yang: Roger's in a black T-shirt and baseball cap, Alan's in white; each is wearing the same moustache, the same sunglasses, and the same wily smirk.

Inside the album, the photographs Alan had selected ranged through every stage of their thirty years together: goofy mug shots from their days in Dan Steinberg's lab at UC–San Diego; Roger and Kathy as new parents, looking a little stunned with Harley in their arms; Harley as a kid with his hair grown down over his forehead; Kimmie, still a tomboy; Roger and Alan on their epic hike from Maroon Bells to Snowmass in Aspen, where they got lost and were gasping for water by the time the six-foot Swedish goddess who rescued them appeared on the trail; Roger and Alan at Gordon conferences in New Orleans and in Orlando; Roger in Rome about to pick a fight with a pair of Swiss Guards in front of St. Peter's; Roger and Alan absorbed in their chess game while sailing in the

Greek Islands; Roger devouring oysters at his favorite shack in New Orleans and mangling crawfish in Orlando; Roger in his Panama hat and spectator shoes; Roger accepting an award from the American Heart Association; Roger arm wrestling with his friend Jake; Roger in his chef's hat, stirring his signature pot of gumbo; me and Roger balancing strawberries on our noses at Alan's fortieth birthday bash; Roger as best man, beaming as Alan and I become man and wife.

On the first page of the album, Alan had written, "When I was a kid, I always had a 'best friend.' We would have adventures, keep secrets, and talk about everything. Above all, we knew how to play and have a lot of fun. As a 'grown up,' I have had the great good fortune of having a best friend in exactly the same way. Roger has been present during my best and worst moments. We have shared all parts of our lives together. We have traveled everywhere. And we know how to have a great time together." Reading the inscription, paging slowly through the album, Roger was so touched, he stopped suddenly with his mouth full, snorted, convulsed, and had to leave the table.

Roger had been given a prognosis of three years; he was now in his ninth. Having watched my brother go through all the classic stages of dying, from anger to acceptance, I kept expecting the pattern to repeat. But it never did, not in Roger's case. Listening to the radio in the bathroom one morning while Alan was shaving and I was brushing my teeth, I heard Garrison Keillor recite a poem that had been written by a woman with terminal cancer. I stopped brushing and thought a minute. "Do you think Roger would like that poem, Alan?" I asked, turning to him. "Do you think I should send it to him?" His answer was always the same. "No. Not yet. He's not there yet."

I wanted Roger to read my memoir before he died, but it wasn't due to be published for another year. I decided that the best way to get it into his hands would be to present it to him as a birthday gift, so I had the manuscript photocopied and spiral bound, wrapped it in gift paper, and brought it with me to Casa del Zorro. For the cover I chose a laminated photograph that Alan had taken of the two of us standing on a street in Capri with our arms wrapped around each other. In the photograph, I am wearing my tiger-striped blouse with the black fishnet eyelet inserts and the racing cougars; Roger is wearing his favorite blue Hawaiian shirt with the big, creamy magnolias. We clashed horribly, and yet we were perfect together. Although I had no way of knowing it at the time, my choice was fortuitous. The gift would soon lead to an end-of-life adventure much more thrilling than any ride on a motorcycle.

A few weeks after leaving the desert, an e-mail message from Roger popped up in my in-box:

> Dear Jeannie,
> I devoured your book while I was traveling to give a talk. I wanted to wait to send you my comments in a manner more commensurate with your beautiful and provocative writing . . . but I just do not have that much time. . . . I particularly enjoyed reading about how you became a liberated American woman while still respecting family and cultural values derived from the old country. And, of course, your book describes one of the most wonderful love stories! I am so happy to have "seen the movie before reading the book!" And your chapter on becoming a poet reminded me of the first time I understood what science means.
>
> I feel privileged to have you and Alan as friends and to have you share your work with me. My only reservation was that after finishing your book, I felt as though I had just tasted a most wonderful and uniquely aged Sauterne, but I wanted MORE!!!!!!!!!!
> With love and best wishes for the success of your book!
> Roger

I was completely thrilled with Roger's wholehearted enthusiasm, although I had to admit to being baffled, at the time, by the connection he had drawn between my poetry and his science. But his appreciation seemed so genuine that it suddenly dawned on me that here was a door I could walk through. "Alan," I asked, "Do you think Roger would be interested in writing his memoir and having me help him?" Alan thought for a moment. "Yes, I think he would like that." Then I asked Roger. He thought it was a good idea too. So, just like that, I became Roger's memoirist.

There was no master plan in the way we worked together. Basically, Roger just talked, I listened, and Alan recorded. Our first session took place on a Sunday morning in San Diego with the three of us sitting around the kitchen table strewn with coffee mugs and the morning paper. While Roger recounted his earliest memories of growing up in Flatbush, the all-Jewish neighborhood in Brooklyn that even as a young child he found stunting and claustrophobic, I took notes and Alan recorded the audio on his computer. That was the first and last time Roger and I were able to sit across from one another, face to face in the same room. All five or six of the subsequent sessions were recorded remotely, with me sitting at home in Madison and Roger in San Diego. We decided on a different theme for each session, and simply allowed one topic to lead us to the next. The videoconferencing system Alan set up from home was clunky, and occasionally broke down altogether, causing some critical losses, and Roger, who was easily fatigued as his pain increased and he became weaker, was forced to cut short a few sessions. Nevertheless, as I listened and took notes over time, I began to discern the outlines of a story that was gathering power, weight, and resonance. Roger's story had integrity, and it rang true. It had an arc and a perceptible through line. It made sense. Above all, it struck me as a quintessentially American story, full of tough guys, guns and outlaws, motorcycle gangs, hairpin turns, razor-thin escapes, and, in the end, redemptive true love. I began to understand that this wasn't just Roger's story, but our story, the story of a whole generation that came of age in the sixties, a generation made up of idealists, hedonists, and anarchists who, no matter how deluded, reckless, or narcissistic, managed to ignite a social revolution, launch the culture wars, and ultimately alter the course of American history. It was a story both shocking and edifying by turns, and I found myself deeply moved by the gift Roger had entrusted to me, and the reciprocal responsibility it carried. Was everyone's life story as worthy of being told, I wondered? And if I didn't tell it, who would? Would anybody ever know that, in spite of his professed hatred for organized religion, he actually had a deeply spiritual side? Roger was "one of the roughs." He needed an amanuensis. "What do you want me to do with all this, Rog?" I asked him after our final session. "Do you want me to write about it?" He thought for a long minute. "Yes," he said.

Flatbush, the Brooklyn neighborhood where Roger was born in 1945, looked and sounded exactly like an Eastern European shtetl. The signs were all written in Hebrew. Everyone spoke Hebrew or Yiddish. For

Roger, it was insufferable. "It's like going to Israel," he ranted. "You go to Flatbush even to this day and you see these people walking around . . . they're wearing their hats and their coats and their earlocks. . . . It looks like the Western Wall! I mean, it's a foreign country there!"

Exposed to orthodoxy at such a young age, Roger became intolerant of all its forms and never lost an opportunity to express his irreverence, no matter how outlandish or absurd. As a token of his scorn, when he finally visited the Western Wall on a trip to Jerusalem, instead of a prayer, he tucked a little box of green peas into a crevice in the Western Wall just so that he could claim that he had "brought peas to the Middle East."

"Ashkenazi Jews," he complained, "they're all related. I had uncles and aunts and cousins and they'd all get together. It was always chicken soup and marzipan, chicken soup and marzipan—just horrible. There was nothing else. *Watch out for the shvartzes! Stay away from the goyim!* Your family was your whole world, and the messages were all about fear. And I wasn't fearful. Pauline, my grandmother, she was five feet tall and weighed 300 pounds. In those days the idea was to get obese. She had huge boobs, and so did my mother, but she never let me nurse. Pauline used to chase me around the house with a spoonful of egg, *You gotta finish your egg! You gotta finish your egg!* God, Ashkenazi Jews are so obsessed with food, and they don't even know how to cook! I was starved for spices."

If it hadn't been for Benjamin Yaeger, Roger's grandfather and his first hero, he would have found nothing to praise in those first five years of his life in Flatbush. But Roger loved tough guys, and Benjamin "was a tough guy, a real tough guy," he told us. "He boxed when he was young. He was maybe 5′ 4″ and he had big arms, big hands, he was like a muscle guy, really fit all his life until the day he died." Benjamin walked everywhere, often with his grandson by his side. They walked together over the Brooklyn Bridge to Manhattan and back again, making frequent stops to kibitz whenever Benjamin bumped into one of his cronies.

"I can remember walking down on the Coney Island boardwalk with him. He used to love to tell me stories. And I remember asking him, "Who is Hitler?" I had a thing about Hitler. And he told me that he was the most despicable person that had ever lived and that he killed our relatives and a lot of other innocent people all over Europe, and I said, "Well, how did he kill them? And he said, "Well, he used to gas 'em and burn 'em to death." And I said, "Well, why didn't they fight? I would fight, Grandpa." And he said, "You don't know what you would have done. You don't know." And I said, "I do know." And I made him a promise that I was always going to be a tough guy. My grandfather had letters that were smuggled out of concentration camps. . . . They knew what was going on in the gas chambers. . . . Do you know that, Alan? They knew what was going on . . . but they just didn't exercise their political muscle in the right way. My grandfather was a Zionist, for sure. . . . He gave tons of money to Israel, tons. . . . I'm sure he felt frustrated. Whatever he did, it wasn't enough, and he could have done more . . . but by then it was too late, it was 1950."

Benjamin had lived for a while in a cardboard box on a New York City street after being kicked out of his home near Berlin when his father died and his mother remarried. He had come over from Germany when he was only thirteen years old, making the arduous voyage in steerage all alone. He started out with nothing, learned the tailoring trade, and eventually made himself a fortune. Your handshake was your signature in those days, and Benjamin had a really strong handshake, and a reputation to match. By the time Roger was born, his grandfather, well respected and well connected, a religious Jew whom everybody knew, was running his own factories. Roger watched his grandfather get up every morning to greet the sun with the tefillin strapped to his forehead, praying in his prayer shawl, and some days Roger prayed right along with him.

Sometimes Benjamin took his grandson to work with him. Roger remembered many women in a big room that was buzzing and whirring with a hundred Singer sewing machines all going at once, and there was his grandfather, presiding over it all, "this incredibly disciplined, hard-working, industrious person who had made his fortune." Once, when the three of us were in New York, near the Tenement Museum on the Lower East Side, we happened to pass a bronze statue of a Jewish tailor in a skull cap stooped over his work. "There's my grandfather!" Roger called out excitedly. We were in what used to be the city's old manufac-turing sector. "And over there, down that street," he said as he waved his arm, "that's where the Triangle Shirt Factory once stood with all those poor young women who were trapped in the fire. They were locked in and they all lost their lives. My grandfather worked for a time in the Triangle Shirt Factory, and he testified on their behalf in the Triangle Shirt Factory trial. That was the trial that changed the labor laws in the State of New York."

Benjamin Yaeger's business was eventually bought out by Jonathan Logan. The family achieved the American Dream in a single generation. They had a big house in Oyster Bay and a chauffeur-driven Pierce Arrow in which Roger's mother was driven to school. Benjamin believed that women were to be worshiped and coddled and, like a lot of Europeans, he didn't trust banks, so he put his money in jewels and made sure that there were diamonds as big as rocks flashing on Pauline's hands. But he lost a pile of money in the late twenties when he invested a million dollars in Chinese silk, and by the time the ship arrived, the stock market had crashed and the silk was worth a pittance. "So, he never recovered the same kind of wealth that he had before the Depression," Roger told us, "but he sent all six of his kids to college. That was my grandfather. His word was law and if you broke the law he'd whack the shit out of you, and that's the way it was."

The one thing Roger didn't like about his grandfather was that he never had any fun. Roger could never remember seeing him laugh. But Benjamin loved cowboys—Tex Ritter, Gene Autry, and Hopalong Cassidy—and he used to like watching cowboy shows on television with his grandson by his side. It was Benjamin, in fact, who drummed into Roger's head the desire to go west. "I swear, my grandfather would have become a cowboy if he'd had the chance," he told us. "And I wanted to go west because of that. I got expelled from school, thrown out of first grade for shooting my six shooters off. I used to love that smell. Even hitting the caps with a rock, I used to love it, those red caps, that was great."

If it hadn't been for Roger's mother, Carolyn, the Davis family might never have escaped from Brooklyn. Carolyn Yaeger was the first woman in her family to go to college. She graduated from Columbia University with a master's degree in education at a time when Columbia was all male and had a Jewish quota to boot, but she got in anyway. "She was just so smart and so well read, you would have loved her," Roger said. "My mother was a member of the Communist Party. My mother smoked dope. My mother had a boyfriend named Hugo, a goy who played the trumpet in the same band as Ozzie and Harriet. I have pictures of her sitting with Hugo and Ozzie and Harriet at the Cotton Club in Harlem that date from the late twenties. But she was so into herself, she didn't even know she had kids. I can remember my mother losing me in downtown Manhattan when I was about four or five. . . . Little kids could ride the subway for free, so I just went under the turnstile and found my way back to Brooklyn." She was just so smart, but she didn't know how to cook, and she was crazy as a loon, and mean . . . *hooooh!* mean, mean. She used to take me shopping, and one day we had just come home, and here I am, right on the stoop of our house, and I have to pee. And she just goes on yakking with our neighbor. I said, "Mommy, I gotta pee." And she just keeps right on yakking. There was this little girl standing there watching the whole thing and she started teasing me. "Oh! You gotta pee! You gotta pee!" So what do you think I did? I peed all over her. . . . My mother was so embarrassed. And so this neighbor lady, she had a basement, this dark basement, and she locked me in the basement! Crazy. Is that crazy? You think that's the way you're gonna break Roger?"

In 1950, when Roger was five years old, the family moved from Brooklyn to Roslyn, a suburb on Long Island. Carolyn had already committed the ultimate transgression in marrying Robert Evan Davis, a goy if there ever was one, and was primed to become the first and only member of her tribe ever to move out of Brooklyn. "Well," Roger explained, "we wanted to get out of the city. But if you want to know what was really going on, my father wanted to extract himself from that Jewish ghetto. And, you know, I can't blame him for that. Because it wasn't just Jewish, it was oppressively Jewish." By this time, Carolyn, having come to equate her family's Judaism with superstition, began to distance herself from her roots. "So, as we extracted ourselves from Brooklyn," Roger said, "we got more and more goyish. We went from being a Jewish family to being only half Jewish, and what's going to happen next? Are we going to become a Christian family? And not just a Christian family, but a family that fosters anti-Semitism."

As if in anticipation of this momentous metamorphosis that was about to overtake the Davis family, Roger's paternal grandmother Bea showed up in their lives like some sort of evil fairy godmother just prior to their exodus from Brooklyn. Having never bothered to marry Roger's grandfather, she arrived with a new husband in tow, a man named Milton Dallin, who was, of all things, a Mormon from Salt Lake City. Beatrice Davis was a suffragette who was active in the Republican Party and openly supported Joe McCarthy. Roger had letters in his possession that had been written to his grandmother by Eisenhower and Joe McCarthy.

"I got up early and she was sleeping in the living room," Roger began, "and she sits me down and tells me about her hero, Charles Lindbergh." The famous American aviator was a Nazi sympathizer who campaigned against the U.S. entry into the war, and openly flaunted the Service Cross of the German Eagle that Hermann Goering had awarded him on Hitler's behalf. Bea must have been appalled at the idea of her son married to a Jewish girl and living in Flatbush in the ample bosom of the Yaeger family. Bent on sabotage, she camped out, doing her utmost to lure her Jewish grandson back into the fold. "And she proceeds to introduce me to Christianity, and she tells me a whole different story of America. She made us watch Bishop Fulton Sheen on television—remember that guy? *Life Is Worth Living*, that was the name of his program. You had to kiss his ring, a real extremist, and there would be my mother, the card-carrying Communist, sitting on the other side of the room, gnarling."

For Roger, it was all rather liberating. Exposed to his goy grandmother's alternate version of reality, however flawed, it dawned on him for the first time in his short life that the world was bigger than Flatbush. The wheels on the freedom train in his little head began to turn, spitting out new thoughts in a narrative that was ultimately subversive: *I want to be an American. I don't like this marzipan crap. I don't like these people talking in this language I can't understand.* "My grandfather used to read *The Forward*," he told us. "You know what *The Forward* is? It's a newspaper that goes backwards! What did I want? I wanted to play football. I wanted to go out west and be a cowboy. I wanted adventure. I didn't want to stick around and be safe and worry about all these goyim who were going to punch you out, or kill you, or burn you, or whatever . . . forget it! I'm not going to do that. And I got out of Brooklyn, didn't I, Alan, and so did you. We escaped!"

Roger was nine years old when the Davis family moved to Glens Falls, near Lake George in upstate New York, where, instead of cowboys, he got Indians. Not just any Indians, but *The Last of the Mohicans.* Built during the time of the Indian Wars before the Revolution, Glens Falls was home to James Fenimore Cooper and the legendary Chief Chingachgook he memorialized, who had raided and scalped the British. By the time the Davis family arrived in 1954, Glens Falls had become a General Electric town. Ronald Reagan came in 1958 to give speeches about the Communist menace, hired by GE. "That's how he got his start in politics—GE gave him his platform."

According to Roger, GE was responsible for polluting the Hudson River and turning it into an ecological disaster, but when the Davises settled on West Mount, outside of town in the early fifties, the place was still largely a wilderness. Living among deer, coyotes, and bears, Roger began to develop a great appreciation for the natural world. He climbed to the top of the falls with his little sister, Leslie. He walked to school and learned how to shoot birds with a slingshot and a .22. But along with wilderness came a lot of prejudice. If the townspeople still harbored a two-hundred-year-old hatred for the British in 1954, imagine how they felt about blacks and Jews. The Davises lost no time in changing their stripes.

"My dad was a frustrated writer with a journalism degree from the University of Wisconsin, who was now working as an advertising marketer for Imperial Wallpaper and writing a column for *Better Homes and Gardens* and *House Beautiful*. He felt that in order to advance his career he needed to join the country club, which was restricted. So on Sundays he took us to the Methodist Church, where my mother became a Sunday school teacher and I was confirmed. One day in tenth grade, my friend Stuart Lazarus asked me if I was Jewish. I said, "Well, my mother's Jewish." I went home and told my mother, and she said, "You shouldn't have said that." So, the next day I told Stewart, "I was just kidding." It was all phony baloney. We went from goyim haters to Jew haters, pretending to be a Methodist family, hiding the booze when the minister came to visit. It was like being forced to live a lie. When my grandparents came to visit, Pauline told me I was going to go to hell because I wasn't growing up to be a true Jew, but my mother said, "Don't worry about it, there's no heaven or hell anyway."

Living in Glens Falls surrounded by so much prejudice and hypocrisy taught Roger to despise all forms of dogma and organized religion with the one notable exception of the God and Country Badge he earned as a Boy Scout. That, he claimed, always guided his life. He and his best friend Paul Ringwood made up their own religion. They called it Benigna. That was their name for God. They practiced Benigna by bowing down to the ground, intoning the sacred name three times, and praying for a miracle, victory in their football games, an upset against a rival, or good golf shots. Paul was raised Catholic, and one Saturday afternoon he persuaded Roger to go to confession with him. When Roger's turn came, he drew back the heavy maroon curtain, stepped inside the confessional, and knelt down in the dark, waiting with baited breath for his chance to tell the priest, "I murdered my mother." But just as the screen slid back, he cracked up laughing and had to bolt, racing out of the church like a bandit.

Roger grew up fast in Glens Falls. Joyce Trazilli, his first girlfriend, taught him how to kiss, but he paid dearly for it when her boyfriend, who was a senior on the football team, beat him up after football practice on the day he caught them making out. Roger learned about sex from Margie, a pregnant pre-teenager his mother rescued from a broken home. Roger liked Margie a lot. He learned how to drink beer and drive a Chevy stick shift, two things he relished doing at the same time, from the boy who knocked her up.

There was a family living next door to the Davises on West Mount that became a kind of second family to Roger, Neal, and Leslie. Roger said that if it hadn't been for the Patricks, all his mother's roots, every bit of Jewishness, would have been washed out of her. Bennett Patrick, Roger's salvation and his role model, was "a real no bullshit guy" who had played baseball for the New York Giants and owned Honingsbaum, the town's major department store. His wife, Harriet, who was Jewish and had worked in vaudeville, had a best friend, a racy redhead named

Lila Libowitz, who was still active in show business. When Lila came to town, the two showgirls kicked up their heels and belted out show tunes, bringing a little bit of the bawdy and naughty into the lives of their straight-laced Methodist neighbors.

But as much as Roger loved the Patricks, his affection never stopped him from stealing their cars. He had keys to all the cars in the neighborhood. And while "Mr. Perfect," his twin brother, Neal, was working weekends at Honingsbaum, learning from Mr. Patrick how to be a businessman, Roger went joyriding with his friend Paul, buying beer with a fake I.D. and getting drunk. If it hadn't been for Paul's father, Charles Ringwood, a judge they called "Political Charlie" who regularly got the boys off their drunk driving charges, Roger would have been in big trouble. But nothing could curb Roger's wild streak. "I just wanted to get out of that town," Roger said with emphasis. "I did not want to be around people who were prejudiced."

As dedicated as Roger was to delinquency, it was no wonder that he was dispatched to the Virginia Military Institute. The year after the family moved from Glens Falls to Delaware, his siblings went off to the University of Delaware while Roger enrolled in VMI. He was proud to find himself in the same lineage with Robert E. Lee and Andrew Jackson—"the toughest of the tough." At VMI he learned to stand at attention for long periods at a time, march under the sweltering sun, swim laps with a heavy pack, and run long distances. As part of their training, VMI rookies were routinely deprived of sleep and forced to hump six miles in the middle of the night with the rat-tat-tat of machine-gun fire rattling overhead. Roger didn't like taking orders, he didn't follow the rules, and he didn't last very long. After a year and a half, he transferred to the University of Delaware to study chemistry. But he never complained about his time at VMI. Kathy credited VMI for the discipline Roger acquired that saw him through his cancer. "It matured me," he acknowledged. "It gave me a goal. I found out how tough I was, mentally and physically, and the confidence I gained put me on this path."

It was no accident that Roger chose to study chemistry. After the move to Delaware, his mother befriended their neighbor, Howard Simmons, a prominent organic chemist who later became the CEO of Dupont.

Howard took a personal interest in Roger, taught him how to smoke cigars and drink scotch, and put him to work in a Dupont laboratory during the summer.

But even as a young child, Roger showed an aptitude for science, taking things apart and putting them back together again. He was a problem solver. In 1957, when the Russians launched Sputnik, Roger was in the seventh grade. Suddenly, there was a national crisis. Too few American kids were studying science. As part of a nationwide campaign to close the gap, President Eisenhower passed the Advanced Science Education Act, and Roger was one of the kids chosen to participate. He knew that half his family had been wiped out; he thought of himself as a patriot and wanted to pay his country back for providing refuge from the Nazis.

But what really drove Roger into science was his hatred for what he called "bullshit." Roger remembered that when he was a kid and the family dog peed on the bed, his mother told him that an old lady had taken the dog to a new home. Roger knew right away that it "was a lousy lie and a bunch of baloney." He felt demeaned by it. With science, he didn't have to rely on the interpretations of adults that, time and again, proved to be untrustworthy. He wanted to figure things out in his own head. Even at a young age he saw right through the twin orthodoxies in which he had been raised. Navigating between distortion and hypocrisy, he was determined not to be caught and dragged into their double whirl-pool. He armed himself with reason, wit, and common sense, and resolved that the only orthodoxy he would ever steer by would be what science alone could provide — "absolute truth, incontrovertible, and experimen-tally provable." Truth would be his Ithaca, the red thread that would guide him home.

In 1969 I wound up in Washington State University, working toward my chemistry Ph.D. on a project sponsored by the U.S. Army. I had always wanted to go west, and Washington State is one of the most beautiful places I've ever been in my life. . . . The trees, the lakes, the rivers are just spectacular. That's why I went there, for its beauty, and the fishing and the hunting. The Evergreen State. But by this time, some of my friends had gotten killed in Vietnam, others had come back seriously wounded—they couldn't talk, or walk—and it was upsetting. I thought the war had no purpose and no end, and was fucking over a lot of people, including me.

"So, after I got to Pullman, I started hanging out at a local bar, where I met a group of faculty members, drinking and shooting pool, and we became friends. Most of them were in the philosophy department, bright, interesting people, probably about five years older than I was. I had been trapped in that narrow, rigid, conservative environment, and, all of a sudden, here I was with people who were very erudite and articulate, and I was trained in chemistry and science. I loved to read and that kind of thing, but I wasn't at that sophisticated level. And I met these people and we just hit it off. . . . It was like, it lifted my soul and opened up my eyes. . . . It was a West Coast experience. And they had this sort of philosophical motorcycle club they called the "Up Against the Wall Mother Fuckers." It wasn't really a gang. Originally, it was just a spoof, a bunch of intellectuals who wanted to ride motorcycles and act like tough guys. The Hell's Angels had taken One Percent as their insignia, because, after Marlon Brando made *The Wild Ones*, somebody claimed that it was really only 1 percent of the motorcycle riding population in the United States who were outlaws. So, we took the Greek symbol for infinity as our insignia. It was like a boys' club. We had them professionally made, and on the back of the jackets, it said, "Up Against the Wall Mother Fuckers."

"So, we had these colors, these jackets, and we used to ride down the road all together, and the cops would stop us and search us, and here we were just university people. That's the way it started out. That's not the way it ended, but that's the way it started out. Initially, we just used to have fun. We used to go to the Coles' house on Saturday night—Bob Cole taught economics and his wife, Johnnetta Cole, was in the anthropology department. She was this real smart black lady who became the first African American woman to be named president of Spelman College. Anyway, they both loved the Porter Wagner program—you remember, like the Grand Ole Opry, with Dolly Parton, and Johnny Cash and all that?

"We used to watch it and make fun of it, and eat pizza, and here we were, all these people sitting around talking politics and literature, real

Americana, you know? I just . . . I grew up. . . . I mean, it was like, wow, this is real college! And I made friends with black people. I mean, I was never a racist. I played football and ran track with black guys, but I never had a real close black friend, and here we were, we shared beers, we smoked joints, we did a lot of things together. It was a very enlightening experience.

"And along with that came a lot of drugs. And I was a chemist, okay? We started off with psilocybin. . . . We would take it and go up into the mountains and spend the whole day in the wilderness just walking around and talking. . . . It changed the way you perceived things, the way you thought about things. . . . I came to realize there was a whole world out there that I had been denied, and I wanted to catch up. This was 1969, remember? The civil rights movement was in full gear. Johnnetta Cole, she was such a radical, she really taught me about racism, about all the missed opportunities, the exploitation, the injustices, and learning about all that first hand, I decided racism was going to be my advocacy. We needed to raise money, so I said, 'Well, why don't we throw some beer bashes? We can get bands to play for free, and charge people. We'll call it the First Annual Gang Rape and Bludgeoning . . . okay?' We became famous for our parties. Gary Larson came to our parties.

"At the First Annual Gang Rape and Bludgeoning, the Unitarian Church gave us their hall for free and a lot of bands wanted to play. We were expecting maybe two hundred people, but instead, maybe fifteen hundred people showed up at five dollars a head. So we raised all this money. We took half of it, I think it was five hundred dollars, and we rode in this column to the County Seat, and gave a check to the old people for new eyeglasses, 'so that the blind could see the truth.' Everything had a little twist to it, okay? We got stopped by the cops, of course, and searched, but then the newspapers were ready for us and took our picture. . . . We made headlines in the Pullman newspaper: 'Mothers Give $500 to Senior Citizen Center.'

"So, the second thing we did. . . . We opened an account in the local bank with the rest of the money, and with that we started the Freedom Bank. That was Teddy Crowell's idea. Teddy was a mathematician. To get a loan, all you had to do was sign up, say how much money you wanted, what you wanted it for, and when you were going to pay it back. There was no end point, no interest; we were not usurers, we were idealists. We were there as a service to the community. If you paid us back before you died, okay. We had maybe $1,500 in the bank and we gave out maybe $300 in the first few weeks. People said they needed the money for tuition, or books, or clothes, or whatever. And then, when they realized that they didn't really have to pay the bank back because that was part of our socialist philosophy, of course, nobody ever paid us back. No way.

"So, let me tell you what happened to the Freedom Bank. I had this really wonderful friend by the name of William O. Ewing III. He came from an old Dutch family that had been in this country for centuries. Bill was in no way an intellectual. Bill was an artist, and not just any artist. He came from the same town as Andrew Wyeth and he learned how to paint like Rembrandt. He was into luminosity, and I helped him make the paint. I had so many good times with Bill, I mean, we were so thick we were like blood brothers. And he protected me. He was maybe one inch taller than me, and one of the few people I couldn't beat at arm wrestling. Bill was the most amoral human being I ever met in my life. He wasn't immoral, but he just didn't give a shit, okay? He stole Rembrandt's notebooks from the Rijksmuseum and got caught. He got put in prison in Amsterdam, but he broke out, of course. He was a real character. So Bill, when he realized that there was nearly $1,200 in the bank, he decided that he needed that money to have his Harley rebuilt. So, really, he stole the treasury. Some people wanted tuition, some people wanted books. Bill, he wanted his Harley redone. That's how I learned how to chop bikes. He knew how to take a Harley apart and put it back together. He was a craftsman, a perfectionist. We did his bike, and then we did my bike. He taught me how to do all these amazing things, how to do body work, how to paint, and how to draw. He had so much patience. He had this real sweet side, but he was incredibly violent too. He had an arsenal like you wouldn't believe. I mean machine guns, I mean brass knuckles, sawed off shot guns."

"So, he was the one who turned the Mothers into a real motorcycle gang?" I asked.

"Yeah, he was the toughest, meanest son of a bitch I ever met in my life. He rode a real Harley chopper, he wore a chrome Nazi helmet, which was probably illegal, and he kept a pair of brass knuckles in his back pocket. Sometimes, when we went into bars, we'd run into the Hell's Angels, and he'd pick out the biggest and the nastiest, and go after him. He'd pick a fight, and he never lost. He would beat him to a pulp, just to show that the Mothers should be respected, okay?

"So, slowly we developed into a real motorcycle gang. We went from magic mushrooms and psilocybin to peyote and LSD, and all of a sudden, speed became the drug of choice, because Bill knew a lot of real heavy dudes who used to come in every now and then from the East Coast. And the next thing you know, we had these real hard-core criminals in our motorcycle club, just because we weren't going to be prejudiced. The one thing you had to have in order to get in was some kind of political principle, some cause that we considered worth fighting for.

"So, one of the people we let in was a guy by the name of Kerrigan Gray. Kerrigan Gray had just gotten out of Walla Walla prison. He was an Irish guy who had done six years for selling marijuana. We were outraged, of course, because what the hell is wrong with marijuana? And Kerrigan Gray, because he kissed the Blarney Stone, was an incredible orator. He'd get on one of those big bullhorns and he knew how to work up a crowd . . . you know how people were in those days . . . and the next thing you know, we started organizing what we thought were important protests against the war. I mean rallies that would encompass the whole university. We marched against the war, and we marched against racism. That's what I was big into. I helped organize a sit-in, and we shut down the university for three days so we could talk about racism, instead of chemistry or sociology or whatever, and within that mix were these real hard-core criminals.

"We started out as a put-on motorcycle club, and the next thing you know we were riding with Hell's Angels, and partying with Hell's Angels . . . and, ah, they were mean. . . .

"That's the way things happened in the sixties. You know, with enough drugs, your mind gets a little twisted about what's acceptable and what's not. Pretty soon, if the cops can bash us over the head, maybe it's okay to bash a cop over the head, right? They were our enemy!

"I decided I needed an officious title. Minister of Defense had a certain noble quality to it, and so I nominated myself Minister of Defense, and by unanimous proclamation I became Minister of Defense, of which the responsibilities were virtually nothing. We never knew exactly how many we were. People would come in, people would leave. One of our people, Joe Schock, was a decorated marine and another great orator. He was so angry, he learned how to put together chemical bombs. So, one day he blew up the Lewiston Armory. Lewiston is a big city in Idaho about thirty miles from Pullman, where the Idaho National Guard's Armory was located. I don't know how many bombs he blew up; it wasn't accurately reported. He blew up tanks and artillery, he started a bunch of fires, and he got caught. I woke up one day and it was all over the newspapers. He did maybe over a hundred thousand dollars worth of damage. Somehow, he knew how to put together a bomb, can you imagine that? Can you imagine me doing anything like that, Jeannie? Apparently, there was a chemist in the motorcycle club who knew how to make bombs. Somehow, Joe Schock figured it out. And he was a real hero, this guy. Here was somebody who came home from Vietnam, saw the truth, and said, you know, we've got to stop this, and that was a very important turning point."

"Did he rat on you, Roger?" I inquired.

"This guy would rather die than rat on anybody. He saw his buddies killed in Vietnam and was trying to exact justice. He was a decorated marine, okay? In fact, the townspeople respected Joe Schock. He was one of them. As it turned out, they were going to put him on trial, and he escaped . . . and has never been heard from again. With enough drugs and whatever, your mind gets a little twisted.

"After Joe Schock got caught and went to jail and got sprung, well, then the motorcycle club started to break up. Actually, they fired Bob Cole and Johnnetta Cole. They were just too radical for the university. And they fired all the professors. Jack Bush got fired. He was in the philosophy department. The first day of class he told his students, 'Just tell me what grade you want and I'll give you the grade, and I don't think this class needs to meet anymore.' So Jack got fired. They couldn't fire me, but, you know, when I went to defend my thesis, my committee never asked me a single question. They just wanted me out of there. I was a really good student, so they couldn't just kick me out without a degree. We got purged eventually. But we went nuts, too.

"You know, apparently, there were people in the motorcycle club who were making this super pure speed and just handing it out. They called it the People's Speed. Apparently, there was a chemist who was doing that, okay? And it was like, word got out and people started coming from all over the country looking for it. It got so hot, pretty soon this person came to his senses and decided it might lead to a lot of trouble, and he got out. But not before he was offered millions and millions of dollars to continue doing it as a profession. This was methyl methedrine, which is like Dexedrine. It probably would have been approved except that it's so addicting. Eventually, you don't eat, and you stay high, and you can exist without any sleep. You can perform incredible physical and mental feats for a short time, but it takes its toll. It's a very dangerous drug with a criminal slant. So, it got this sort of nasty criminal slant to it, this motorcycle club, and then, you know, bit by bit we lost a lot of the professors, more and more of the Hell's Angels types showed up, and pretty soon there were guys who actually stole other people's motorcycles. That's when I sort of bowed out.

"It was just sort of a very interesting experience for me to see how you could go from being very idealistic, and naive, and generous, accepting all sorts of behaviors, and how, pretty soon, the bad behaviors sort of take over, and you lose the goodness . . . you know, the idealism. It really became a hard-core criminal kind of thing that I thought was dangerous. There was a time when I was half in and half out. . . . I didn't know if I was a real biker or if I was a Mother . . . and it was a little bit scary sometimes. . . . People were carrying guns, and shooting guns . . . oh, yeah. I once took Kathy to one of these parties and I thought, I wonder if we're going to get out of here without Kathy getting raped, okay? I saw the handwriting on the wall.

"Jeannie, I used to shoot up both arms, jump on my Harley, and go weaving in and out of traffic at a hundred and ten miles an hour! I thought I was invincible. I used to shoot pool for money. Once, I got into a barroom brawl. In Pullman, after shooting up and jumping on my

Harley, I went to this bar. I challenged the table and told this guy, 'Let's play for five bucks,' and I was so focused, I ran the whole table. I stood up and said, 'Game's over. Pay up!' Everybody was crowding around. And the guy said, 'No, I'm not gonna pay up.' And I said, 'Whad'ya mean? We were playing for five bucks. That was the deal. You gotta pay up.' And I turned to another guy who was watching the whole thing, and I said, 'You remember that. We were playing for five bucks.' And the guy I was playing with takes a swing at me, and I ducked. Then he picks up a pitcher of beer and hits me smack in the middle of my forehead, cracks my head open. . . . Jeez, I was going to kill him . . . it was a real barroom brawl . . ."

"Who won?" I asked.

"I think it was pretty much a standoff, but I came home with my head twice as big as normal, blood all over me, and Kathy said, 'What happened to you?' My God, it was crazy stuff like that, hard living, and I started asking myself, do I really want to be a biker? You could really get hurt, probably lose a lot of IQ, too.

"But you know, it wasn't all bad. There was a good side, too. I cherish these experiences. I drank coffee with Allen Ginsberg, and I drank tea with Ken Kesey. It was in 1969. . . . Ken Kesey—he wrote *One Flew Over the Cuckoo's Nest*, and he lived just outside of Eugene, Oregon. He had this school bus he fixed up that was painted all over with flowers, and they called themselves the Merry Pranksters, Ken Kesey, Allen Ginsberg, and some guy who was one of the Chicago Seven. They used to go up and down the Pacific Northwest and just stop off and meet people and have these little parties, or whatever. And the Merry Pranksters showed up on campus one day. I see this guy walking down the street wearing stars and stripes and a top hat. Did you ever see that hat, that Ginsberg hat? And I said, 'I know you, how do I know you?' It was Allen Ginsberg, and I followed him, and we ended up having coffee and doughnuts. That's the way it was in the sixties. It wasn't a big deal, it just happened. It was like going from one adventure to another."

Roger's adventures took a serious turn when he started wearing a gun. It was legal to carry a gun in Washington in those days. "Packing" was considered a birthright in the west, so long as you didn't hide it. He had suffered a serious pummeling in that barroom brawl, and he and Bill and Jack talked about taking revenge. That was when Kathy was getting ready to walk out. "I didn't want to get caught in the middle of drugs and guns," she said. Kathy was a good influence on Roger. She had grown up among loggers and trappers in Olympia, a true daughter of the Northwest, part Italian, part French Canadian, part Nez Perce. Roger had always dreamed of a girl like her, someone with her feet planted firmly on American ground. He told her she was his Pocahontas and his Sacajawea all rolled into one. They met in the summer of '69, the year Kerrigan Gray had shoot-outs with the police and Joe Schock blew up the Armory.

I had been watching her. I was walking down campus one day, feeling pretty good, and I saw this woman with this shape. She had on these tight, black-and-white pin-striped pants that showed off the curve of her butt, and she had these long, lithe legs, and she was just prancing along. I turned to this guy I was with, and I said, 'Did you see that woman? That is the most beautiful woman I have ever seen.' And I kept running into her. I'd wave to her, I'd smile at her. If I was on my motorcycle, I'd beep, or something. I'm not even sure she noticed me. She worked weekends as a cocktail waitress at this bar I sometimes went to. One night, when I was with my same friend, I spotted her. 'Wow, there's that girl again!' I said. 'Would I like to meet her!' This went on for maybe six months. One day, I walked into the student union cafeteria, where there was this doughnut shop, and there she was, sitting all by herself, drinking coffee. She was the only one in the whole place. I saw my chance. It was still sort of summer, and I had on this straw hat. I went up to her, tipped my hat, and said, 'Pardon me, Ma'am, is this seat taken?' And she said, 'Go ahead.'"

According to Kathy, "He was fair and freckled with red hair and a huge, thick, handlebar moustache. He was well muscled with a huge upper body and six-pack. He had big shoulders and arms, but his hands were soft. He wore a denim vest studded with VMI brass pins and old Boy Scout patches," and as Kathy remembered it, instead of a straw hat, Roger was wearing "a peaked leather cap with a big red star pinned on the front." That night she took him to the Mushroom House, an art installation made out of chicken wire and stucco. They sat inside where there was only room for two, and smoked grass together and talked. Later on, they went to the Dairy Queen. Neither of them had any money, so they pooled their change and ordered a hot fudge sundae to share and five cents worth of extra fudge. "They really layered it on," Kathy said.

They slept together that night but they didn't make love. In fact, Kathy strained their relationship to the breaking point by holding off for a month or more. Meanwhile, the two of them went backpacking together and had all sorts of adventures. "I wanted to get to know her," Roger said. When they finally did become lovers, it was as if a key had finally found the perfect lock. "It was the most incredible sex I've ever had with anyone in my entire life," Roger said. "But it took me a long time, years, maybe ten years, before I could actually believe that someone that perfect would be my woman, would form a real lasting bond with me that I could trust." Forgiveness had a lot to do with it, on both sides. That was the one thing Roger learned in Sunday school that stuck. He was big on forgiveness, just as he was big on love.

It was 1968, the year after the Summer of Love. Charles Manson was on the loose following his murder rampage. Charles Manson communes were becoming popular in Pullman, where there was a flourishing drug scene. All this made Kathy nervous. Roger was living with one of the Mothers in Stu Thomas's basement when he met Kathy. He and Kathy used to crash there, listening to the Doors and the Rolling Stones. Kathy was afraid of the Mothers at first. They looked a lot like the Hell's Angels and the Highwaymen, the two nasty gangs she went out of her way to avoid. But she wasn't afraid of Roger. His bravery fortified her. When she figured out that the Mothers were really a motorcycle club and not a gang, she relaxed somewhat, but stayed circumspect. "I could see that some of the Mothers were jerks and pathological liars, that they were into petty thievery and other drug-related crime. Bill Ewing and Jack Bush moved in with Roger in the fall and talked Roger into shooting speed. People came over every night and that's when I threatened to move out. I said to Roger, 'You're drinking and drugging every night. How do you ever expect to finish your Ph.D.?'" The turning point came when Roger got into the brawl at the bar. But by that time, Roger himself wanted out. It was a narrow escape, based on sheer luck.

Roger continued: "There was this guy in the Ph.D. program who was a very conservative Vietnam vet. He and I used to vie with each other to see who was the best student. That's why he respected me. Otherwise, he would have thought I was some hippie jerk or something. One day, he let me know that his next door neighbor was the chief of police, and that they were investigating me. They were getting ready for a raid, and if I didn't do something, I was going to wind up in prison. This was in 1970, I guess. So I went home and cleaned out everything I owned, and I buried it in the backyard. All sorts of stuff, a lot of drugs as well. And, sure enough, I got picked up! And they found a little teeny marijuana butt in the ashtray of my car, which I think was planted. They said, 'You're under arrest and you're going to jail, but if you allow us to search your house, and you're clean, we'll let you off.' I don't think they had enough evidence for a search warrant. So, I was clean. I was prepared for this. The first thing they did was bust into the apartment, and there was Kathy. She was half naked and she got mad at me for that. They searched, and searched, and searched, and found nothing. I might even have had guns. I mean, I was doing all sorts of stuff in those days. And that's when Kathy sort of put the hammer down. And she was right. She told me I had to change my ways, or she was out of there. But I knew I had to change my ways. I wasn't completely crazy. I was only semi-crazy.

"Well, it was a crazy time! At so many points along the way I could have been lost. I was so young. I didn't know what I wanted, or why I even chose to get a degree in chemistry. And then, I mean . . . how my brain got twisted. . . . I went from being this conservative Boy Scout to knowing people who did hard time! One guy I knew was an armed robber. He might even have been a murderer, for all I knew. But after you got under that tough guy façade, they were just people who had made the wrong decisions, or big mistakes; they got caught, they went a little bit overboard. You could justify how they had become criminals. There are people in prison, and the difference between them and you isn't that big a deal. I could have been one of them. . . . *There, but for the grace of God . . .* they taught me that. I grew up in this little society where, you know how Jews are, especially Ashkenazi Jews, and especially Ashkenazi Jews from Germany. That was my mother's family, and my father's family was tight-ass conservative Christian . . . give me a fuckin' break, you know? . . . so when you're a kid you grow up thinking, Jeez, there's too much prejudice, and that's a bunch of crap. There are so many interesting people in the world, it's really not black and white, or good and bad. . . ."

"So what did you learn from all this, Roger?" I asked.

"What did I learn? I think it made me a much better person, and that it saved my soul. I learned I wanted to do something with my life. I was originally just going to work for Dupont and play golf. I could have been a really successful Duponter. That's not what I chose. . . . My advisor introduced me to a problem and let me have carte blanche. He was running a lab with a lot of resources, but he was distracted. His marriage was falling apart. He invited me over once, and his wife thought I was a Hell's Angel and told him he was never to invite me again. I worked and worked in the lab, and within three to five months, I made this compound that was so unstable it would change color, from white to blue to yellow. All molecules have an intrinsic energy. I used to dream about molecules. In a low-energy state they're stable; in a high-energy state they fly apart. I learned how to manipulate these molecules in a very specific way. . . . Fortunately, my advisor didn't get in my way. 'I can't give you a Ph.D. in a year,' he told me. 'Why don't you pick another problem?' I did that one, too. I was so dedicated to solving these problems, I became married to my work. I took LSD and climbed Kamiak Butte—"

"What's Kamiak Butte?" I interrupted.

"It's one of the oldest geological formations in the west, a big butte in the middle of nowhere like an island. . . . It goes up about a thousand feet and looks out over all these fields where there was once an ancient sea. When I reached the summit I sat there, looking out over those rolling wheat fields. It opened up my thinking. I knew within two weeks I had a solution, and it worked, and I published the paper. Once you learn how to solve a problem, it's like learning how to write a poem, it's like a flower, something beautiful, something worthy. It's amazing how much energy you have when you're on the right path. . . . You revise and revise . . . be honest . . . see what's really there . . . and that's the way you do science, the same way you write a poem. You have to be emotionally honest to write a good poem—you taught me that—and to do science, you have to be intellectually honest.

"I look at it more in a spiritual sense—having respect for nature in all its capricious vagaries, the forces that cause all of us to be here. The world wasn't created for man to understand. If humans can't predict, it's because we don't have enough understanding. My hunch is that we never will. There will always be questions, but that's what separates us from nature. I think if people could understand science more, and what drives scientists, they would appreciate what it means to be human. I look upon this as the highest form of endeavor that humans can evolve to, the great human enterprise. Love is unique to humans. I believe we're all gods. That's what God is. We are gods. We create the universe through our perception, through our understanding. Religion is human consciousness relating to the physical world . . . magnetic waves, radio waves, frequencies, whatever. . . .

"I finished up this research and published some papers and the guy who was my advisor . . . he was never there, he was having an affair with a woman who lived in Potlatch, Idaho, and that's when Kathy and I left Pullman. We moved out to Bill Ewing's. He had a farm he rented with horses and about five acres of marijuana way out in Potlatch, and it just so happened that it was right next door to where my advisor's girlfriend was living. The chemistry department called me in. They wanted me to graduate because they were afraid I was going to cause a scandal. At my oral, they said, 'Roger, whatever you wrote, we're sure it's great. . . . You have all these papers . . . you're a really good student . . . we don't even need to go over it . . . you passed.' So we lived on this farm in Idaho. We had a wonderful time, and then I got a post-doc lecturer position in the chemistry department at the University of Colorado, so we packed up and moved to Denver, and that was the end of the Mothers.

When we got to Denver, Kathy got sick. She had Graves' disease, and I didn't think I wanted to get married, so she went back to her mother and I spent the next three months, I mean, I was wild. I was screwing every woman I could get my hands on. I mean, like exotic dancers and strippers . . . and I was this teacher, and I used to have these young honeys throwing themselves at me. . . . So, did I think about teaching? After about three months of that, or four months, or six months, that's when I decided that I really wanted to live with Kathy. I missed her. So I wanted to get all that out of my system. Right after my fling, I

proposed to Kathy on the phone. And around that same time, that was
when I decided I didn't want to be an organic chemist anymore. I decided
it was a dirty occupation. Organic chemists made napalm, they made
explosives, and they were polluting. Remember that chemical company
in Buffalo, New York, that contaminated the ground water and caused
all those birth defects?"

"Love Canal?"

"And then that town in India where all those people died overnight?"

"Bhopal?"

"It was all around the same time."

"There was this guy who worked next to me in the lab in Denver. He
left, and went to medical school, and I stayed in touch with him and got
interested in it myself. I never took a biology course in my life. I didn't
even know what biochemistry was. All of a sudden, I was going to be a
biochemist. Crazy! Just crazy! There's no harder way to do it. I just
studied, I read like mad. I can learn anything, but on my own terms, in
my own way.

We got married in June of '72 on a ferry boat in the Puget Sound,
and everyone, including the pilot of the boat, got so high on this super
grass that a friend of mine brought that the boat crashed into the pylons
and tore out the dock. So that was the end of our wedding. We had a
good time, and we lived happily ever after, with a few bumps along the
road . . . ha! ha! . . . and the Mothers did show up for my wedding. That
was the last time I ever saw them."

"So, Roger, are you telling me that you were really an outlaw?"

"Oh, yeah! You know that. My mother used to tell me that I was
going to end up in prison. I believed her, right? I have far exceeded my
expectations. I know I exceeded my mother's! I'd say it's been a slow
evolution to turn me into something. I never had the great expectations
that a lot of people have. That wasn't me. I was just trying to prove my
mother's prophecy wrong. I never thought life would turn out so good. I
never thought I'd become a good person. You know, it's been a great trip.

"Once I learned that Kathy loved me for who I was, for what I was,
that gave me so much power. In other words, I knew who I was in my
own mind, but people didn't necessarily accept that. I don't play the
game at all. I don't try to charm or cajole people. Everyone has told me

that. I'm going to do it my way. But once it was clear that Kathy accepted me for who I am, that she could love me even though I'm a screw-up like that . . . and it's harder to get my stuff published . . . wow, that gave me the strength to really exercise this Roger Davis, the scientist, the father, whatever. . . . Once I figured it out . . . that allowed me to express my full personality."

"You're pretty special, Roger," I said, "You were always a wild man and an outlaw, and that's the stamp you put on your career as a scientist."

"Absolutely. These super scientists from Texas, they call me a renegade. That's their exact word. I mean, they respect me and they read my papers, but I don't even know what renegade means. . . . What the heck is a renegade?"

"It means someone who gets things done outside the parameters of the law, or outside the herd. . . . Here, let me look it up. I have a dictionary right here. *Renegade: one who rejects a religion, a cause, an allegiance . . . or one group for another . . . a deserter . . . a rebel . . . to become an outlaw . . .*"

"It's more fun, right?"

"That's so interesting . . . *from medieval Latin . . .* renegare, *to deny*. Roger, you've earned it well . . ." And here Roger responded with a phrase he had made all his own.

"*Il piacere e tutta mio,*" he said, meaning the pleasure is all mine. It was the closest he ever came to mastering a little bit of Italian.

The irony in Roger's life story was that it was idealism, however misguided, that led him astray, just as it was idealism that plucked him back from the brink. Like his mother before him, the socialist who sheltered the pregnant Margie and once adopted two orphan boys from Naples, Roger had a passion for social justice. The Freedom Bank, the marches for racial equality that he organized, the university sit-ins he led, even the Peoples' Speed and the collusion with ex-cons and outlaws was all conceived and set on fire in the collective brain of a generation bent on changing the world.

But before Roger told me his life story, I never thought of him as an idealist. To me, he was always a wise guy who loved to play the class clown. He and Alan took excessive pride in their irreverence, and as a team they were incorrigible. How many times had Alan regaled me with the story of the prank Roger pulled, getting a group of pilgrims to kneel down with him in the crypt of St. Peter's in Rome, craning for a view in the murky dark of the reliquary that held the saint's bones when he called out, "Look! I see some bones! I see a box! And it says, 'Kentucky Fried Chicken'!" Another time, he spoiled my rapture in one of those tiny chapels that dot the hills all over the Greek islands when he barged through the door, shouting, "*Sacre Coeur!*"

But the real shocker came on the big island in Hawaii when the four of us were exploring an active volcano, creeping our way, inch by inch, across long, livid tongues of undulating lava. Far below us, at what seemed an almost unfathomable depth, a fiery inferno worthy of Dante was blazing away. I caught glimpses of it through the occasional crack in the lava's surface, and was quaking with fear. To me, it was easy to understand why the Hawaiians had once thrown live pigs and other offerings into the fire pit to appease Pele, the goddess of the volcano. Imagine my horror when I looked up, and there was Roger standing on a ledge with his back turned and his pants pulled down, yelling, "Take that, Pele!"

When Roger and I once got lost together in Capri, I got a glimpse of the better angles of his nature. It was on a Sunday afternoon in May. The four of us were on our way to da Gelsomina, a restaurant famous for its homemade ravioli, overlooking the Bay of Naples, and accessible only by foot. It was an easy stroll through the countryside along the Via Migliara, a lovely woodland path no wider than the chariot wheels that once whisked the Emperor Tiberius around the island. Kathy and Alan sprinted out of sight on their long legs while Roger and I sauntered along at our usual leisurely pace, enjoying the beauty of the golden green, sun-drenched afternoon.

By the time we reached da Gelsomina our spouses were nowhere to be found. Looking about, we happened to notice a sign on the opposite side of the path that was half hidden in the foliage behind a wire wicker fence. What appeared to be a map was marked with colored trails going off in different directions. It was framed in wood and looked hand painted, with a legend in the upper left-hand corner. A red arrow near the bottom pointed the way to a "Bel Vedere," a scenic overlook, and the words

"Parco Filosófico" were printed in bold across the top. Oddest of all were two little blue books dangling from the wire fence by two pieces of knotted, cotton string, one in German and the other in Italian. I looked at the Italian title and read *Sagezza occidentále*. "Roger," I said excitedly, "that means Wisdom of the West!" It dawned on me that these were guide books, and that we were standing at the entrance to a philosophers' park, one of those rare gems tourists sometimes stumble on that never make it into the guide books. The whole thing had a charming, naive quality about it that struck me as peculiarly Italian. Who in the world would have gone to all this trouble?

"Look, Roger," I said, following with my finger the gold path that led to the right. "This path says "Realismo," and this other one, the blue one that goes to the left, says "Idealismo." Realism or Idealism. Which one shall we choose?" Kathy and Alan, having arrived independently at this same spot only a few minutes earlier, had both chosen the gold path, the one marked Realism, as we would later discover. Alan would return with a quote from T. S. Eliot he had scribbled on a piece of scrap paper: "Where is the wisdom we have lost in knowledge?" But Roger and I, kindred blithe spirits that we were, set off along the blue trail, the one marked Idealism.

It was steep, leading diagonally up a grassy embankment. Scrambling up the ragged incline, we soon began to notice that the path was studded here and there with tiles. The tiles were set in stone close to the ground, each one displaying a bilingual quotation from one of the great western philosophers, beginning with Plato, St. Thomas, and St. Augustine. Clambering over rocks and stones, ducking under overhanging branches, we felt like kids on a treasure hunt, making our way from one tile to the next, seeking out each inscription. Roger took my picture; I was seated on a bench with my arm inclined around a tile that bore a saying from Seneca in Latin: *Omne hoc quod vides, quo divina atque humana conclusa sunt, unum est: membra sumus corporis magni.* "All this that you see before you, encompassing the divine and the human, is one: and we are members of a great body."

As we climbed higher, it soon became apparent that very few lovers of wisdom had ventured this far along the trail, judging from its state of neglect. Overgrown with thickets and thorns, rugged and broken, the path was almost impossible to follow. The higher we climbed, the more obscure it grew until, nearing the top of the cliff, we found ourselves reading inscriptions from Nietzsche, Marx, and Wittgenstein, the blue trail having somehow gotten mixed up with the gold. As things grew more and more difficult to decipher, we happened on a clearing with yet another sign at the entrance. "Campo Reale di Meditazione," I read aloud. "Roger, this is a place for realists to rest and meditate. There must be something like it somewhere around here for idealists like us. But I don't see anything, do you?"

Neither of us ever found it. As a matter of fact, like so many things Italian, the pattern of the whole park seemed to defy logic. It was a philosophers' jumble. In the maze, it was easy to become separated, and, in fact, we did lose track of one another. Feeling oddly bereft, I wandered alone for a while, searching for Roger, wondering if we would ever be reunited. Although neither of us knew it, we were both, in our separate ways, approaching the highest point on Anacapri. When I finally reached the plateau at the summit where the trail opens up, I followed it, and found him.

The scene was stunning. His back was turned and his hands, as usual, were in his pockets. Standing on the edge of a sheer precipice, gazing out over the sea, he was plunged in a deep reverie. Seabirds were wheeling and tumbling in great soundless spirals all around him, veering off by mere inches from the cliff face, and beyond, the sky was a gauzy blue. Roger had found the way to his own Campo di Ideale Meditazione. This was the Bel Vedere di Migliara that was promised by the red arrow on the sign below. Unwittingly, we had blundered onto a rocky outcropping a full nine hundred and ninety feet above the sea, a headland so exalted that here, at this ethereal height, the sea, the sky, and the air all seemed to interpenetrate and blur together.

Fearful of the height, and anxious not to disturb Roger's reverie, I approached ever so gingerly and peeked out over the edge. There was no barrier. It would have been so easy to fall. It made me feel giddy just to glimpse the surf so far below us as it dimly thundered and crashed against the rocks, sending up a rainbow mist in the sunlight. And that is where I want to leave him, this man who repudiated all religion but who once professed, "I believe we are the gods. . . . We bring the universe to consciousness. . . . That's what God is." One week before Roger died, Alan asked him, "Roger, how do you want to be remembered?" "Truth," he responded. It was science that led Roger not just to the place of truth, but to the vanishing point where truth deposits us. Standing there on that headland jutting out into the Mediterranean, he was no longer the bull trapped in the labyrinth. He was Daedalus, the scientist, readying himself to test his last fabulous hypothesis.

❧

Roger died on June 17, 2008. The following August, Alan and I flew to Aspen to meet Kathy, Kimmie, and Harley at the Kern Lipid Conference that Roger cofounded. Alan felt terrible about having missed Roger's memorial service. To make up for it, he organized a second service to be held in the rotunda as a special afternoon session. By three o'clock the place was packed. Kimmie, who had just been officially inducted into medical school, delivered a brave eulogy. I recited Dylan Thomas's poem "Do Not Go Gentle into That Good Night," and Alan gave a very personal remembrance, beginning with his tribute, "When I was a boy, I had a best friend . . ." as the same set of photographs he had once assembled for Roger's birthday flashed, magnified, on the video screen behind him.

The next day Alan and I joined Kathy, Kimmie, and Harley as we boarded the bus that would take us up to Maroon Bells, carrying Roger's ashes. It was already late in the day by the time we arrived. As we entered the clearing, the sun was beginning to sink behind the twin peaks that give the mountain its name, and I caught a flash in the corner of my eye that must have been the tuft of a whitetail, startled into hiding. There had been a lot of rain that summer, and we could hear the distant roar of the White River as we started toward the lake. It might have been the slanting angle of the sun, or maybe the thin air, but whatever the cause, the scene that spread itself before us, electric and surreal, fairly screamed with color, it seemed so alive: the meadow at the end of summer was a riot of sunflower gold, fuchsia, and fireweed; the twin peaks, backlit by the setting sun, an almost shocking magenta; the lake, streaked with a mossy neon green, deepened to black in the inky shadows of the evergreens on the far side. As we gathered by the edge of the lake, I heard a faint crackle, and realized it was the sound of the parchment paper as Kathy opened, ever so carefully, the folds that held Roger's ashes. As Kathy tossed the first handful high into the air above the lake, Kimmie sat down on a rock, covered her face, and began to sob. Harley, standing on a bank a little farther off, said simply, "Good-bye, Papa."

Afterward, we left the lake and followed the stream toward the mountains, drawn by the silvery music that grew louder and more insistent until, by the time we reached the footbridge over the river, it fairly thundered and broke up, tumbling and crashing over branches and boulders, sending up a powerful spray. I had once heard that the dead can hear us from the other side if only we shout loudly enough. So we stood on that bridge, all five of us, and yelled "Rogerrrrrrrr" at the top of our lungs over the river's roar as we flung the rest of the ashes over the railing, and watched, riveted, as the motes were briefly borne aloft in the updraft, drifted, fell apart, and were finally carried downstream, lost in the torrent.

There was a chill in the air and dew was beginning to gather as we started back, walking Indian file in silence through the darkening valley, past the lake that was becoming opaque, and the pines on the hill, now more shadow than shape. Looking down at my feet, moving one after the other along the dirt path as I thought about Roger, a phrase from the end of Whitman's great poem came back to me . . . *look for me under your bootsoles* . . . and then another . . . *lacy jags . . . the vapor and the dusk . . . I depart as air . . . in the last scud of day* . . . as slowly, bit by bit, in no necessary order, the poem began assembling itself out of the dim recesses of my memory . . . *I too am not a bit tamed . . . I bequeath myself to the dirt . . . failing to fetch me . . . keep encouraged . . . missing me one place, search another* . . . and on it went, gathering itself fragment by fragment, piecing itself into a whole. As we walked out onto the road, caught the last bus, and wound our way back down the mountainside, it kept on singing to me, the song of Roger's self.

9

Selected Poems

1970–2002

January Thaw

These days hang
like gray socks filling up
with snow. I am
empty inside them, hollow
as the small caves
of boots
left side by side
to stiffen in the hall.

This is the month
of mud and rain-soaked stumps.
Knucklebones, thin fingers
of snow litter the yard.
A trail of chicken's feet,
fish heads, rinds
and oyster shells leads down
to the ravine. Snow

sticks in shadow
like a corpse of rags.

In the bottom of the night
my grandmother inhabits
the body of a hound. Long
tongues of hair leap and
twist in the air around her face.
In my arms she rolls wild eyes,
howls, drools, whimpers
once, and dies.

Troubled Sleep

Nightmare fumes around my face like camphor in a sac.
Your shoes are open graves I stumble on.
Your socks, dead birds to gather up.

This is the bottleneck. With every breath
I draw, the rings
constrict. Beside me in the bed
you're like a third rail, rigid with current.

I listen to your mutterings, sort through gibberish
for signs. You thrash, cry out, wrestle with the sheet.
Underneath the El, the house shakes . . .

I dream my mother's dream
from my grandmother's bed: the eels are all
escaping from the kitchen sink.

A blue volt wracks the sky
arcing you awake. Our eyes meet.
The light fails. We plunge through tunnels
pitched headlong. Brakes squeal like pigs.

Waking Early after Heavy Snow

While we slept, the snow
fell and pinned us to the bed, sealing
our eyes
shut, filling up
the dreaming holes of our mouths.

Waking numb, we find our bodies
tangled
like wet rope, dense
as bushes deep in the ravine,
each twig
thick as a thumb.

We wait. Slugs of light
slide through the venetian blind,
assemble slowly
on the rug, lengthen, grow fat.

At last we stagger, tug up the window
lids, letting in the white
eyes of day. The woods
sway and start to fall apart, piece
by white piece.

We fumble with spoons, bowls, eggs
and struggle, like those crocuses
that let their saw teeth part
too soon, and have to fight
all day to hold up
heavy yellow cups half filled with snow.

The Zealot

Everything was wet. The pitcher sweated.
Wooden doors swelled up like thumbs.
Saliva pooled from the tongues of the cats.
Even the beeswax candles melted
and keeled over. Only he
stayed dry as a snake, his neck blackening all summer.

I spent whole days comatose, feet propped over the bed
imagining cool layers of white plaster under the white wall.
Mornings I'd wake to the empty rooms and find him
crouched over pots and jars, mixing potions in the garden.
I'd watch his fingers flick and dart among the slick leaves
prying squash blossoms open, shaking out pollen.

Water trickled through the beds. The sky often rippled
and cracked open as I lay among the sheets.
He glided through the heat like an Ethiopian.
Oblivious to all rumblings, he went on tying up tomatoes
until they tottered seven feet over that rank, slippery acre.

The garden festered by caprice, overspreading strings,
trellises he set like traps, violating shapes
he teased and fretted. The pitch of the katydids
rose to a scream as warnings came crackling over the radio.

Screwball! the neighbors taunted, but joined him
with smudge pots, tattered blankets and torches.
Yelling all night through teeth clenched like Klansmen
they staved off the inevitable.
Then, it was hopeless.

Rummaging one afternoon, obsessed with loss, his eyes lit
on the zinc trough in the basement. He hauled it up
two floors, rigging ropes and pulleys, hoisting

pebbles by the bucketful. I cringed
as each bucket swung through the window like a wrecker's ball.
He carried in the plants themselves at last
crowing over his plot to outwit nature.

All that winter on the pea-green porch, peppers and tomatoes
sickened and wasted. Flesh molded to vine.
Drooping, fuzzy at first, the coils and goosenecks stiffened.
Each softening cheek stretched to a leathery hide.
Tendrils grew into horns and talons.
They oozed, dripped, gave off fetid vapors.

He never let anything die.

Of Bread

It doesn't matter that the house isn't locked.
Without you, it's empty as an oven
of its loaves.

I want neither your ham nor your cheese
nor your oysters and white
wine.

I want the yeast of you, making me rise
'til I split, two halves
in your teeth

and the butter melting, the hot bran
your yam-yellow light spilling
your honey seeping all through the comb

Not this house with its darkening oak.
Not that table laid with its cold
plates.

Sailing to America

Why have I called you "Mother"
In my sleep?
                    Robin Morgan

In the bath, you stroke my breasts
furrowing the mounds where sparrows nest
you blaze a set of tracks
through wave on wave of prairie grass
brush forth, back
back, forth—
my breasts
turn into boys on board a ship
emigrants, each with a cap.
Together by the rail we stand transfixed
sure of nothing but this steady tow
that laps, laps
sucking at our sides—
Someone who loved us once is calling, calling
like a mother from another life—
we ride each wave, whitecaps crest
foam up like cream,
O what a rich ocean this is! Her voice
tilts us to the wind, curls our sails crisp
calling, calling, pulling us
until it stops.
We find ourselves offshore
craning for a view: it lies before us—
America
two leagues off.

Postpartum

for Giancarlo

Stunned, like a fish by a blow
I lie in the green
near bottom
spinning a fin
belly lolling toward the sun

far, far above, you flit through the cage
of weeds
that was your mother, your swamp

we've changed places, you and I
you took the air
bursting into light like a swallow from a barn
now it is I who thrash and thump about down here in the blood-
blind clubfoot dark

your hands wave above the crib, white moths
fanning back the dark . . .

oh my berry, my sweet black frog, we are lost
holding each other's trembling
like an old man's hands

Nursing My Child through His First Illness

Basilicata, 1974

1

Sleepless he rages, fists on the rails
howling for hours . . .

This, the old dream to be martyred
the calling denied
floats up, a kidney in a bowl
carried to the altar, St. Agatha's breasts
Ophelia's face

the procession of virgins advances, she carries
a candle
she wears a white dress

a thimble rolls out of my grandmother's coffin
I am bound on the hoop sewn into my hem

This is the way, each moment
I mount
ever higher, the life
of the flesh
falls away

knock knock knock

upstairs, the invalid thumps with his cane
from the bed

knock knock knock

in his three-legged
crib, the infant stands up.

2

I live alone on the edge of town
I keep my father's house

Remember, O most gracious virgin mary
never was it known that anyone who fled to thy protection
was left
unaided . . .

Skull-bald, these mountains hang over us
massive and terrible
leaning like great-aunts over an infant's cradle.

3

teeth descend from the cave roof in rows
Mouth
under the Mountain

O mother of the word incarnate
before thee I stand
sinful and sorrowful

a tower extrudes from a hill
salt
laps at the edge, uneasy

my darling, I'll croon to you, I'll coo
I'll carry you for hours
your wails
splash my sides like a tide of acid
you wear me away all white

the sea sucks up, shudders
subsides to a hiss

starfish slide
dead crabs float
belly up
the moon spins upside down
I'll croon, I'll coo, I'll carry you for hours

all the rock pools give up their ghosts
in the sun
white algae heaps up in pockets
airy
weightless
I drift, I rove, I carry you for hours

O Mountain, O Rose, O Gold

knock knock knock

pocked, pitted, this blister of rock

white algae heaps up in pockets
despise not my petition
hear me, O Mother
Answer.

Crossing the Great Divide

> Your real country is where you're heading
> not where you are.
>
> Rumi

Maratea, Basilicata

1

Hooked in this space between sea and sky
like a hammock
pitched from a cliff
I stare out at the day, death in the corners of its eyes.

Only the goat-hoofed, the cloven
survive in this place
scrambling for toeholds, hanging in the crags.

The gecko clings with tacky feet to the stucco wall.
Stupefied at noon,
he curves around a roof beam
abandoning his long body to its love for the hot dark.

I let myself down, inch by inch.
On the ledge, white wine withers in the glass.
I live in the holes.

Life slows to a lizard's pulse
a hot stone,
I hold the quick between my thumbs, stroking its throat.

2

The sea asleep, brassy serpent
sullen in the shallows now
a muddy swell
slithering through trees below.

I shall live out my life rejoicing
ribboning under the jagged shadow of the hawk.

There is no reason for this joy
eagle-bald, knifing through me like a canyon.

There is nothing in this landscape that defines me.

3

Freed from the past with its priest's hands
we are grails
crossing a great divide,
below us, the abyss, ahead, the dense glass—
Believing we will crash, we are passed
whole
through the rose
the blue
the needle's eye of God.

August I

Cicadas chew the eye of noon.
Joe-pye
high as I am.
Orioles in soundless pairs over the goldenrod
rise.

The air, stabbed like a saint with sorrow and desire
shrills.
This is the sound love makes.
Love's apple
lets go the bough,
drops
to earth with a *thump*, round and rosy-cheeked.
My mother's dead three weeks.

August II

The hollyhocks unbuttoning behind the house
fumble with their stiffened shirts.
They crash and fall like drunks across the drive.

Somebody throws the dice hard.
Walnuts pock the roof.
Grasshoppers thrum their thighs like punk guitars

as the din, ratcheting upwards, tightens like a scrotum
and it's hard to breathe the thick air
plush as plum-skin.

The cat twitches its ears at twilight, a black spot
pinned into quivering gold, holding alive
the light that dies in the rabbit's eyes.

I slip a mask inside my mother's coffin.

Mater Dolorosa

I

Mother most sad
Mother most silent
Mother afflicted
Mother demented
Mother transfixed with grief
Mother given to the Lutherans
Mother bereft of her children
Mother left to die alone

Mirror of patience
Seat of wisdom
Well of calm
Smiling tiger
Lady from Niger
Eye of the storm

We children, that you might hear us
We children, that you might spare us
We children, that you might bring us with you into heaven
    to share in the company of your mother
      and your sister and your brother and our father

From your wrath, deliver us
From your scorn, deliver us
From your mop and pail, deliver us
Mother, have mercy
Mother, have mercy
Mother, have mercy
Remember us, O Mother
Now and at the hour of our death.

II

Grassy Mound
Chicken Little
Clammy brow
Mother of the clean sheet
Hole where I came out
Hole where my sister came out
Hole where my brother came out
Mouth that my father kissed
Mexican Hairless
Font of bliss

Blue Rose
Baby rose
Pressed rose
Primrose
Rock rose
Rosey the Riveter

III

Steam iron
Sweating kettle
Rising scum
Rocking cradle
Boiled egg
Rusty ladle
Mother of vapors and rubs
She who kept us alive
She who did not dash our brains out.

Broken tooth
Pearly gate
Bloody root
Mother of maggots and moths
We praise you, we bless you, we call your name.

Mother of lineaments and cloths
Mother of iodine
Mother of gauze
She who bound up our wounds
She who painted our thumbs
Mother of ovens and stoves
Rubber glove
Mother of cloves
Mother of the clean steps
Hear me, look on me, remember me, O Mother
Now and at the hour of our death.

IV

Rosy ghost
Vapor trail
Baby's breath
Face veil
Freight cargo
Mother lode
Flashgun
Silver bullet
Screaming Mimi
Loose cannon
Shining path
Vacuum cleaner
Third rail

A River of Ice and Sapphires

My father's ram's-head ring she always wore
spilled from her hand to the floor
one day as she lay dying,
but the marbles in the blue glass jar beside her bed
stayed, like the eyes in her head.

Those eyes! Cracked sapphires.
I love those eyes!
You can't have them, she said.

That was no surprise.
Hadn't she come from a tribe that kept what they prized?
Hadn't she once told me about the old lady
who locked herself in when the house caught fire
and died with her fists full of jewels?

Fire and ice twitched together
in my mother's head where a dangerous river
would sometimes start to melt and move,
like the day she slammed the iron down hard,
and started to curse. *God Almighty!* The iron reared,
hissing and snorting on her upraised arm like a thunderhead.
I felt the steam kiss my cheek.
I was a child.
I hardly looked at the iron.
It was the ice in her eyes that held me riveted.

Stop looking at me! I can hear my brother cry.
You've been looking at me all my life!
Hawkeye, I called her.
That gaze went through you like a laser.

But I couldn't get enough of it.
I kept hovering, hoping that a fish or a star

might slide through, something with flash
to warm myself by.

Staring into those eyes, I started out across the Ohio,
the river melting and rushing downstream,
the current hurrying me under.
Whatever it was held me up, willy-nilly, wasn't me.
I would have gladly drowned drinking that water.

Three days before my mother died, her mind cleared.
Her cheeks and forehead shone like snow on silver.
Oh, how beautiful you are! Look! How beautiful!
I kept exclaiming standing beside her.
She gave no sign she knew me.
And then without any warning, her eyes locked mine.

Like the thousand slippery dimes my father once poured
into my outstretched hands, I gasped at the force
of that surge. Our two densities met and merged
emptying into one another beyond mother or daughter,
her blue into my brown, and we flowed that way together
until I felt everything she had ever withheld
flood into me,
faith, fortune, forgiveness,
as I swam through the blue electric river of my mother.

Bacchus at St. Benedict's

1

Three days after I settled in at the monastery
Bacchus paid me a visit in late afternoon.

I had been waiting all day under the slick leaves of the oaks,
pacing from porch to pool in the heat.
Even the great bell lost its claim on my mind.
I was tuned
to a subtler meld—the faint crush
of gravel on the dirt road.

He was out in a flash, teeth, shades,
sun shining through his red hand, upraised.
It gleamed, waving the wine.
"*I found a 1983 botrytis Sémillon!*" he sang
to someone who'd been chanting psalms three days.

2

The first surge was the pool, waking up
to his wide plunge.
Big-eyed, I watched the water seize,
rocked to its knees.

We set out along a meadow sliced by swallows
when the sky was turning ruddy.
The road, studded with apple, pear, and mulberry,
veered, and we lost
the red, dipping
into shade below the Sisters' cemetery.

He nodded at the oratory, approved
the icons, but when we came
upon the chapel, and I explained

holy wine inside the tabernacle,
he had to be restrained, thinking
In there, at least, I'll find a decent wineglass!

3

On the porch, he poured the Sémillon,
then a Gewürztraminer
he matched with salmon, pink slabs
of watermelon, white rinds
lined with green grinning from black plates.
Delicacies he presented two at a time,
now a crown of garlic
now a round of bread . . .

He was ceremonious, stirring the strawberries,
his red hand cool,
too classy to disgrace this novice.
It was she, in fact, who finally did it,
setting down her glass to pose the question,
"How long before we take off our clothes?"

4

Midmorning the day after, he's gone in a spurt of gravel.
It's noon before I can resume my life of measure
heeding the bell that calls us to chapel,
thinking on death every day.

Jesus and Bacchus, Jesus and Bacchus, what am I doing?
I'm writing a poem about the god of wine.
Does a wine thief wound the barrel?
Does it matter which vat
we dip from (*red or white?*)
if it's rapture
we're after, why not be drunk by noon?

Happiness

It was Swami Satchidananda who set her straight.
You are the source of your own happiness, he told her
out of the blue, looking her straight in the eye
and tapping it into her chest.

Then came the bridegroom, pressing his suit.
Are you capable of happiness? he quizzed her.
This was serious. He had put it to the test.
She checked the box marked *Yes*.
A choice. A deliverance.

All this came as a great surprise
to one who had pressed her face against the glass.
Happiness had passed her by like the boys on their Flexible Flyers.
It was a shock to have it show up now like her mother in a nightgown
standing on the school bus steps waving a lost lunch.

Once, in the middle of the night, lightning had struck the iron lamp
on her desk, summoning her father to the threshold like Zeus.
If happiness came at all, she thought it might come like that,
a thunderclap that would strike hard,
or bounce around on the ground like pearls and be briefly lost.

The wonder was that it would have so little to do with sex
or God; be more like a game of connect-the-dots or
pick-up sticks she might have played with a friend
sitting cross-legged on the bare wooden floor.

That it would return her to the peace of pebbles in her father's yard
where she had played as a child under the leafy ears of the oaks;
to a sky the ragman tented with his cry each spring
restoring columbine and larkspur to the fieldstone wall.

That maybe—ah, now here's a thought—it had been there all along,
a plane invisible above the clouds
that went on humming on those summer afternoons,
droning on over the bounce of a red rubber ball,
the crash of jacks on gray plank boards,
the perfect ring a tumbler left, lifted from the silt.

That it would forgive the day she squatted in the shade
of Mrs. C.'s garden, too busy to run indoors,
thinking that the little pile she'd left
steaming under a still-swaying branch of bleeding heart
was soft and brown and beautiful as the chestnut nose
    on the ragman's horse.

 Jean Feraca, Wisconsin Public Radio's Distinguished Senior Broadcaster, is host and executive producer of *Here on Earth: Radio Without Borders*. She won an Ohio State and Gabriel Award for her *Women of Spirit* radio series on female leaders in the early Christian Church, and the National Telemedia Council's Distinguished Media Award for her radio advocacy of people with mental illness, and the 2011 Gabriel Award for "Muslims, Mosques, and American Identity," a program in the series Inside Islam. A resident of Madison, Wisconsin, she is author of three collections of poetry: *South from Rome: Il Mezzogiorno*, *Crossing the Great Divide*, and *Rendered into Paradise*. Jean is a recipient of *The Nation*'s Discovery Award and a National Endowment for the Arts Fellowship, and two of her poetry books were finalists for the Pushcart Prize. *I Hear Voices: A Memoir of Love, Death, and the Radio* was selected as the 2007 winner of the Kenneth Kingery/August Derleth Nonfiction Book Award, sponsored by the Council for Wisconsin Writers. It was also named an Outstanding Book by the American Association of School Librarians, and one of the year's Best Books for General Audiences by the Public Library Association.